Readings from
**SCIENTIFIC
AMERICAN**

IMAGE, OBJECT, AND ILLUSION

With Introductions by
Richard Held
Massachusetts Institute of Technology

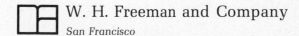

W. H. Freeman and Company
San Francisco

Cover design from "Multistability in Perception" by Fred
Attneave. Copyright © 1971 by Scientific American, Inc.
All rights reserved.

All of the SCIENTIFIC AMERICAN articles in IMAGE,
OBJECT, AND ILLUSION are available as separate
Offprints. For a complete list of more than 975 articles
now available as Offprints, write to W. H. Freeman
and Company, 660 Market Street, San Francisco,
California 94104.

**Library of Congress Cataloging
in Publication Data**

Held, Richard, comp.
  Image, object, and illusion.

  1. Optical illusions—Addresses, essays, lectures.
I. Scientific American. II. Title. (DNLM:
1. Illusions—Collected works. WW103 H474i)
QP495.H35   612'.84'08   74–11012
ISBN 0–7167–0505–2
ISBN 0–7167–0504–4 (pbk.)

Printed in the United States of America

9 8 7 6 5

PREFACE

Illusions of the senses have for us the same appeal as a magician's tricks. They contradict our everyday experience; they defy, and yet demand, rational explanation. For some thinkers they have raised questions about reality itself. How can the observer be sure that everything he senses is not illusory? Of course, even if it were, we would still have the problem of why some aspects of perception are called illusions—in the narrow sense—although others are not. Why do we consider that some perceived images veridically represent external objects but that others do not? The answer depends, as I believe the following articles demonstrate, upon what we assume is the necessary correspondence between certain of the properties of the object (such as wavelength of reflected light, measured size, geometric shape) and those of its perceived image (color, apparent size, form). In many instances the assumed correspondence may hold and we regard the perceptions as veridical. If, however, one or more of these assumed correspondences proves incorrect, we term the perception an illusion. Accordingly, the illusions simply indicate the inadequacies of the assumed correspondences. They can be likened to the visible tops of icebergs; they indicate hidden regions of ignorance about the workings of perceptual processes.

Some illusions are fascinating because they show us in a particularly clear way the workings of our own perceptual processes. The works of certain artists, such as Escher, play on such themes, but most compelling in this respect are the reversible figures. A cube appearing to extend toward the observer may suddenly switch its orientation and appear to extend away from him. The observer need not have performed any particular action and certainly the cube did not change. Then to what must this change be attributed? Obviously, some alteration in the observer himself has occurred, implicating a perceptual process that has at least two states, each corresponding to a different appearance of the figure. We expect that such a perceptual process is, in turn, the expression of an underlying neural mechanism. An understanding of such mechanisms, which is still quite remote, can be expected to yield the ultimate explanation of sensory illusions. In the meantime, they serve as fascinating challenges.

May 1974   *Richard Held*

CONTENTS

Note on cross-references: References to articles included in this book are noted by the title of the article and the page on which it begins; references to articles that are available as Offprints, but are not included here, are noted by the article's title and Offprint number; references to articles published by SCIENTIFIC AMERICAN, but which are not available as Offprints, are noted by the title of the article and the month and year of its publication.

IMAGE, OBJECT, AND ILLUSION

INTRODUCTION

Disentangling mental images from actual objects in the world has pre-occupied natural philosophers from their earliest writings to the present. Most commentators agree that unless the perceived image has some clearcut relation to what is in the world we would be subject to dangerous deception. Yet, each of us is familiar with optical or other sense illusions; and we may even believe that although they deceive us about the world, at the same time they reveal truths about the working of our minds. If we accept this paradox, then what is the relation between image and object? What is the significance of illusions of the senses? The articles in this collection present a variety of modern approaches to the question posed in a context of scientific inquiry.

Obviously, there can be nothing problematic about the relation between the object and its image in the mind until we seek to identify the two with each other according to specific and immutable characteristics. The revolution in science that began in the seventeenth century has provided precise accounts of the properties of certain objects and events of the physical world. An example of this physical specification was Johannes Kepler's influential account of the formation of the optical image by a lens (discussed in the article of Neisser entitled "The Processes of Vision"). By showing how light reflected from an object forms an image on the retina of the observer's eye, Kepler provided a model for relating objects to their sensed images. The retinal image is essentially a point-for-point copy of the object although it is inverted because of the manner in which the light rays cross in their passage through the lens system of the eye (see the diagram by Descartes, p. 10). As Neisser points out, it is easy to assume that the mental image is, in turn, a similar copy of the retinal image, reinverted so that its orientation is the same as that of the object. This copy theory dominated theories of perception until recent times. As a consequence, writers on the senses assumed that specific local (punctate) properties of the percept could always be identified with their corresponding loci on the object.

Consider an example of the above reasoning. Assume that there are two identical red rectangular objects equally distant from the observer (such as are seen in Gregory's railway track figure, p. 51). Their perceived images might be expected to have identical corresponding properties. One might expect to see them as two rectangles of equal length, and if the amount of light reflected from each rectangle were the same, they might be expected to appear equal in hue. However, if it is not immediately apparent to the reader, a few minutes spent scanning the articles in this volume will convince him that changing only the surroundings of the rectangles may be enough to change their appearance both in size and color. Observations of this kind force us to acknowledge that we cannot assume that a simple correspondence obtains between the local properties of an object and those of an image.

The apparent color of an object depends in part upon the brightness of what surrounds it (as Ratliff and Wallach show in their articles); and its apparent size upon the arrangement of edges in its neighborhood (as Gregory shows). Recognition that one cannot identify properties of the image with simple corresponding properties of the object—or rather with the sensory stimulation originating at the object—leads to a search for those properties of stimulation which will produce the appropriate perception. As Neisser writes, "The first problem . . . is . . . the discovery of the stimulus." Accept this view and we are confronted with a challenging scientific problem, as yet without a general solution. The illusions can now be regarded as at least as important as "valid" images. When Purkinje, the renowned Czech physiologist of the nineteenth century, said, "Deceptions of the senses are the truths of perception," he meant that illusions call to our attention the workings of the visual system, whereas normal perception fails to do so. Following his own dictate, Purkinje discovered several important phenomena in vision that bear his name.

The workings of the visual system can be expressed as rules or laws relating properties of sense stimulation to percepts. The physiology underlying some of these rules has become known; for others it is still not understood. Once we recognize that the perceptual system has laws of its own the original problem is inverted. Instead of trying to find images in the mind which correspond to simple physical descriptions of aspects of the world, such as light intensity and wave length, measured distance, and motions, we must find ways of so partitioning the properties of the physical world as to yield measures which can be related to perceptual descriptions. The task of discovering the stimulus becomes, in effect, that of discovering how the stimulus influences the workings of the perceptual system.

The Processes of Vision

by Ulric Neisser
September 1968

Light enables us to see, but optical images on the retina are only the starting point of the complex activities of visual perception and visual memory

It was Johannes Kepler who first compared the eye to a "camera" (a darkened chamber) with an image in focus on its rear surface. "Vision is brought about by pictures of the thing seen being formed on the white concave surface of the retina," he wrote in 1604. A generation later René Descartes tried to clinch this argument by direct observation. In a hole in a window shutter he set the eye of an ox, just in the position it would have had if the ox had been peering out. Looking at the back of the eye (which he had scraped to make it transparent), he could see a small inverted image of the scene outside the window.

Since the 17th century the analogy between eye and camera has been elaborated in numerous textbooks. As an account of functional anatomy the analogy is not bad, but it carries some unfortunate implications for the study of vision. It suggests all too readily that the perceiver is in the position of Descartes and is in effect looking through the back of his own retina at the pictures that appear there. We use the same word—"image"—for both the optical pattern thrown on the retina by an object and the mental experience of seeing the object. It has been all too easy to treat this inner image as a copy of the outer one, to think of perceptual experiences as images formed by the nervous system acting as an optical instrument of extraordinarily ingenious design. Although this theory encounters insurmountable difficulties as soon as it is seriously considered, it has dominated philosophy and psychology for many years.

Not only perception but also memory has often been explained in terms of an image theory. Having looked at the retinal picture, the perceiver supposedly files it away somehow, as one might put a photograph in an album. Later, if he is lucky, he can take it out again in the form of a "memory image" and look at it a second time. The widespread notion that some people have a "photographic memory" reflects this analogy in a particularly literal way, but in a weaker form it is usually applied even to ordinary remembering. The analogy suggests that the mechanism of visual memory is a natural extension of the mechanisms of vision. Although there is some truth to this proposition, as we shall see below, it is not because both perception and memory are copying processes. Rather it is because *neither* perception *nor* memory is a copying process.

The fact is that one does not see the retinal image; one sees with the aid of the retinal image. The incoming pattern of light provides information that the nervous system is well adapted to pick up. This information is used by the perceiver to guide his movements, to anticipate events and to construct the internal representations of objects and of space called "conscious experience." These internal representations are not, however, at all like the corresponding optical images on the back of the eye. The retinal images of specific objects are at the mercy of every irrelevant change of position; their size, shape and location are hardly constant for a moment. Nevertheless, perception is usually accurate: real objects appear rigid and stable and appropriately located in three-dimensional space.

The first problem in the study of visual perception is therefore the discovery of the stimulus. What properties of the incoming optic array are informative for vision? In the entire distribution of light, over the retina and over a period of time, what determines the way things look? (Actually the light is distributed over two retinas, but the binocularity of vision has no relevance to the variables considered here. Although depth perception is more accurate with two eyes than with one, it is not fundamentally different. The world looks much the same with one eye closed as it does with both open; congenitally monocular people have more or less the same visual experiences as the rest of us.)

As a first step we can consider the patterns of reflected light that are formed when real objects and surfaces are illuminated in the ordinary way by

PERCEPTION OF SIZE relies heavily on cues provided by a textured surface. These five disks, if seen alone, would appear to lie

sunshine or lamplight. J. J. Gibson of Cornell University, who has contributed much to our understanding of perception, calls this inquiry "ecological optics." It is an optics in which point sources, homogeneous fields and the other basic elements of classical optics rarely appear. Instead the world we ordinarily look at consists mostly of *surfaces*, at various angles and in various relations to one another. This has significant consequences for the visual input.

One of these consequences (the only one we shall examine here) is to give the visual field a microstructure. Most surfaces have some kind of texture, such as the grain in wood, the individual stalks of grass in a field or the weave in a fabric. These textures structure the light reaching the eye in a way that carries vital information about the layout of environmental objects. In accordance with the principles of perspective the texture elements of more distant surfaces are represented closer to one another on the retina than the elements of surfaces nearby. Thus the microstructure of a surface that slants away from the observer is represented on the retina as a gradient of density—a gradient that carries information about the orientation of the surface.

Consider now an ordinary scene in which discrete figures are superposed on textured surfaces. The gradient of increasing texture density on the retina, corresponding to increasing distance from the observer, gives a kind of "scale" for object sizes. In the ideal case when the texture units are identical, two figures of the same real size will always occlude the same number of texture units, regardless of how far away either one may be. That is, the relation between the retinal texture-size and the dimensions of the object's retinal image is invariant, in spite of changes of distance. This relation is a potentially valuable source of information about the real size of the object—more valuable than the retinal image of the object considered alone. That image, of course, changes in dimension whenever the distance between the object and the observer is altered.

Psychologists have long been interested in what is called "size constancy": the fact that the sizes of real objects are almost always perceived accurately in spite of the linear dependence of retinal-image size on distance. It must not be supposed that this phenomenon is fully explained by the scaling of size with respect to texture elements. There are a great many other sources of relevant information: binocular parallax, shifts of retinal position as the observer moves, relative position in the visual field, linear perspective and so on. It was once traditional to regard these sources of information as "cues" secondary to the size of the object's own retinal image. That is, they were thought to help the observer "correct" the size of the retinal image in the direction of accuracy. Perhaps this is not a bad description of Descartes's situation as he looked at the image on the back of the ox's eye: he may have tried to "correct" his perception of the size of the objects revealed to him on the ox's retina. Since one does not see one's own retina, however, nothing similar need be involved in normal perceiving. Instead the apparent size of an object is determined by information from the entire incoming light pattern, particularly by certain properties of the input that remain invariant with changes of the object's location.

The interrelation of textures, distances and relative retinal sizes is only one example of ecological optics. The example may be a misleadingly simple one, because it assumes a stationary eye, an eye fixed in space and stably oriented in a particular direction. This is by no means a characteristic of human vision. In normal use the eyes are rarely still for long. Apart from small tremors, their

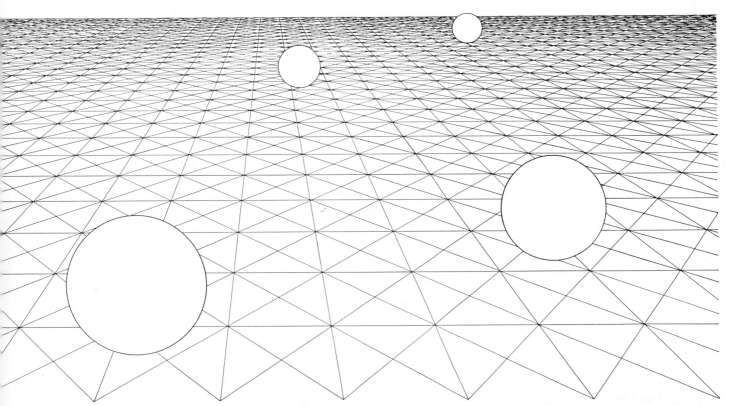

in one plane and be of different sizes. Against this apparently receding surface, however, they seem to lie in five different planes. Since each disk masks the same amount of surface texture, there is a tendency to see them as being equal in size. This illustration, the one at the bottom of the next two pages and the one on page 8 are based on the work of J. J. Gibson of Cornell University.

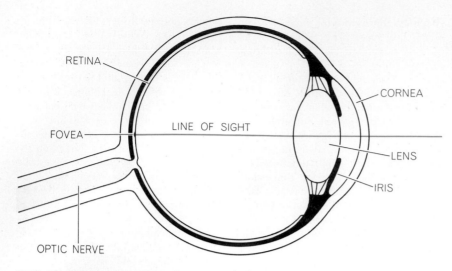

RETINA

FOVEA

LINE OF SIGHT

CORNEA

LENS

IRIS

OPTIC NERVE

SITE OF OPTICAL IMAGE is the retina, which contains the terminations of the optic nerve. In the tiny retinal depression known as the fovea the cone nerve endings are clustered. Their organization and dense packing make possible a high degree of visual acuity.

most common movement is the flick from one position to another called a "saccade." Saccades usually take less than a twentieth of a second, but they happen several times each second in reading and may be just as frequent when a picture or an actual scene is being inspected. This means that there is a new retinal image every few hundred milliseconds.

Such eye movements are necessary because the area of clear vision available to the stationary eye is severely limited. To see this for oneself it is only necessary to fixate on a point in some unfamiliar picture or on an unread printed page. Only a small region around the fixation point will be clear. Most of the page is seen peripherally, which means that it is hazily visible at best. Only in the fovea, the small central part of the retina, are the receptor cells packed close enough together (and appropriately organized) to make a high degree of visual acuity possible. This is the reason one must turn one's eyes (or head) to look directly at objects in which one is particularly interested. (Animals with non-foveated eyes, such as the horse, do not find this necessary.) It is also the reason why the eye must make several fixations on each line in reading, and why it roves widely over pictures.

Although it is easy to understand the function of saccadic movements, it is difficult or impossible to reconcile them with an image theory of perception. As long as we think of the perceiver as a homunculus looking at his retinal image, we must expect his experience to be one of almost constant interruption and change. Clearly this is not the case; one sees the page or the scene as a whole without any apparent discontinuity in

space or time. Most people are either unaware of their own eye movements or have erroneous notions about them. Far from being a copy of the retinal display, the visual world is somehow *constructed* on the basis of information taken in during many different fixations.

The same conclusion follows, perhaps even more compellingly, if we consider the motions of external objects rather than the motions of the eyes. If the analogy between eye and camera were valid, the thing one looked at would have to hold still like a photographer's model in order to be seen clearly. The opposite is true: far from obscuring the shapes and spatial relations of things, movement generally clarifies them. Consider the visual problem presented by a distant arrow-shaped weather vane. As long as the weather vane and the observer remain motionless, there is no way to tell whether it is a short arrow oriented at right angles to the line of sight or a longer arrow slanting toward (or away from) the observer. Let it begin to turn in the wind, however, and its true shape and orientation will become visible immediately. The reason lies in the systematic distortions of the retinal image produced by the object's rotation. Such distortions provide information that the nervous system can use. On the basis of a fluidly changing retinal pattern the perceiver comes to experience a rigid object. (An interesting aspect of this example is that the input information is ambiguous. The same retinal changes could be produced by either a clockwise or a counterclockwise rotation of the weather vane. As a result the perceiver may alternate between two perceptual experiences, one of which is illusory.)

Some years ago Hans Wallach and D. N. O'Connell of Swarthmore College showed that such motion-produced changes in the input are indeed used as a source of information in perceiving; in fact this kind of information seems to be a more potent determiner of what we see than the traditionally emphasized cues for depth are. In their experiment the subject watched the shadow of a wire form cast on a translucent screen. He could not see the object itself. So long as the object remained stationary the subject saw only a two-dimensional shadow on a two-dimensional screen, as might be expected. The form was mounted in such a way, however, that it could be swiveled back and forth by a small electric motor. When the motor was turned on, the true three-dimensional shape of the form appeared at once, even though the only stimulation reaching the subject's eyes came from a distorting shadow on a flat screen. Here the kinetic depth effect, as it has been called, overrode binocular stereoscopic information that continued to indicate that all the movement was taking place in a flat plane.

In the kinetic depth effect the constructive nature of perception is particularly apparent. What one sees is somehow a composite based on information accumulated over a period of time. The same is true in reading or in any instance where eye movements are involved: information from past fixations is used together with information from the present fixation to determine what is seen. But if perception is a temporally extended act, some storage of information, some kind of memory, must be involved in it. How shall we conceive of this storage? How is it organized? How

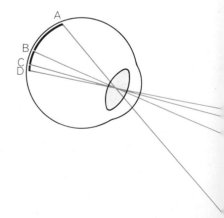

A
B
C
D

CONTRACTION OF IMAGE takes place as the distance between the viewer and the long does it last? What other functions might it serve?

With questions like these, we have moved beyond the problem of specifying the visual stimulus. In addition to identifying the sources of information for vision, we want to know how that information is processed. In the long run, perhaps, questions about processes should be answered in neurological terms. However, no such answers can be given at present. The neurophysiology of vision has recently made great strides, but it is still not ready to deal with the constructive processes that are central to perception. We shall have to be content with a relatively abstract account, one that does not specify the neural locus of the implicated mechanisms.

Although seeing requires storage of information, this memory cannot be thought of as a sequence of superposed retinal images. Superposition would give rise only to a sort of smear in which all detail is lost. Nor can we assume that the perceiver keeps careful track of his eye movements and thus is able to set each new retinal image in just the right place in relation to the older stored ones. Such an alignment would require a much finer monitoring of eye motion than is actually available. Moreover, the similar synthesis of information that is involved in the kinetic depth effect could not possibly be explained that way. It seems, therefore, that perceiving involves a memory that is not representational but schematic. During a series of fixations the perceiver synthesizes a model or schema of the scene before him, using information from each successive fixation to add detail or to extend the construction. This constructed whole is what guides his

movements (including further eye movements in many cases) and it is what he describes when he is being introspective. In short, it is what he sees.

Interestingly enough, although the memory involved in visual synthesis cannot consist simply of stored retinal afterimages, recent experiments indicate that storage of this kind does exist under certain circumstances. After a momentary exposure (too short for eye movement) that is followed by a blank field the viewer preserves an iconic image of the input pattern for some fraction of a second. George Sperling of the Bell Telephone Laboratories has shown that a signal given during this postexposure period can serve to direct a viewer's attention to any arbitrary part of the field, just as if it were still present.

The displays used in Sperling's experiments consisted of several rows of letters—too many to be reported from a single glance. Nevertheless, subjects were able to report any *single row*, indicated by the postexposure signal, rather well. Such a signal must come quickly; letters to which the observer does not attend before the brief iconic memory has faded are lost. That is why the observer cannot report the entire display: the icon disappears before he can read it all.

Even under these unusual conditions, then, people display selectivity in their use of the information that reaches the eye. The selection is made from material presented in a single brief exposure, but only because the experimental arrangements precluded a second glance. Normally selection and construction take place over a series of glances; no iconic memory for individual "snapshots" can survive. Indeed, the presentation of a

second stimulus figure shortly after the first in a brief-exposure experiment tends to destroy the iconic replica. The viewer may see a fusion of the two figures, only the second, or an apparent motion of the figures, depending on their temporal and spatial relations. He does not see them separately.

So far we have considered two kinds of short-term memory for visual information: the iconic replica of a brief and isolated stimulus, and the cumulative schema of the visible world that is constructed in the course of ordinary perception. Both of these processes (which may well be different manifestations of a single underlying mechanism) involve the storage of information over a period of time. Neither of them, however, is what the average man has in mind when he speaks of memory. Everyday experience testifies that visual information can be stored over long periods. Things seen yesterday can be recalled today; for that matter they may conceivably be recalled 20 years from now. Such recall may take many forms, but perhaps the most interesting is the phenomenon called visual imagery. In a certain sense one can see again what one has seen before. Are these mental images like optical ones? Are they revived copies of earlier stimulation? Indeed, does it make any sense at all to speak of "seeing" things that are not present? Can there be visual experience when there is no stimulation by light?

To deal with these problems effectively we must distinguish two issues: first, the degree to which the mechanisms involved in visual memory are like those involved in visual perception and, second, the degree to which the perceiver

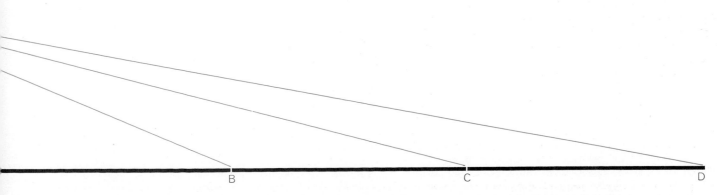

object in view increases. The texture elements of a distant surface are also projected closer together than similar elements nearby. Thus a textured surface slanting away from the viewer is represented optically as a density gradient (*see illustration on next page*).

is willing to say his images look real, that is, like external things seen. Although the first issue is perhaps the more fundamental—and the most relevant here—the second has always attracted the most attention.

One reason for the perennial interest in the "realness" of images is the wide range of differences in imaging capacity from person to person and from time to time. When Francis Galton conducted the first empirical study of mental im-

agery (published in 1883), he found some of his associates skeptical of the very existence of imagery. They assumed that only poetic fancy allowed one to speak of "seeing" in connection with what one remembered; remembering consisted simply in a knowledge of facts. Other people, however, were quite ready to describe their mental imagery in terms normally applied to perception. Asked in the afternoon about their breakfast table, they said they could see it clearly, with

colors bright (although perhaps a little dimmer than in the original experience) and objects suitably arranged.

These differences seem to matter less when one is asleep; many people who report little or no lifelike imagery while awake may have visual dreams and believe in the reality of what they see. On the other hand, some psychopathological states can endow images with such a compelling quality that they dominate the patient's experience. Students of per-

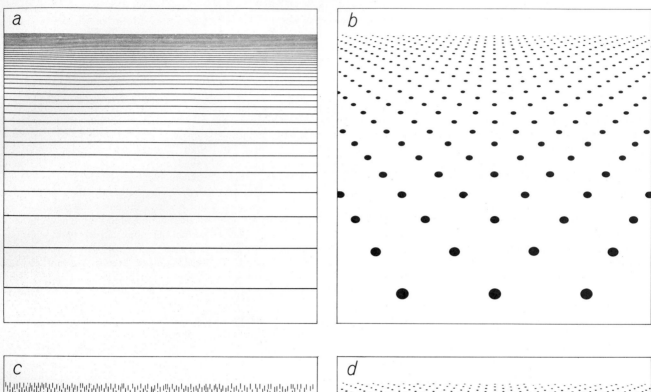

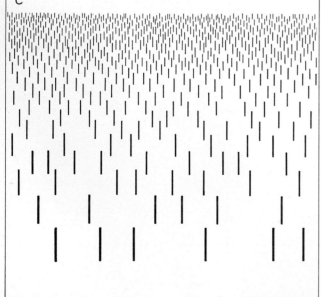
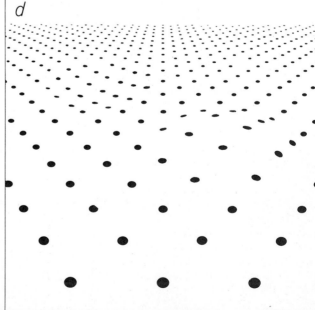

DENSITY GRADIENTS convey an impression of depth. Depending on the size, shape and spacing of its textural elements, the gradient may create the impression of a smooth flat surface (*a, b*), a rough flat surface (*c*) or a surface broken by an elevation and a depression (*d*). Like the gradients depicted, the textured surfaces of the visual world (by structuring the light that falls on the retina) convey information concerning the orientation of the surface. Textured surfaces also provide a scale for gauging the size of objects.

cception have often disregarded dreams and phantasms, considering them "hallucinatory" and thus irrelevant to normal seeing. However, this is a difficult position to defend either logically or empirically. Logically a sharp distinction between perception and hallucination would be easy enough if perceptions were copies of the retinal image; hallucinations would then be experiences that do *not* copy that image. But since perception does more than mirror the stimulus (and since hallucinations often incorporate stimulus information), this distinction is not clear-cut. Moreover, a number of recent findings seem to point up very specific relations between the processes of seeing and of imagining.

Perhaps the most unexpected of these findings has emerged from studies of sleep and dreams. The dreaming phase of sleep, which occurs several times each night, is regularly accompanied by bursts of rapid eye movements. In several studies William C. Dement and his collaborators have awakened experimental subjects immediately after a period of eye motion and asked them to report their just-preceding dream. Later the eye-movement records were compared with a transcript of the dream report to see if any relation between the two could be detected. Of course this was not possible in every case. (Indeed, we can be fairly sure that many of the eye movements of sleep have no visual significance; similar motions occur in the sleep of newborn babies, decorticated cats and congenitally blind adults.) Nevertheless, there was appreciably more correspondence between the two kinds of record than could be attributed to chance. The parallel between the eye movements of the dreamer and the content of the dream was sometimes striking. In one case five distinct upward deflections of the eyes were recorded just before the subject awoke and reported a dream of climbing five steps!

Another recent line of research has also implicated eye movements in the processes of visual memory. Ralph Norman Haber and his co-workers at Yale University reopened the study of eidetic imagery, which for a generation had remained untouched by psychological research. An eidetic image is an imaginative production that seems to be external to the viewer and to have a location in perceived space; it has a clarity comparable to that of genuinely perceived objects; it can be examined by the "*Eidetiker*," who may report details that he did not notice in the original presentation of the stimulus. Most *Eidetikers*

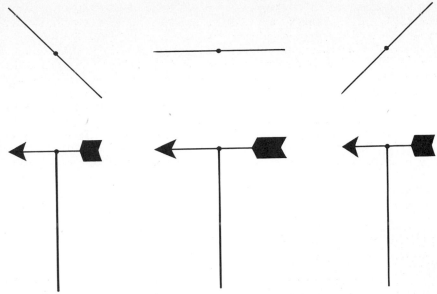

AMBIGUOUS VISUAL INPUT can arise from a stationary weather vane. The weather vane in three different orientations is shown as it would be seen from above (*top*) and in side view (*bottom*). If the vane begins to rotate, its real length will become apparent.

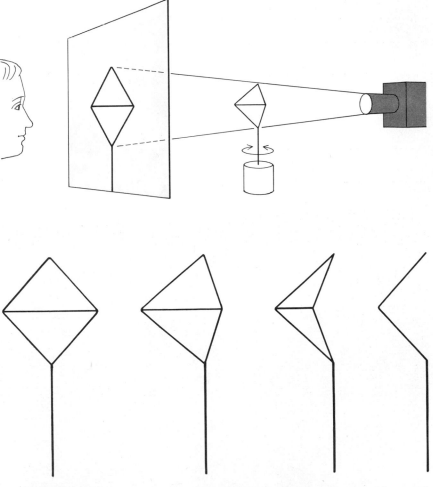

KINETIC DEPTH EFFECT shows how movement can endow perceived objects with three-dimensional shape. The shadow of a bent wire form (*shown at bottom in four different orientations*) looks as flat as the screen on which it is cast so long as the form remains stationary. When it is swiveled back and forth, the changing shadow is seen as a rigid rotating object with the appropriate three-dimensionality. The direction of rotation remains ambiguous, as in the case of the weather vane in the illustration at top of the page.

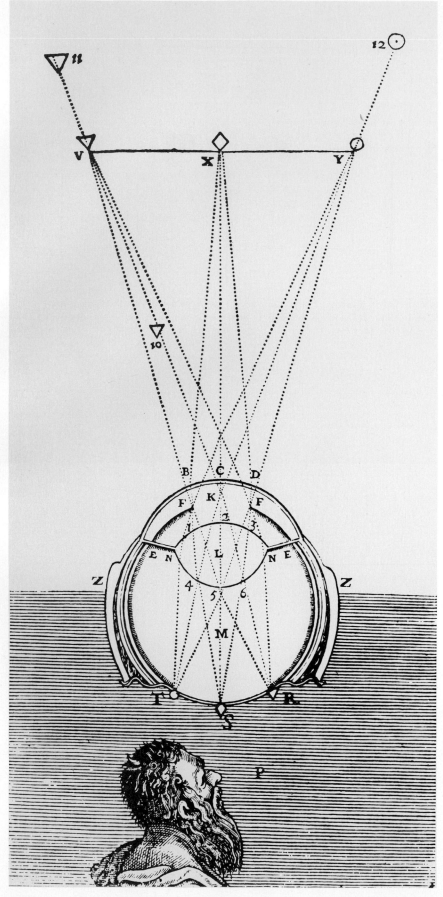

OPTICAL ANALYSIS BY DESCARTES included an experiment in which he removed the eye of an ox, scraped the back of the eye to make it transparent and observed on the retina the inverted image of a scene. The illustration is from Descartes's essay *La Dioptrique*.

are children, but the developmental course of this rather rare ability is not well understood. What is most interesting about these images for the present argument is that the *Eidetiker* scans them with his eyes. Asked about a detail in one or another corner of the image, he moves his eyes to look at the appropriate part of the blank wall on which he has "projected" it. That is, he does just what anyone would do who was really looking at something.

Are these esoteric phenomena really relevant to the study of vision? It might be argued that they do not provide a safe basis for inference; dreaming is a very special physiological state and eidetic imagery is restricted to very special types of people. It is not difficult, however, to show that similar processes occur in persons who do not have vivid visual imagery at all. A simple demonstration suggested by Julian Hochberg of New York University helps to make this point: Try to remember how many windows there are in your own house or apartment.

If you have never considered this question before, it will be hard to find the answer without actively looking and counting. However, you will probably not need to look at the windows themselves. Most people, even those who say they have no visual imagery, can easily form and scan an *internal representation* of the walls, counting off the windows as they appear in them. This process evidently uses stored visual information. It seems to involve mechanisms much like those used for seeing and counting real windows.

We can draw three conclusions from this demonstration. First, seeing and imagining employ similar—perhaps the same—mechanisms. Second, images can be useful, even when they are not vivid or lifelike, even for people who do not have "good imagery." Third, mental images are constructs and not copies. This last point may have been obvious in any case—you might just as well have been asked to imagine a gryphon and to count its claws—but it bears further emphasis. All the windows could not have been optically imaged on the retina simultaneously, and they may not even have appeared there in rapid succession. The image (or series of images) developed in solving this problem is new; it is not a replica of any previous stimulus.

The first two of these points have received additional confirmation in a recent experiment by Lee R. Brooks of McMaster University, whose method puts imagery and visual perception in direct competition. In one of his studies the subjects were shown a large block *F* and told to remember what it looked like. After the *F* was removed from view they were asked to describe the succession of corner points that would be encountered as one moved around it, responding "Yes" for each point that was either on the extreme top or the bottom of the *F*, and "No" for each point in between. This visual-memory task proved to be more difficult when the responses were made by *pointing* to a printed series of yeses and noes than when a spoken "Yes" or "No" was allowed. However, the difficulty was not intrinsic to the act of pointing; it resulted from the conflict between pointing and simultaneously visualizing the *F*. In another of Brooks's tasks the subjects had to respond "Yes" for each noun and "No" for each non-noun in a memorized sentence.

In this case they tended to rely on verbal-auditory memory rather than visual memory. As a result spoken response was the more difficult of the two.

We would not have been surprised to find a conflict between visually guided pointing and corner-counting on an *F* the viewer was *looking at*. After all, he could not be expected to look in two places at once. Even if the *F* had appeared on the same sheet of paper with the yeses and noes, interference would have been easy to understand: the succession of glances required to examine the corners of the *F* would have conflicted with the visual organization needed to point at the right succession of responses. What Brooks has shown, rather surprisingly, is that this conflict exists even when the *F* is merely imagined. Visual images are apparently produced by the same integrative processes that

make ordinary perception possible.

In short, the reaction of the nervous system to stimulation by light is far from passive. The eye and brain do not act as a camera or a recording instrument. Neither in perceiving nor in remembering is there any enduring copy of the optical input. In perceiving, complex patterns are extracted from that input and fed into the constructive processes of vision, so that the movements and the inner experience of the perceiver are usually in good correspondence with his environment. Visual memory differs from perception because it is based primarily on stored rather than on current information, but it involves the same kind of synthesis. Although the eyes have been called the windows of the soul, they are not so much peepholes as entry ports, supplying raw material for the constructive activity of the visual system.

COLOR AND CONTRAST

I

COLOR AND CONTRAST I

INTRODUCTION

An object is visible if it either reflects or emits an amount of light that differs from that of its surroundings. The difference defines the borders of the object. The most primitive property of an image is its boundedness, and since we cannot conceive of a visible entity without boundaries, the formation of a boundary, or edge, from the light-defined border is the all-important beginning of the process of defining an image.

In accord with the old image-copy theory, we might suppose that an image will appear brighter or dimmer than its surroundings in proportion to the difference in amount of light received at the eye from these sources. Moreover, the image ought to have an edge at, and only at, the places where there is a corresponding border of the object which produces a sharp gradient in the distribution of light energy on the retina. However, neither of these suppositions is necessarily true. Dark and bright strips—called Mach bands, after their discoverer, and discussed at length by Ratliff—appear in places in the image which do not exactly correspond with gradients of light energy. Areas having different luminances may appear with the same brightness: the so-called contrast phenomenon discussed extensively by Wallach. As Ratliff's beautiful examples show, a region which is actually dimmer than an adjacent surround may nevertheless appear brighter.

In further contradiction of the copy theory, Fabio Metelli in his article, "The Perception of Transparency," gives examples which show that a single region of color may be perceived as divided into two overlapping objects. These examples of perceived transparency present us with the paradox that unlike two objects, two images may occupy the same place at the same time.

A plausible physiological account of the existence of Mach bands can be given in terms of lateral inhibition (see Ratliff's article). A similar process may underlie the contrast effects described by Wallach. Metelli's transparency phenomena, however, require an explanation in which the extraction of contour and its organization into form precedes the operation on color. This requires a considerably more complex physiological model.

Contour and Contrast

by Floyd Ratliff
June 1972

We see contours when adjacent areas contrast sharply. Surprisingly, certain contours, in turn, make large areas appear lighter or darker than they really are. What neural mechanisms underlie these effects?

Contours are so dominant in our visual perception that when we draw an object, it is almost instinctive for us to begin by sketching its outlines. The use of a line to depict a contour may well have been one of the earliest developments in art, as exemplified by the "line drawings" in the pictographs and petroglyphs of prehistoric artists. We see contours when there is a contrast, or difference, in the brightness or color between adjacent areas. How contrast creates contours has been thoroughly studied by both scientists and artists. How the contour itself can affect the contrast of the areas it separates has been known to artists for at least 1,000 years, but it is relatively new as a subject of scientific investigation. Although the psychophysiological basis of how contrast enables the visual system to distinguish contours has been studied for the past century, it is only in the past few years that psychologists and physiologists have started to examine systematically the influence of contour on contrast.

You can readily observe how the visual system tends to abstract and accentuate contours in patterns of varying contrast by paying close attention to the edges of a shadow cast by an object in strong sunlight. Stand with your back to the sun and look closely at the shadow of your head and shoulders on a sidewalk. You will see a narrow half-shadow between the full shadow and the full sunlight. Objectively the illumination in the full shadow is uniformly low, in the half-shadow it is more or less uniformly graded and in the full sunlight it is uniformly high; within each area there are no sharp maxima or minima. Yet you will see a narrow dark band at the dark edge of the half-shadow and a narrow bright band at its bright edge. You can enhance the effect by swaying from side to side to produce a moving shadow.

These dark and bright strips, now known as Mach bands, were first reported in the scientific literature some 100 years ago by the Austrian physicist, philosopher and psychologist Ernst Mach. They depend strictly on the distribution of the illumination. Mach formulated a simple principle for the effect: "Whenever the light-intensity curve of an illuminated surface (whose light intensity varies in only one direction) has a concave or convex flection with respect to the abscissa, that place appears brighter or darker, respectively, than its surroundings" [*see bottom illustration on next page*].

The basic effect can be demonstrated by holding an opaque card under an ordinary fluorescent desk lamp, preferably in a dark room. If the shadow is cast on a piece of paper, part of the paper is illuminated by light from the full length of the lamp. Next to the illuminated area is a half-shadow that gets progressively darker until a full shadow is reached. Ideally the distribution of light should be uniformly high in the bright area, uniformly low in the dark area and smoothly graded between the bright and the dark areas [*see top illustration on next page*]. If you now look closely at the edges of the graded half-shadow, you see a narrow bright band at the bright edge and a narrow dark band at the dark edge. These are the Mach bands. Their appearance is so striking that many people will not believe at first that they are only a subjective phenomenon. Some will mistakenly try to explain the appearance of the bands by saying they are the result of multiple shadows or diffraction.

Exact psychophysical measurements of the subjective appearance of Mach bands have been made by Adriana Fiorentini and her colleagues at the National Institute of Optics in Italy. Their technique consists in having an observer adjust an independently variable spot of light to match the brightness of areas in and around the Mach bands. In general they find that the bright band is distinctly narrower and more pronounced than the dark band. The magnitude of the effect, however, varies considerably from person to person.

Since Mach bands delineate contours we expect to see, only a careful observer, or someone who has reason to objectively measure the light distribution at a shadow's edge, is likely to realize that the bands are a caricature of the actual pattern of illumination. Artists of the 19th-century Neo-Impressionist school were unusually meticulous in their observations, and this was reflected in much of their work. A good example is Paul Signac's "Le petit déjeuner." In this painting there are numerous contrast effects in and around the shadows and half-shadows. Particularly striking is how some of the shadows are darkest near their edges and quite light near

NEO-IMPRESSIONIST PAINTER Paul Signac was a meticulous observer of the contrast effects in shadows and half-shadows. On the opposite page is a portion of his "Le petit déjeuner" (1886–1887). Note how the shadow is darker near the unshaded tablecloth and lighter next to the dark matchbox. Similar effects can be found in other shadows. The effects change when the painting is viewed from various distances. The painting is in the Rijksmuseum Kröller-Müller at Otterlo in the Netherlands and is reproduced with its permission.

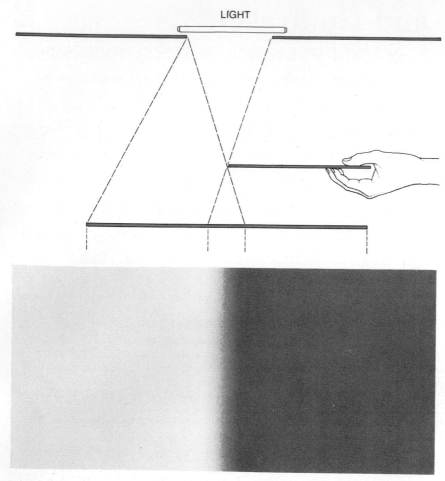

LIGHT

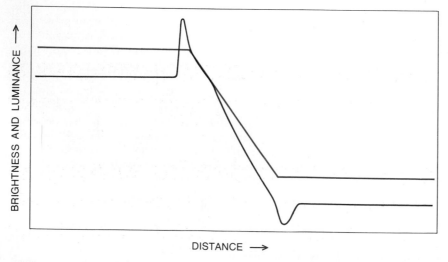

MACH BANDS can be produced with light from an ordinary fluorescent desk lamp (*upper illustration*). Place a sheet of white or gray paper on the desk and the light about a foot or so above it. Covering the ends of the lamp, which usually are not uniformly bright, may enhance the effect. Turn out the other lights in the room and hold an opaque card an inch or less above the paper. Various positions should be tried for optimum results. Note the narrow bright line and the broader dark line at the outer and inner edges of the half-shadow; these are the Mach bands. The lower illustration is a photograph of a half-shadow produced by the method described. The reproduction of the photograph does not retain all the characteristics of the original because of losses inherent in the reproduction process.

OBSERVED BRIGHTNESS CURVE obtained by psychophysical measurements (*black line*) has two sharp flections, one corresponding to the bright band and the other to the dark band. Measurement of actual luminance (*colored line*) across a half-shadow region reveals that the effect lies in the eye of the beholder and is not an objective phenomenon.

the object casting the shadow. Where Signac saw contrast he painted contrast, whether it was objectively present in the original scene or not. The effects we see in his painting depend of course partly on what Signac painted and partly on how our own eyes respond to contrast. When we view Signac's painting, our own eyes and brain further exaggerate the contrast he painted. As a result the painting appears to have even more contrast than the original scene could have had.

Without precise physical and psychophysical measurements it is difficult to tell how much of the contrast we perceive is objective and how much is subjective. Adding to the confusion is the fact that the subjective Mach bands can seemingly be photographed. All the photograph does, however, is to reproduce with considerable fidelity the original distribution of light in a scene, and it is this distribution of light and dark that gives rise to the subjective Mach bands. Moreover, the photographic process can itself introduce a spurious enhancement of contrast. Edge effects that closely resemble Mach bands can arise as the film is developed. Unlike Mach bands, they are an objective phenomenon consisting of actual variations in the density of the film, and the variations can be objectively measured.

On many occasions scientific investigators have mistaken Mach bands for objective phenomena. For example, shortly after W. K. Röntgen discovered X rays several workers attempted to measure the wavelength of the rays by passing them through ordinary diffraction slits and gratings and recording the resulting pattern on film. Several apparently succeeded in producing diffraction patterns of dark and light bands from which they could determine the wavelength of the X rays. All, however, was in error. As two Dutch physicists, H. Haga and C. H. Wind, showed later, the supposed diffraction patterns were subjective Mach bands.

As early as 1865 Mach proposed an explanation of the subjective band effect and other contrast phenomena in terms of opposed excitatory and inhibitory influences in neural networks in the retina and the brain. The means for direct investigation of such neural mechanisms did not become available, however, until the 1920's, when E. D. Adrian, Y. Zotterman and Detlev W. Bronk, working at the University of Cambridge, developed methods for recording the electrical activity of single nerve cells. The basic excitatory-inhibitory principle

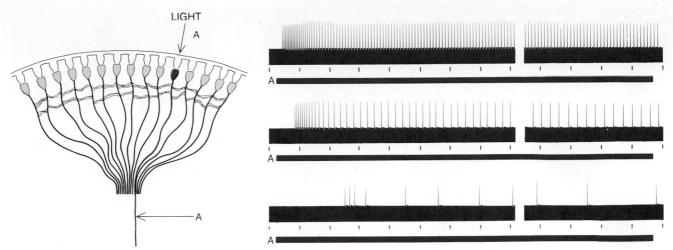

RATE OF DISCHARGE of nerve impulses produced by steady illumination of a single receptor, A, in the eye of the horseshoe crab *Limulus* is directly related to the intensity of the light. The nerve fibers from the receptor are separated by microdissection and connected to an electrode from an amplifier and a recorder.

The top record shows the response of A to steady, high-intensity light. The middle record shows the response to light of moderate intensity, and the lower record the response to low-intensity illumination. Duration of the light signal is indicated by the colored bar. Each mark above the colored bar indicates one-fifth of a second.

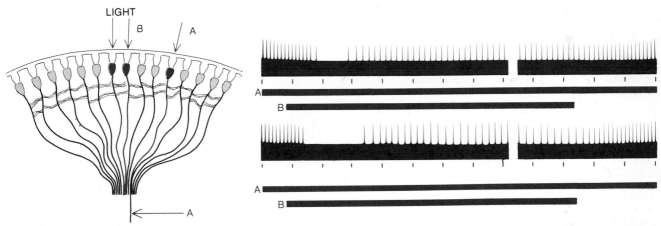

INHIBITION of receptor, A, steadily exposed to moderate illumination is produced when neighboring receptors, B, are also illuminated. The beginning and the end of the records show the initial and final rate of impulses by A. The colored bars indicate duration of light signals. The upper record shows the effects on A of moderate-intensity illumination of B. The lower record shows the effect on A of high-intensity illumination of B. The stronger the illumination on neighboring receptors, the stronger the inhibitory effect.

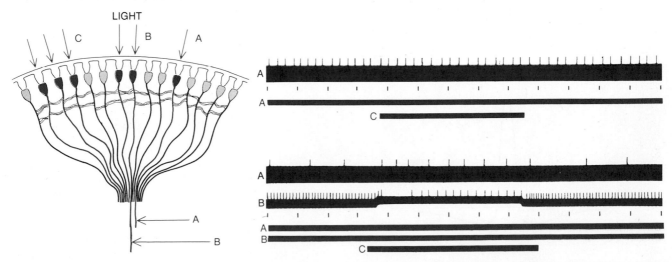

DISINHIBITION of receptor A occurs when the inhibition exerted on it by the B receptors is partially released by illuminating the large area C. The upper record shows that A's activity is not affected when C also is illuminated because of the distance between them. The first part of the lower record shows the inhibitory effect of B on A, then the inhibition of B when C is illuminated and the concomitant disinhibition of A. When the illumination of C stops, B returns to a higher rate of activity and resumes its inhibition of A.

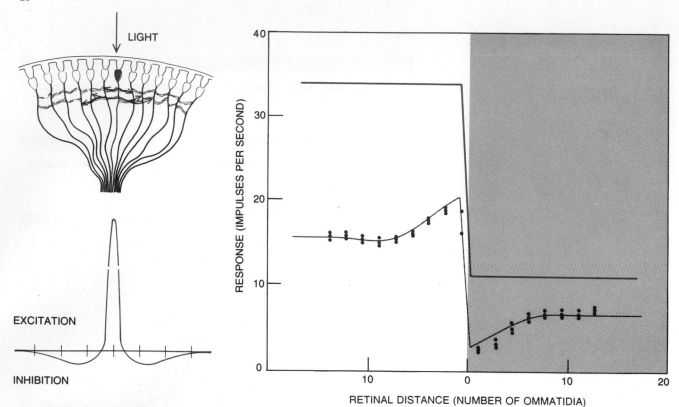

LIGHT

EXCITATION

INHIBITION

RESPONSE (IMPULSES PER SECOND)

40

30

20

10

0

10   0   10   20

RETINAL DISTANCE (NUMBER OF OMMATIDIA)

LATERAL INHIBITION in the eye of the horseshoe crab is strongest between receptors a short distance apart and grows weaker as the distance between receptors increases. Below the eye section is a graph of the type of excitatory and inhibitory fields that would be produced by the illumination of a single receptor. The colored line in the graph on the right shows what the retinal response would be to a sharp light-to-dark contour if lateral inhibition did not occur. The points on the graph show responses actually elicited by three scans of the pattern across the receptor in an experiment by Robert B. Barlow, Jr., of Syracuse University. The thin line shows the theoretical responses for lateral inhibition as computed by Donald A. Quarles, Jr., of the IBM Watson Research Center.

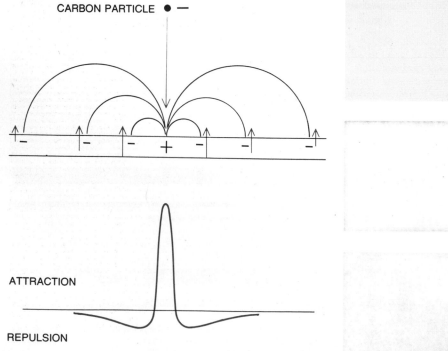

CARBON PARTICLE ● ─

− − − + − − −

ATTRACTION

REPULSION

EDGE EFFECT in xerographic copying is the result of the shape of the electrostatic field (which is quite similar to that of the "neural" field in the top illustration) around a single charged point on the xerographic plate (*upper left*). The first panel on the right shows the original pattern. The middle panel shows a Xerox copy of the original. Note how contrast at the edges is greatly enhanced. The bottom panel shows a Xerox copy made with a halftone screen placed over the original so that the pattern is broken up into many dots.

has been demonstrated to be essentially correct in experiments that H. K. Hartline and I, together with our colleagues, have carried out over the past 20 years.

We measured the responses of single neurons in the compound lateral eye of the horseshoe crab *Limulus*. (The animal also has two simple eyes in the front of its carapace near the midline.) The lateral eye of the horseshoe crab is comparatively large (about a centimeter in length) but otherwise it is much like the eye of a fly or a bee. It consists of about 1,000 ommatidia (literally "little eyes"), each of which appears to function as a single photoreceptor unit. Excitation does not spread from one receptor to another; it is confined to whatever receptor unit is illuminated. Nerve fibers arise from the receptors in small bundles that come together to form the optic nerve. Just behind the photoreceptors the small nerve bundles are interconnected by a network of nerve fibers. This network, or plexus, is a true retina even though its function is almost purely inhibitory.

Both the local excitatory and the extended inhibitory influences can be observed directly. A small bundle of fibers from a single receptor is separated by microdissection from the main trunk of the optic nerve and placed on an electrode. In this way the nerve impulses generated by light striking the receptor can be recorded. Weak stimulation produces a low rate of discharge; strong stimulation produces a high rate. These responses are typical of many simple sense organs.

In addition to the excitatory discharge there is a concomitant inhibitory effect. When a receptor unit fires, it inhibits its neighbors. This is a mutual effect: each unit inhibits others and in turn is inhibited by them. The strength of the inhibition depends on the level of activity of the interacting units and the distance between them. In general near neighbors affect one another more than distant neighbors, and the stronger the illumination, the stronger the inhibitory effect. We discovered that such an organization can produce a second-order effect that we call disinhibition. If two sets of receptors are close enough together to interact, they inhibit each other when both sets are illuminated. Now suppose a third set of receptors, far enough away so that it can interact with only one of the two sets of receptors, is illuminated. The activity of the third set will inhibit one set of the original pair, which in turn reduces the inhibition on

FILTER produced by lateral inhibition at low spatial frequencies and the lack of resolving power of the retina at high spatial frequencies causes intermediate spatial frequencies to be the most distinctly seen. The width of the vertical dark and light bands decreases in a logarithmic sinusoidal manner from the left to the right; the contrast varies logarithmically from less than 1 percent at the top to about 30 percent at the bottom. The objective contrast at any one height in the figure is the same for all spatial frequencies, yet the spatial frequencies in the middle appear more distinct than those at high or low frequencies; that is, the dark lines appear taller at the center of the figure. The effects of changes in viewing distance, luminance, adaptation and sharpness of eye focus can be demonstrated by the viewer.

MACH BAND PHENOMENON created with horizontal lines is shown here. In the illustration at left the black lines are a constant thickness from the left side to the midpoint and then thicken gradually. When the illustration is viewed from a distance, a vertical white "Mach band" appears down the middle. In the illustration at right the horizontal black lines are a constant thickness from the right side to the midpoint and then thin out. When viewed from a distance, the illustration appears to have a vertical black band down the middle.

CRAIK-O'BRIEN EFFECT (this example is known as the Cornsweet illusion) is the result of a specific variation of luminance at the contour, which makes the outer zone appear slightly darker even though it has the same luminance as the inner zone. The effect here is less than in the original because of difficulty in reproducing the actual intensity relations.

RAPID ROTATION of this disk will create the Cornsweet illusion. The white spur creates a local variation near the contour between the two zones that causes the apparent brightness of the inner zone to increase. In the same way the dark spur creates a local variation that causes the outer zone to appear darker. Except in the spur region the objective luminance of the disk when it is rotating is the same in both the inner and the outer region.

the remaining set, thus increasing their rate of discharge [*see bottom illustration on page 19*]. Following the discovery of disinhibition in the eye of the horseshoe crab, Victor J. Wilson and Paul R. Burgess of Rockefeller University found that some increases in neural activity (called recurrent facilitation) that had been observed in spinal motoneurones in the cat were actually disinhibition. Subsequently M. Ito and his colleagues at the University of Tokyo observed a similar type of disinhibition in the action of the cerebellum on Deiter's nucleus in the cat.

The spatial distribution and relative magnitudes of the excitatory and inhibitory influences for any particular receptor unit in the eye of *Limulus* can be represented graphically as a narrow central field of excitatory influence surrounded by a more extensive but weaker field of inhibitory influence [*see top illustration on page 20*].

As Georg von Békésy has shown, the approximate response of an inhibitory network can be calculated graphically by superimposing the graphs for each of the interacting units, each graph scaled according to the intensity of the stimulus where it is centered. The summed effects of overlapping fields of excitation (positive values) and inhibition (negative values) at any particular point would determine the response at that point. In the limit of infinitesimally small separations of overlapping units, this would be mathematically equivalent to using the superposition theorem or the convolution integral to calculate the response. In fact, these inhibitory interactions may be expressed in a wide variety of essentially equivalent mathematical forms. The form Hartline and I used at first is a set of simultaneous equations—one equation for each of the interacting receptor units. Our colleagues Frederick A. Dodge, Jr., Bruce W. Knight, Jr., and Jun-ichi Toyoda have since that time expressed the properties of the inhibitory network in a less cumbersome and more general form: a transfer function relating the Fourier transform of the distribution of the intensity of the stimulus to the Fourier transform of the distribution of the magnitude of the response. This in effect treats the retinal network as a filter of the sinusoidal components in the stimulus, and can be applied equally well to both spatial and temporal variations. The overall filtering effect of the *Limulus* retina is to attenuate both the lowest and the highest spatial and temporal frequencies of the sinusoidal components.

It has long been known that spatial and temporal filtering effects of much the same kind occur in our own visual system. The main characteristics of the spatial "filter" can be seen by viewing the test pattern devised by Fergus W. Campbell and his colleagues at the University of Cambridge [see top illustration on page 21].

Even without considering the filter-like properties of neural networks it is possible to see how the subjective Mach bands can be produced by the interaction of narrow fields of excitation and broad fields of inhibition. Near the boundary between the light and dark fields some of the receptors will be inhibited not only by their dimly lit neighbors but also by some brightly lit receptors. The total inhibition of these boundary receptors will therefore be greater than the inhibition of dimly lit receptors farther from the boundary. Similarly, a brightly lit receptor near the boundary will be in the inhibitory field of some dimly lit receptors and as a result will have less inhibition acting on it than brightly lit receptors farther away from the boundary. Because of these differential effects near the boundary the response of the neural network in the *Limulus* retina will show a substantial maximum and minimum adjacent to the boundary even though the stimulus does not have such variations.

Opposed excitatory and inhibitory influences can mediate some highly specialized functions in higher animals. Depending on how these opposed influences are organized, they can detect motion, the orientation of a line or the difference between colors. No matter how complicated the visual system is, however, the basic contrast effects of the excitatory-inhibitory processes show up. For example, recent experiments by Russell L. De Valois and Paul L. Pease of the University of California at Berkeley show a contour enhancement similar to the bright Mach band in responses of monkey lateral geniculate cells. The simple lateral inhibition that produces contrast effects such as Mach bands may be a basic process in all the more highly evolved visual mechanisms.

Contrast phenomena are by no means found only in the nervous system. Indeed, contrast is found in any system of interacting components where opposed fields of positive (excitatory) and negative (inhibitory) influences exist. Whether the system is neural, electrical, chemical or an abstract mathematical model is irrelevant; all that is needed to produce a contrast effect is a certain distribution of the opposed influences. A familiar example is the contrast effect in xerography. The xerographic process does not reproduce solid black or gray areas very well. Only the edges of extended uniform areas are reproduced unless some special precautions are taken. This failing is inherent in the basic process itself. In the making of a xerographic copy a selenium plate is first electrostatically charged. Where light falls on the plate the electrostatic charge is lost; in dark areas the charge is retained. A black powder spread over the plate clings to the charged areas by electrostatic attraction and is eventually transferred and fused to paper to produce the final copy.

The electrostatic attraction of any point on the plate is determined not by the charge at that point alone but by the integrated effects of the electrostatic fields of all the charges in the neighborhood. Since the shapes of the positive and negative components of the individual fields happen to be very much like the shapes of the excitatory and inhibitory components of neural unit fields in the retina, the consequences are much the same too [see bottom illustration on page 20]. Contours are enhanced; uniform areas are lost. To obtain a xerographic copy of the uniform areas one merely has to put a halftone screen over the original. The screen breaks up the uniform areas into many small discontinuities, in effect many contours.

Similar contrast effects are seen in photography and in television. In photography a chemical by-product of the development process at one point can diffuse to neighboring points and inhibit further development there, causing spurious edge effects; in television the secondary emission of electrons from one point in the image on the signal plate in the camera can fall on neighboring points and "inhibit" them, creating negative "halos," or dark areas, around bright spots. The similarity of the contrast effects in such diverse systems is not a trivial coincidence. It is an indication of a universal principle: The enhancement of contours by contrast depends on particular relations among interacting elements in a system and not on the particular mechanisms that achieve those relations.

How a contour itself can affect the contrast of the areas it separates cannot be explained quite so easily. This effect of contour on contrast was first investigated by Kenneth Craik of the University of Cambridge and was described in

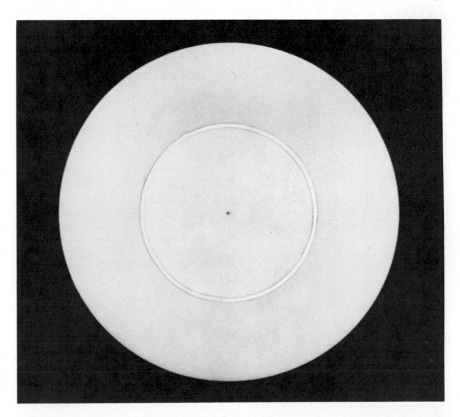

SOURCE OF CRAIK-O'BRIEN EFFECT can be demonstrated by covering the contour with a wire or string. When this is done, the inner and outer regions appear equally bright.

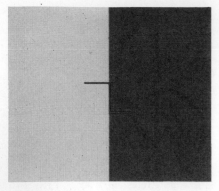
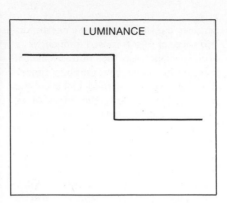
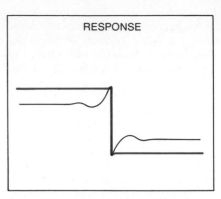

STEP PATTERN of illumination (*left*) also has a step-pattern luminance curve (as measured by a photometer) across the contour. A computer simulation of the response of the *Limulus* eye to the pattern (*black curve at right*) shows a maximum and a minimum that are the result of inhibitory interaction among the receptors. The colored curve at right shows how the pattern looks to a person; the small peak and dip in the curve indicate slight subjective contrast enhancement at the contour known as "border contrast."

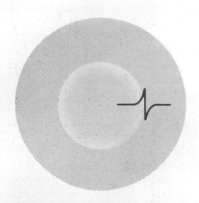
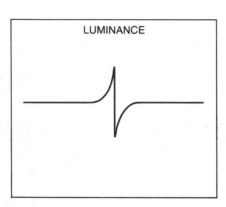
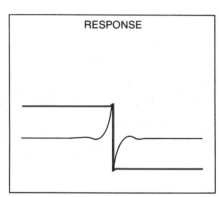

LUMINANCE on both sides of the Craik-O'Brien contour is the same but the inside (here simulated) is brighter. The human visual system may extrapolate (*colored curve*) from the maximum and minimum produced by inhibitory processes (*black curve at right*).

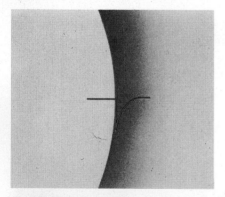
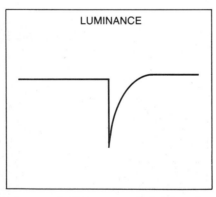
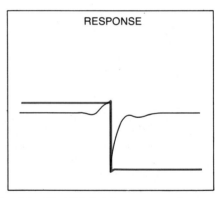

DARK SPUR between areas can create brightness reversal. Objectively the area at left of the contour is darker than the area at far right, but to an observer the left side (here simulated) will appear to be brighter than the right side. This brightness reversal agrees with the extrapolation (*colored curve*) from the maximum and minimum produced by inhibitory processes (*black curve at right*).

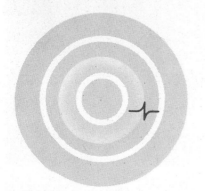
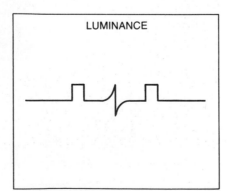
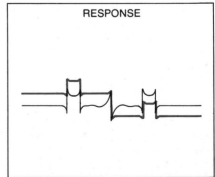

TWO BANDS OF LIGHT of equal intensity are superimposed on backgrounds of equal luminance separated by a Craik-O'Brien contour. The lights add their luminance to the apparent brightness (*colored curve*) and one band appears brighter than the other.

his doctoral dissertation of 1940. Craik's work was not published, however, and the same phenomenon (along with related ones) was rediscovered by Vivian O'Brien of Johns Hopkins University in 1958. The Craik-O'Brien effect, as I shall call it, has been of great interest to neurophysiologists and psychologists in recent years.

A particular example of this effect, sometimes called the Cornsweet illusion, is produced by separating two identical gray areas with a special contour that has a narrow bright spur and a narrow dark spur [see top illustration on page 22]. Although the two uniform areas away from the contour have the same objective luminance, the gray of the area adjacent to the light spur appears to be lighter than the gray of the area adjacent to the dark spur. When the contour is covered with a thick string, the grays of the two areas are seen to be the same. When the masking string is removed, the difference reappears but takes a few moments to develop. These effects can be very pronounced; not only can a contour cause contrast to appear when there actually is no difference in objective luminance but also a suitable contour can cause contrast to appear that is the reverse of the objective luminance.

With the choice of the proper contour a number of objectively different patterns can be made to appear similar in certain important respects [see illustrations on opposite page]. It is reasonable to assume that in all these cases the dominant underlying neural events are also similar. With the mathematical equation for the response of a Limulus eye one can calculate the neural responses to be expected from each type of pattern when processed by a simple inhibitory network. When this is done, one finds that the calculated responses are all similar to one another. Each has a maximum on the left and a minimum on the right. Furthermore, there is a certain similarity between the calculated neural response and the subjective experience of a human observer viewing the patterns: where the computed response has a maximum, the pattern appears brighter on that side of the contour; where the computed response has a minimum, the pattern appears darker on that side of the contour. Indeed, merely by extending a line from the maximum out to the edge of that side of the pattern and a line from the minimum out to the edge of that side of the pattern one obtains a fair approximation to the apparent brightness. This correspon-

dence suggests that opposed excitatory and inhibitory influences in neural networks of our visual systems are again partly responsible for creating the effect. Even so, much would remain to be explained. Why should the influence of the contour be extended over the entire adjacent area rather than just locally? And why do three distinctly different stimuli, when used as contours, produce much the same subjective result?

The answer to both of these questions may be one and the same. Communication engineers have experimented with a number of sophisticated means of data

compression to increase the efficiency of transmitting images containing large amounts of redundant information. For example, if a picture is being transmitted, only information about contours need be sent; the uniform areas between contours can be restored later by computer from information in the amplitudes of the maxima and minima at the contours. By the same token signals from the retina may be "compressed" and the redundant information extrapolated from the maximum and the minimum in the neural response. Such a process, which was postulated by Glenn A. Fry

KOREAN VASE from the 18th century provides an excellent example of the effect of a dark spur between areas. The moon appears to be brighter than the sky directly below it, but the actual luminance is just the reverse. If only a portion of the moon and an equal portion of the sky about one moon diameter below it are viewed through two identical small holes in a paper so that the dark contour is masked, the moon appears darker than the sky.

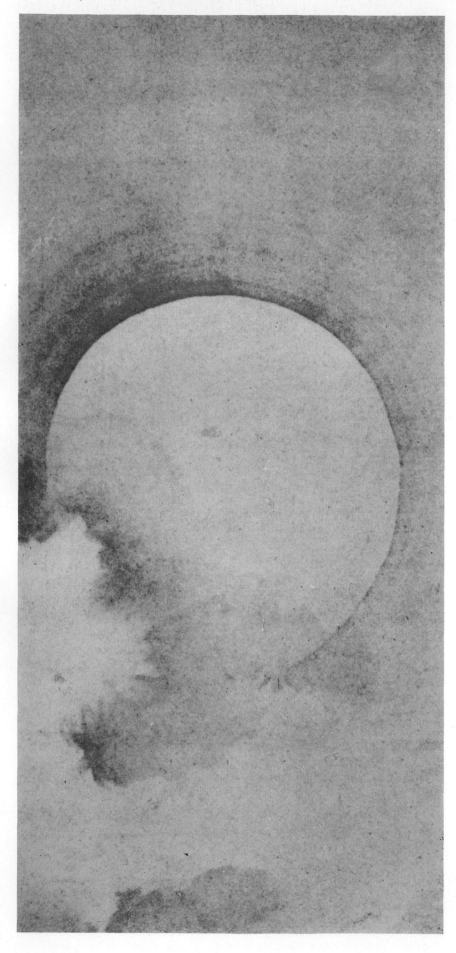

of Ohio State University many years ago, could explain the Craik-O'Brien effect.

What the actual mechanisms might be in our visual system that could "decode" the signals resulting from data compression by the retina and "restore" redundant information removed in the compression are empirical problems that have not yet been directly investigated by neurophysiologists. The problem as I have stated it may even be a will-o'-the-wisp; it is possible that there is no need to actually restore redundant information. The maximum and minimum in the retinal response may "set" brightness discriminators in the brain, and provided that there are no intervening maxima and minima (that is, visible contours) the apparent brightness of adjacent areas would not deviate from that set by the maximum or the minimum.

Some evidence that apparent brightness is actually set by the maximum and minimum at a contour or discontinuity and is then extrapolated to adjacent areas can be found in experiments conducted by L. E. Arend, J. N. Buehler and Gregory R. Lockhead at Duke University. They worked with patterns similar to those that create the Craik-O'Brien effect. On each side of the contour they produced an additional band of light. They found that the difference in apparent brightness between each band of light and its background depended only on the actual increment in luminance provided by the band, but that the apparent brightness of the two bands in relation to each other was determined by the apparent brightness of the background. For example, if two bands of equal luminance are superimposed on two backgrounds of equal luminance that are separated by a Craik-O'Brien contour, one of the bands of light will appear brighter than the other [*see bottom illustration on page 24*]. A number of related phenomena, in which contrast effects are propagated across several adjacent areas, are under investigation by Edwin H. Land and John H. McCann at the Polaroid Corporation. These experi-

JAPANESE INK PAINTING, "Autumn Moon" by Keinen, has a moon that objectively is only very slightly lighter than the sky. Much of the difference in apparent brightness is created by the moon's contour. The extent of the effect can be seen by covering the moon's edge with string. The painting, made about 1900, is in the collection of the late Akira Shimazu of Nara in Japan.

ments lend further support to the general view outlined here.

Of course, the human visual system is far too complex for the simple notion that apparent brightness is determined by difference at contours to be the whole story. Nonetheless, the general idea contains at least the rudiments of an explanation that is consistent with known physiological mechanisms and with the observed phenomena. Several entirely different distributions of illumination may look much the same to the human eye simply because the eye happens to abstract and send to the brain only those features that the objectively different patterns have in common. This type of data compression may be a basic principle common to many different kinds of neural systems.

Even if the cause of the Craik-O'Brien effect is in doubt, the effect itself is incontrovertible. Although the effects of contour on perceived contrast are relatively new to the scientific community, the same effects have long been known to artists and artisans. One can only speculate on how the effects were discovered. Very likely they emerged in some new artistic technique that was developed for another purpose. Once such a technique had been perfected, it doubtless would have persisted and been handed down from generation to generation. Furthermore, following the initial discovery the technique would probably have been applied in other media. In any event such techniques date back as far as the Sung dynasty of China (A.D. 960–1279), and they are still employed in Oriental art. For example, in a Japanese ink painting made about 1900 a single deft stroke of the brush greatly increases the apparent brightness of the moon [see *illustration on opposite page*]. If the contour is covered with a piece of string, the apparent brightness of the moon diminishes and that area is seen to be very little brighter than its surround.

A similar effect is found in a scene on an 18th-century Korean vase [see *illustration on page 25*]. Here the moon is actually darker than the space below it. Measurements of a photograph of the vase with a light meter under ordinary room lights showed that the luminance of the moon was 15 foot-lamberts and the space one moon diameter below was 20 foot-lamberts. The contour effect is so strong that the apparent brightness of the two areas is just the reverse of the objective luminance.

The contour-contrast effect can be produced on a ceramic surface by still another technique. This technique was

CHINESE TING YAO SAUCER is an example of the famous Ting white porcelain produced in the Sung dynasty of about A.D. 1000. Although the entire surface is covered with only a single creamy white glaze, the incised lotus design appears brighter than the background because of the incisions, which have a sharp inner edge and a graded outer edge, producing exactly the kind of contour that creates an apparent difference in brightness.

developed more than 1,000 years ago in the Ting white porcelain of the Sung dynasty and in the northern celadon ceramics of the same period. In the creation of the effect a design was first incised in the wet clay with a knife. The cut had a sharp inner edge and a sloping outer edge. The clay was then dried and covered with a white glaze. The slightly creamy cast of the glaze inside the cuts produces the necessary gradient to create the Craik-O'Brien effect. The result is that the pattern appears slightly brighter than the surround [see *illustration above*]. Since the effect depends on variations in the depth of the translucent monochrome glaze, it is much more subtle than it is in the Japanese painting and in the Korean vase. But then subtlety and restraint were characteristic of the Sung ceramists.

These examples of the effects of contrast and contour from the visual sciences and the visual arts illustrate the need for a better understanding of how elementary processes are organized into

complex systems. In recent years the discipline of biology has become increasingly analytical. Much of the study of life has become the study of the behavior of single cells and the molecular events within them. Although the analytic approach has been remarkably productive, it does not come to grips with one of the fundamental problems facing modern biological science: how unitary structures and elementary processes are organized into the complex functional systems that make up living organs and organisms. Fortunately, however, we are not faced with an either-or choice. The analytic and the organic approaches are neither incompatible nor mutually exclusive; they are complementary, and advances in one frequently facilitate advances in the other. All that is required to make biology truly a life science, no matter what the level of analysis, is to occasionally adopt a holistic or organic approach. It is probably the elaborate organization of unitary structures and elementary processes that distinguishes living beings from lifeless things.

3

The Perception of Neutral Colors

by Hans Wallach
January 1963

*What makes a surface gray and why does it stay gray
even when the illumination changes? Apparently the
ratio between adjacent light intensities governs the
perceived lightness of an achromatic color*

Most investigations of color perception deal with the relation between the spectral composition of light—the assortment of wavelengths in it—and the color sensations it evokes. But there is a family of colors the quality of which does not depend on wavelength or combinations of wavelengths. These are the achromatic, or neutral, colors—white, the various grays and black—which differ from one another only in degree of lightness or darkness. The scale of lightness, in other words, is the only dimension of the neutral colors, although it is one dimension (along with hue and saturation) of the chromatic colors as well. The perception of neutral colors is therefore a basic problem in visual perception that needs to be understood in its own right and that at the same time has implications for color vision in general.

The fact that lightness does not depend on a property of light itself is not only a semantic paradox but also a major complication in the study of neutral-color perception. Light can appear dim or bright but not light or dark. It can be blue or yellow or red but not gray. Lightness or darkness is a property of surfaces, and the investigator of neutral-color perception must concern himself with white or gray or black surfaces. Now, the physical property of a surface that corresponds to a perceived neutral color is reflectance. A surface deserves to be called white if it reflects diffusely about 80 per cent of the visible light of any wavelength that falls on it, and it is called black if it reflects only 4 or 5 per cent of the incident light. The various shades of gray range between these extreme reflectance values. The big problem in understanding the perception of neutral colors is that the amount of light reflected by a neutral surface depends not only on its reflectance but also on the intensity of the illuminating light. As the illumination varies over a broad range, the intensity of the light reflected by a surface of a given neutral color will vary just as much. The light message that is received from a reflecting surface is therefore an ambiguous clue to its reflectance—to its "actual" color.

How then can one account for the fact that perceived neutral colors are usually in good agreement with the reflectance of the surface on which they appear—that a dark gray object, for example, tends to look dark gray in all sorts of light? This "constancy" effect, as psychologists call it, can be simply demonstrated by an experiment that David Katz, a German psychologist, devised more than 30 years ago. Two identical gray samples are fastened to a white background and a screen is so placed that it casts a shadow on one of the samples and on its surround [see *illustration below*]. The sample in the shadow does indeed appear to be a somewhat darker gray than the sample in direct illumination. That is to say,

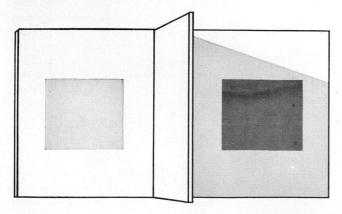 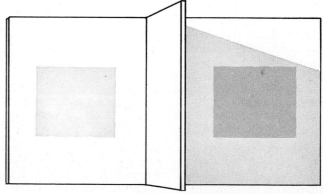

CONSTANCY of neutral colors is demonstrated by this experiment. When one of two identical gray samples is placed in shadow, it looks to an observer only a little darker than its brightly illuminated counterpart although, as the drawing shows, it reflects a lot less light (*left*). The color of the shadowed sample is then lightened until it looks the same as the well-lighted one; it still reflects much less light (*right*). In each situation constancy is at work, making the grays appear more equal than the actual light intensities they reflect would warrant. The drawing reproduces these actual light intensities, not the apparent colors of the samples.

IMPRESSIVE DEMONSTRATION of constancy can be given with the setup illustrated in the top photograph. A dark gray sample suspended before a light-colored wall is illuminated by a projection lantern. When the sample hangs alone, any change in room illumination or lantern intensity changes its apparent color. At the bottom left, for example, it appears almost white. But if a white surround is placed behind the sample within the lantern beam, the sample immediately looks gray again (*bottom right*). It stays gray in spite of changes in the lantern intensity or room illumination. The bottom photographs simulate the apparent colors of the sample.

constancy is not complete. But the shadowed sample by no means looks as much darker as the difference in the actual light intensities reflected by the two samples would warrant, which is to say that there is a constancy effect. When the shadowed sample is replaced by a patch of lighter gray so chosen that the two surfaces appear to be the same in spite of their different illuminations, the shadowed sample will still reflect a good deal less light than the directly illuminated one. This difference in the actual light intensity compatible with apparent equality of color represents the constancy effect. Any explanation of this effect must account eventually not only for its presence but also for its incompleteness as demonstrated in the first part of the experiment.

For a long time the standard explanation of constancy has been that the viewer takes illumination into account when he evaluates the intensity of the light reflected by a surface. The difficulty with this is that illumination is never given independently. It manifests itself only by way of the light that the various surfaces in the visual field reflect. One variable, the intensity of the reflected light, depends on both the incident illumination and the reflectances of the surfaces—and is in turn the only direct clue to both of these factors.

The Katz demonstration had the virtue of simulating the conditions under which constancy occurs in everyday life, but it is not amenable to as much manipulation as an experimental situation worked out by Adhémar Gelb of the University of Frankfort. In my laboratory at Swarthmore College some 15 years ago we undertook to explore with Gelb's setup some of the inconsistencies of the orthodox explanation of constancy.

We suspend a dark gray sample some distance from a light-colored wall and illuminate it with a projection lantern so placed that the bright spot formed where the beam hits the wall is concealed behind a door or curtain. With the room nearly dark, the dark gray sample appears brightly luminous, provided that it is perfectly flat and evenly illuminated so that no shiny high lights show. As the general illumination—and hence the illumination on the light wall behind the suspended sample—is raised, the luminous appearance of the sample disappears and it becomes a white surface. Remember that the sample is really dark gray; in this situation constancy is clearly absent. A further

increase in room illumination changes the appearance of the sample to a light gray. Obviously the wrong illumination is being taken into account! The light reflected by the dark sample is being evaluated in terms of the general illumination on the wall; the strong light from the projector is being ignored. The reason for this, proponents of the standard explanation would say, is that the strong light from the lantern is visible on only one object, the dark gray sample, the surround of which reflects only the dimmer general illumination; constancy would be restored if the light from the lantern showed in the surround. And so it is. When a piece of white cardboard, somewhat larger than the sample but small enough to fit into the beam, is hung behind the dark sample, the sample looks dark gray. The orthodox explanation is that the white cardboard surround makes it possible to take into account the effect of the lantern light on the intensity of the light reflected by the dark sample.

What happens when we vary the intensity of the lantern beam? With the gray sample alone intercepting the beam, every reduction in the intensity of the light causes a change in the apparent color of the sample, which can be altered in this manner all the way from white to dark gray. With constancy restored by the addition of the white cardboard, however, the same changes in light intensity hardly affect the color of the sample and its surround. The sample remains dark gray and the surround white, although the latter looks more or less strongly luminous as the lantern light is varied. This "luminousness" is a special aspect of neutral-color perception, as will be seen; in so far as the neutral colors as such are concerned, however, the combination of dark gray surface with white surround is resistant to changes in illumination.

It is difficult to see how this demonstration of constancy can be explained by any mechanism that takes the illumination into account. The amount of light the white cardboard reflects, after all, gives information about the intensity of the illumination only when the cardboard is correctly assumed to be white. But there is no cue for such an assumption. What if the cardboard were not white? As a matter of fact a surround of any other color fails to produce constancy, that is, to cause a dark gray sample to be perceived as dark gray. If, with the walls of the room dark, the white cardboard is replaced by a medium gray one, the surround again appears luminously white in the lantern beam, whereas the dark gray sample looks light gray. Although the color is now incorrectly perceived, the combination of sample and surround is still resistant to illumination changes. The intensity of the beam can be moved through a broad range and the sample remains light gray.

If taking illumination into account is not the explanation of constancy, what is? Some years ago Harry Helson, then at Bryn Mawr College, proposed an entirely different approach, invoking the mechanism of adaptation by which the eye adjusts itself to wide variations in the amount of light available. To account for the fact that constancy prevails when different illuminations are visible simultaneously, he suggested that incoming light intensities are evaluated in terms of a "weighted average" of stimulation in different parts of the retina, the light-sensitive screen at the back of the eye. It seems to me that there is implicit in this notion of regional adaptation an assumption of some sort of interaction of processes arising in different parts of the retina, and such interaction would appear to be a requirement in any explanation of constancy. Helson's explanation was advanced as part of a general theory of sensation that has been quite successful, and he did not describe a specific mechanism for interaction.

Speculating on the observations just described, in which the combination of gray sample and cardboard background proved resistant to changes in illumination, I wondered if a ratio effect might be at the heart of the matter. Since any neutral surface reflects a constant fraction of the available illumination, the light intensities reflected by two different surfaces under the same illumination should stand in a constant ratio no matter how the illumination is changed. If one could demonstrate that perceived neutral colors depend on the ratio between the light intensities reflected from adjacent regions, all the foregoing observations, and in fact neutral-color constancy in general, would be explained. The following experiments show that this is indeed the case.

The first experiment calls for a darkened room, a white screen and two identical slide projectors the light intensity of which can be altered by measured amounts. In an otherwise dark room one lantern projects a disk of light on the screen and the other lantern a ring of light that fits closely around the disk. The light intensity of the disk is kept constant; variation of the intensity of the ring then changes the appearance of the disk through the entire range of neutral colors. When the ring intensity is half or a quarter that of the disk, the disk looks white. When the ring intensity is higher than that of the disk, the disk becomes gray. Its shade deepens from light to medium to dark gray as the ring light is made first twice as intense as and then four and eight times more intense than the light in the disk. When the relative intensity of the ring is raised still further, the disk even appears black. This experiment shows clearly that the neutral color of an area does not depend on the intensity of the reflected light as such, because with the intensity of the illumination of the disk held constant its color nevertheless ranges all the way from white to black as the intensity of its surround is increased. Obviously what matters is the relation of the intensity of the light reflected from the disk to the intensity of the light reflected from the surrounding ring.

Another experiment demonstrates that a particular gray is produced largely by a specific ratio between the intensity of the ring and that of the disk. A second pair of lanterns is added to project an identical ring-and-disk pattern on a second screen. If the ring and disk in each pattern are illuminated with the intensities in the same ratio but with the absolute intensity in one pattern reduced to, say, a third or a quarter of the intensity in the other, almost the same gray is perceived in both disks. Whenever the intensity of one of the disks is varied until the grays of the two disks appear to be truly equal, the disk intensities turn out to be almost equal fractions of the intensities in their respective rings.

The discovery that the various gray colors depend approximately on the ratio between light intensities stimulating adjacent regions of the retina goes a long way toward explaining neutral-color constancy in general. The ratio principle can account for the observed constancy in the Katz experiment, where a sample in shadow is compared with one in direct illumination. The combination of sample and background is resistant to differences in illumination because the ratio between the intensities reflected by sample and background is constant. It will be recalled, however, that constancy was not complete in the Katz experiment. A ring-and-disk demonstration explains this also. The ratio principle operates best only when the ring and disk are presented against

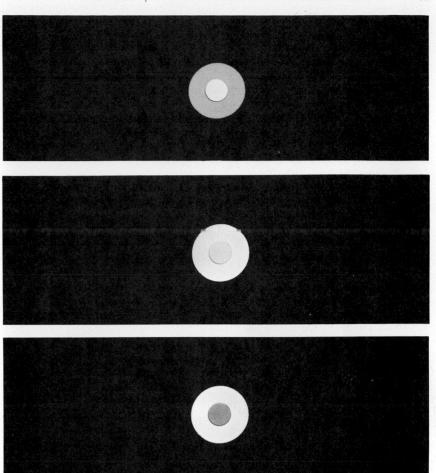

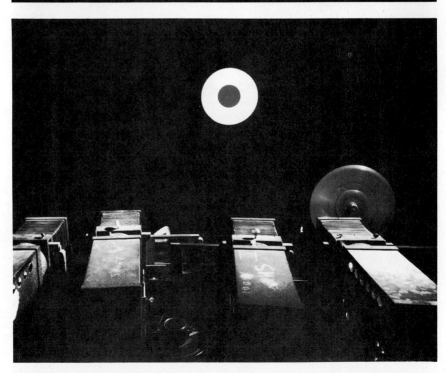

NEUTRAL-COLOR PERCEPTION depends largely on the ratio between two different light intensities in adjacent regions, as demonstrated with a ring-and-disk pattern projected by two lanterns in a dark room. In this experiment the light in the disk is kept constant but the ring light is increased, changing the appearance of the disk from white to dark gray. The ring-to-disk ratios are (*top to bottom*) one to three, two to one, four to one and eight to one. These photographs show how the ring and disk colors appear to an observer.

a dark background or when the ring is enlarged to fill the whole visual field. If, instead, the ring is surrounded by an area of still higher intensity, the disk assumes a darker color. And this is in essence what happens in the Katz setup: the gray sample and background in the shadow correspond to the disk and ring, and the portion of the background that remains under direct illumination corresponds to the outer region of still high-

er illumination that makes a disk appear darker. It is largely because the shaded region and the area under direct illumination are adjacent that constancy is incomplete. Were they widely separated, as they are in the presentation of two ring-and-disk patterns, much better constancy would result, because the ratio principle would then operate as nearly perfectly as it did in the projector experiments.

Although perception of illumination may not be very accurate and does not account for the constancy of neutral colors, it cannot be denied that people do perceive conditions of illumination. A room looks generally brighter near the window than it does far from the window; there is a bright area on the wall near a lighted table lamp and there are shadows on other walls; one side of the house across the street appears brightly

RATIO PRINCIPLE is confirmed by projecting a second pattern from two more projectors. The ratio between ring and disk light intensities is made the same in both patterns but the absolute intensities in the pattern at the left are four times greater than those at the right. In spite of the variation in absolute intensity, the grays perceived in the two disks look remarkably similar to an observer. The photograph, however, approximately reproduces the true light intensities rather than the apparent disk colors.

illuminated by the sun. How, in view of the ratio principle, is one to account for the fact that the shadow on the gray wall does not look exactly like a darker gray or black but has a somewhat translucent appearance; that the wall near the lamp does not seem to be lighter in color but merely looks brighter and less opaque; that the sunlit wall of the house looks outright luminous? All of these examples have one thing in common: the typical quality of a surface of neutral color is either completely replaced by a luminous appearance or is modified in the direction of what can be considered a partially luminous quality. The two-projector experiment, as already noted, also produces examples of this luminousness and of a translucent quality in the grays that is the low-intensity counterpart of the same effect.

When the intensity of the light reflected from the disk is two to four times higher than the intensity of that reflected from the ring, the disk looks white; when the intensity of the disk is lower than that of the ring, the disk looks gray or black depending on the ratio between the two intensities. If the intensities of ring and disk are reversed, however, the appearance of the ring is very different from that of the disk under corresponding conditions. Under illumination of the higher of the two intensities, the ring appears not white but plainly luminous, like the glass globe of a not too bright lamp. Under illumination of the lower intensity the ring does look gray, but the gray has a peculiar quality. It lacks the opaqueness of an ordinary surface; it seems rather to be somewhat translucent, as if there were a light source behind it. As a matter of fact it resembles an extended shadow, which also lacks the opaqueness of a dark surface color, although to a lesser degree. With the ring eliminated altogether, the dark region surrounding the disk does not look like an opaque black surface but like a dark expanse. The distinction between the two kinds of darkness is pointed up vividly when the disk is eliminated and a ring of light is projected alone on a dark field. The area inside the ring has a black surface color quite different from the dark expanse outside the ring.

Several factors seem to account for the sensation of luminosity. The larger of two contrasting areas, in the first place, tends to appear luminous. In our experiments the ring was usually larger than the disk. With the ring reduced in width so that its area is smaller than

that of the disk, the appearance of luminosity and translucence transfers to the disk. The degree of contact between two surfaces reflecting different light intensities also plays a part in this effect. Surrounded completely by the ring, the disk tends to look more like an opaque surface. The ring, which tends to assume the luminous quality, is in contact with the disk on one side only and is bordered on its outer perimeter by the darkness of the room, from which there is minimum stimulation. Lack of contact also explains the luminousness or translucence observed when the disk or the ring is presented alone.

To isolate the effect of difference in contact we have projected two sets of bars, one from each lantern, so that bars of high and low intensity alternate in the pattern on the screen. The two outside bars, one white and one gray, appear somewhat luminous, whereas all the other bars show opaque colors. Since the areas of each bar and of each intensity are exactly equal, the luminous look can only be attributed to the diminished contact of the outer bars with areas of different intensities. A special case of reduced contact occurs when an intensity gradient replaces the sharp border between two areas of different intensities. Such gradients appear in the penumbrae of shadows, where the grays assume the quality of translucence that belies the opacity of the surface under inspection.

Regardless of size or degree of con-

LUMINOUS QUALITY is produced by a reduction in the degree of contact with an area of contrasting light intensity. In this pattern of bars of alternating high and low intensity, the two outside bars look somewhat luminous to an observer (the effect is not apparent in a photograph) because they have only half as much contact with contrasting bars.

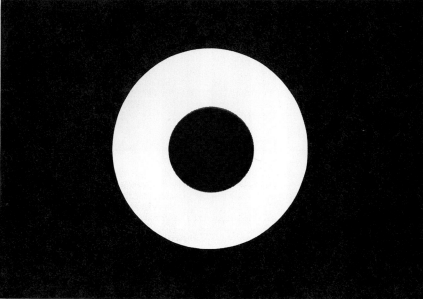

CHROMATIC COLORS also vary in lightness depending on the intensity of the illumination in an adjacent region. The experiment simulated here shows how the appearance of a disk of orange light changes with the intensity of a neutral surround. In this case increasing the intensity of the ring changes the apparent color of the disk to brown.

tact, when the intensity difference becomes greater than about four to one, the area of higher intensity becomes somewhat luminous as well as white; with very large differences it loses all whiteness. An illuminated disk in an otherwise dark field never looks white or gray; depending on its intensity, it is brightly or dimly luminous. The most familiar illustration of this laboratory finding is the contrast between the appearance of the moon by day and by night. In a bright blue sky the moon looks white. As the setting of the sun reduces the intensity of the blue sky the moon's light becomes relatively more intense and the moon appears more and more luminous, even though the intensity of the light arriving from the direction of the moon certainly does not increase.

It can be concluded, therefore, that a region reflecting the higher of two light intensities will appear white or luminous, whereas an adjacent region of lower intensity will appear gray or black. Every change of the intensity ratio causes a change in the color of the area of lesser intensity along the scale of grays. As for the area of higher intensity, it ap-pears white when the intensity ratio is small and becomes luminously white and finally luminous as the ratio is increased. If the contact between surfaces of different intensities is reduced, neutral colors become less dense and opaque and even somewhat luminous. The same effect is seen in a region that is larger than an adjacent one of different intensity.

It seems to me that these facts can be explained by considering that stimulation with light gives rise to two different perceptual processes. One process causes luminousness and the other produces the various opaque colors. The first process is directly dependent on intensity of stimulation and the state of adaptation of the eye. The second is an interaction process: an area of the retina that receives a higher intensity of stimulation induces a sensation of gray or black in a neighboring region of lower intensity, with the particular color roughly dependent on the ratio of the two intensities; conversely, the region stimulated at a lower intensity induces a white color in the region of higher intensity. If the intensity ratio is too high, however, if the relative size of the inducing surface is too small or if the contact between two regions of different intensities is too small, the interaction process may give way to the process that gives rise to the sensation of luminosity, or the sensation of color and luminosity may be experienced simultaneously.

The processes of neutral-color perception have their counterparts in the perception of chromatic colors. This is not surprising; the neutral colors are continuous with the chromatic colors: for any sample of a greatly desaturated chromatic color a closely similar gray can be found. A final experiment with the two projectors demonstrates that the lightness of chromatic colors depends on a relation between the intensities of stimulation in neighboring regions. When a disk of chromatic light is surrounded by a ring of white light, variation in the intensity of the latter changes the lightness of the chromatic color in the disk. In this way a bright pink, for example, can be changed to a dark magenta. The same experiment performed with a yellow or orange disk yields a surprising result: surrounding the disk with a ring of high-intensity white light transforms the disk into a deep brown. This serves to demonstrate that brown is a dark shade of yellow or orange. It also dramatizes the point that the shades and tints of chromatic colors, as well as the neutral colors, are the result of an interaction process.

Even the luminous appearance that results from stimulation with light from a neutral surface has its counterpart in the sensation of chromatic colors. For many years psychologists have distinguished a number of "modes of appearance" of chromatic colors, including surface colors, expanse colors and aperture colors. Surface colors are the opaque colors of objects, the hued counterparts of the neutral surface colors. Expanse colors, of which the clear blue sky is a good example, occur in extended homogeneous regions and lack the density and opaqueness of surface colors. That is, expanse colors have a luminous appearance, which may be caused by a relatively high intensity of stimulation or because they are greatly extended in relation to an adjacent region of different intensity. Aperture colors are observed when one looks through a hole in a screen at a chromatic surface some distance beyond the screen. Under these conditions the surface is transformed into a seemingly transparent chromatic film stretched across the hole.

The aperture mode has been attributed to the peculiarities of the laboratory arrangement in which it is usually observed. It can be shown, however, that this effect too is a product of specific ratios of stimulation intensities. The "transparent film" appears only when the intensity of the light reflected from the chromatic surface seen through the hole is high in relation to that of the light reflected from the screen. Raising the illumination on the screen transforms the film into a surface color, so that the hole comes to look like a piece of colored paper attached to the screen.

Such a change can be observed easily out of doors on a clear morning. Cut a small hole in a large sheet of white cardboard. Hold the sheet up so that the sky is visible through the hole. The sky will appear in the hole as a blue transparent film. Now turn until the white cardboard reflects the direct light of the sun. When the cardboard is brightly illuminated, the hole seems to be replaced by an opaque bluish-gray patch, notable for its lack of saturation. This transformation of the strongly saturated expanse color of the sky into a surface color of medium lightness by the provision of a relatively large surface of contrastingly high light-intensity shows how desaturated the blue of the sky really is. It suggests that the sky looks very blue not only because the blue wavelengths of sunlight are scattered by the atmosphere but also—and perhaps largely—because the sky is so bright.

4

The Perception of Transparency

by Fabio Metelli
April 1974

Certain mosaics of opaque colors and shapes give rise to the impression of transparency. A simple theoretical model predicts the conditions under which perceptual transparency will occur

What do we mean when we say that something is transparent? Actually the term has two meanings. If we are referring to the fact that light can pass through a thing or a medium, then the meaning of "transparent" we intend to convey is physical; if, on the other hand, we mean to say that we can see through something, then the meaning we intend to convey is perceptual. The distinction would not be very important if physical and perceptual transparency were always found together. Such, however, is not the case. Air is physically transparent, but normally we do not speak of "seeing through" it. Nor do we always perceive plate glass doors, since we occasionally run into them. It seems useful, therefore, to give a more precise definition of the perception of transparency: One perceives transparency when one sees not only surfaces behind a transparent medium but also the transparent medium or object itself. According to this definition, air and plate glass are not perceptually transparent unless there is fog in the air or there are marks or reflections on the glass.

The fact that physical transparency is not always accompanied by perceptual transparency can be demonstrated. Take a square of colored transparent plastic and glue it onto a larger square of black cardboard. Provided that the layer of glue is spread evenly, the plastic no longer is perceived as being transparent; it appears to be opaque. Changing the color of the cardboard, say from black to white, does not alter the effect [*see top illustration on facing page*].

There also are instances where physical transparency is absent and perceptual transparency is present. Wolfgang Metzger of Münster has shown that mosaics of opaque cardboard can give rise to a perception of transparency even though there are no elements in the mosaic that are physically transparent [*see second illustration from top on facing page*]. These two examples make it clear that physical transparency is neither a necessary nor a sufficient condition for the perception of transparency. Physical transparency cannot explain perceptual transparency.

What causes perceptual transparency? As with other visual phenomena, the causes must be sought in the pattern of stimulation and in the processes of the nervous system resulting from retinal stimulation. Light reaches the retina only after having passed through several transparent mediums (air and the transparent mediums of the eye). The input to the retina, however, does not contain specific information about the characteristics of the transparent layers through which the light has traveled and been filtered. The perception of transparency is thus not the result of filtration; it is a new fact originating in the nervous system as a result of the distribution of the light stimuli acting on the retinal cells.

Perceptual transparency depends on the spatial and intensity relations of light reflected from a relatively wide field and not on light reflected only from a local area. This can be demonstrated by juxtaposing two sets of squares that do not appear to have any transparent areas [*see third illustration from top on facing page*]. The juxtaposition produces a change from apparent opacity to transparency even though the light reflected from each region has not changed.

The conditions under which transparency is perceived have been studied by several eminent investigators, beginning in the 19th century with Hermann von Helmholtz and his contemporary Ewald Hering. They were at odds on almost all points. In his treatise on physiological optics Helmholtz described the perception of transparency as "seeing through" and studied it with a simple device in which images of two strips of paper of different colors were perceived one behind the other. The colors were superposed by reflection and transparency. Similar dual images can be found on windows under certain conditions, for example in the evening when one looks outside and sees both the reflection of the illuminated room and the external landscape.

Hering denied the possibility of seeing one color behind another. He argued that when light reflected by two different colors reaches the same retinal region, an intermediate or fusion color will be perceived. He supported his argument with new observations. When an observer concentrated only on the region where the two color images were superposed, just one color, the fusion color, was perceived.

In 1923 the German psychologist W. Fuchs was able to solve the Helmholtz-Hering controversy. He showed that both colors are perceived only when the transparent object and the object seen through it are perceived as independent objects. If the region of superposition of the two objects is isolated (even if it is just by the attitude of the observer), then only the fusion color is perceived. In the following years important findings were made by the Gestalt psychologist Kurt Koffka and some of his students at Smith College. B. Tudor-Hart showed that transparency on a totally homogeneous ground is not possible (for example the transparent plastic on a black cardboard). In 1955 Gaetano Kanizsa of the University of Trieste pointed out that whereas investigators had been concentrating only on the region of superposition of two figures, the conditions for perceiving transparency also applied to the regions in which the background could be seen through the transparent surface. The fact that this point had been neglected indicates that transparency on a figure is much more evident than transparency on the background [see bottom illustration at right].

The early investigators worked with filters or transparent objects, but after it became clear that physical transparency is not essential for the perception of transparency the use of physically transparent objects was generally abandoned. A number of investigators worked with the episcotister: a wheel with sectors cut out. The wheel generates a strong impression of transparency when it is rotated at high speed [see top illustration on following page]. This technique enables the experimenter to independently vary the size of the missing sectors (which affects the degree of transparency) and the color of the remaining sectors (which determines the color of the transparent layer).

In my own work I have used the mosaic method developed by Metzger because it offers a means of independently varying the color, the size and the shape of each region of a configuration. With this method it is easy to demonstrate that transparency depends on form as well as on color [see middle illustration on following page].

There are three main figural conditions for perceiving transparency in overlapping figures: figural unity of the transparent layer, continuity of the boundary line and adequate stratification. Let us examine each condition in turn.

When the unity of the central region of a transparent shape is broken, the perception of transparency is lost [see bottom illustration on following page]. On the other hand, modification of the shape that does not break up figural unity will not cause transparency to be lost. Figural unity of the transparent layer alone, however, is not sufficient to give rise to the perception of transparency. The boundary that divides the figure into two regions (one light and one dark) must be perceived as belonging to the opaque regions. A break in the continuity of the boundary line where it intersects the transparent layer can destroy the transparency effect. Abrupt changes in the boundary at points other than this intersection do not hinder the perception of transparency [see top illustration on page 39].

We have defined the perception of transparency as seeing surfaces behind a transparent medium or object. This means that the layer having the condi-

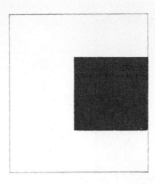

COLORED SQUARES OF TRANSPARENT PLASTIC glued onto a black cardboard (*left*) or a white one (*right*) no longer appear to be transparent. This demonstrates that perceptual transparency is not possible when the underlying field is homogeneous.

MOSAIC METHOD for constructing a figure with perceptual transparency out of opaque pieces is depicted. There is a strong impression of transparency in the central region where the two rectangles overlap. The method was originally developed by Wolfgang Metzger.

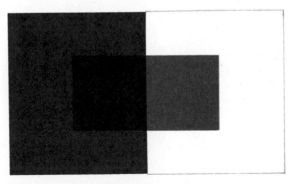

CHANGE FROM OPACITY TO TRANSPARENCY is obtained when the two figures depicted in the illustration at the top of the page are juxtaposed in the manner shown here.

TRANSPARENCY EFFECT is much more evident on an opaque figure than on the background, but conditions required to perceive transparency are the same in both instances.

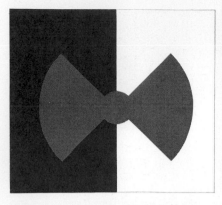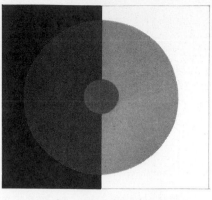

EPISCOTISTER is a wheel with cutout sectors (*left*). When the wheel is rapidly rotated with a suitable background behind it, a strong impression of transparency is created (*right*).

PERCEIVED TRANSPARENCY of the gray circle (*figure at left*) can be abolished either by an abrupt change of form (*middle*) or by an alteration in the color relations (*right*).

FIGURAL UNITY OF THE TRANSPARENT LAYER is a necessary condition for perceiving transparency (*top left*). When the unity of the shape is broken, the transparency effect is lost. Changes in the shape, however, do not destroy transparency (*bottom right*).

tions necessary to become transparent must be located on or above the surface of the opaque object. It is not sufficient, however, for one surface to be perceived as being on top of another in order to obtain the effect of transparency. It is possible to perceive different strata in figures where no transparency is seen [*see bottom illustration on facing page*]. In order to create adequate stratification for transparency the underlying regions must appear to meet under the whole of the transparent layer.

Let us take as a model a figure in which the underlying region is composed of two squares, one black and one white. On these are superposed two smaller squares, one light gray (over the white) and the other dark gray (over the black) [*see illustration on page 41*]. When all the figural and color conditions for transparency are met, then the gray regions appear to be a single transparent surface. (Unbalanced transparency is possible, but here we shall for the most part discuss cases where the transparent layer appears to be uniform.)

How is it that two shades of gray give rise to the same shade of gray in the transparent layer that is perceived? This phenomenon has been described as a case of perceptual scission, or color-splitting. The original gray is called the stimulus color. With the perception of transparency the stimulus color splits into two different colors, which are called the scission colors. One of the scission colors goes to the transparent layer and the other to the surface of the figure below. In 1933 Grace Moore Heider of Smith College formulated the hypothesis (and gave an experimental demonstration) that there is a simple relation between the stimulus and the scission colors: when a pair of scission colors are mixed, they re-create the stimulus color.

The process of color scission works in a direction opposite to that of color fusion. The law of color fusion, also known as Talbot's law (although it actually goes back to Isaac Newton), enables us to predict what color will be perceived when two colors are mixed. The same law, as Heider demonstrated, can be used to describe the color scission that gives rise to transparency. Since measuring chromatic colors such as yellow, red and blue is relatively complex, we shall limit our discussion to the achromatic colors (white, gray and black), which can be measured in a simple way. The achromatic colors vary only in one dimension: lightness. They can be defined by their albedo, or coefficient of reflectance: the percentage of light they reflect.

Every surface absorbs and reflects part of the light falling on it. An ideal white that reflects 100 percent of the light falling on it would have a reflectance of 100; an ideal black that absorbs 100 percent of the light falling on it would have a reflectance of zero. These limits are never reached; a piece of white cardboard typically has a reflectance of about 80 and a piece of black cardboard a reflectance of about 4. Grays have a reflectance ranging from 4 to 80.

A device for studying color fusion is the color wheel. Two or more colors are placed on the wheel, which is then rotated rapidly. The fusion color perceived depends on two factors: the component colors and the proportions in which they are mixed [see illustration on following page]. With achromatic colors the resulting fusion color can readily be predicted, but with color scission there is a great variety of ways in which the stimulus color can split. How can we determine how much of the stimulus color will go to the transparent layer and how much to the opaque layer?

Let us consider first the transparent layer. By way of example imagine what happens when you add a dye to a glass of water. As more dye is added the water becomes less transparent and objects seen through the water become less visible. It is therefore plausible that in the scission process the greater the proportion is of color going to the transparent layer, the less its perceived transparency will be.

Now let us consider the opaque surface. Suppose that as you view it through a glass of water it is painted with a dye. Obviously the visibility of the opaque surface will increase as more dye is put on it.

The limiting case in the scission process is when all the color goes to one layer. If all the color goes to the transparent layer, it becomes opaque. If all the color goes to the underlying surface, then the transparent layer becomes invisible. Transparency is perceived only when there is a distribution of the stimulus color to both the transparent layer and the opaque layer. Moreover, transparency varies directly with the proportion of color going to the opaque layer. As more color goes to the opaque layer, less goes to the transparent one and the more transparent it appears. The proportion of color going to the opaque layer, which is described by an algebraic formula, can therefore be regarded as an index of transparency.

With achromatic colors it is possible to

BOUNDARY LINE must appear to belong to the underlying opaque regions and must be visible through the transparent layer for transparency to be perceived (*top left*). Sudden change of the boundary line at the points of intersection causes transparency to be lost (*top right and bottom left*), but in other locations, even in the region that appears to be transparent, it can make abrupt changes without affecting the transparency (*bottom right*).

STRATIFICATION OF SURFACES is another necessary condition for the perception of transparency. If the light gray and the dark gray regions of a figure are perceived as being two different strata, figural unity is lost and transparency is not perceived (*top left*). Another example of inadequate stratification is when the gray regions appear to have an opaque layer above them (*top right*). The underlying opaque regions must meet under the whole of the gray regions in order for transparency effect to occur (*bottom left and right*).

derive a second algebraic formula that states a relation between the reflectances of the surfaces involved and the color of the transparent layer [*see illustration on facing page*]. If the reflectances of the four surfaces in the figure are known, then the index of transparency can be calculated and the relative lightness of the transparent layer can be predicted. Such predictions are possible when (in most cases, as it happens) the transparent layer is perceived to be uniform in color as well as in the degree of transparency;

in other words, the transparent layer is a perceptual unit, not divided by the boundary belonging to the opaque layer below.

The validity of the theoretical algebraic formulas can be tested by taking our model figure and altering the color (black, gray and white) of individual regions. When the reflectance values of the gray squares are very different, the calculated coefficient of transparency is large and therefore transparency should be readily perceived. When the gray re-

gions are similar, the coefficient is very small and transparency usually is not perceived. Some necessary color conditions of transparency can be deduced from the theoretical formulas. Transparency is possible only when the darker gray square is on the darker underlying surface and the lighter gray square is on the lighter underlying surface. If these conditions are not met, transparency cannot be perceived. Finally, the difference of reflectance of the colors in the transparent layer must always be less

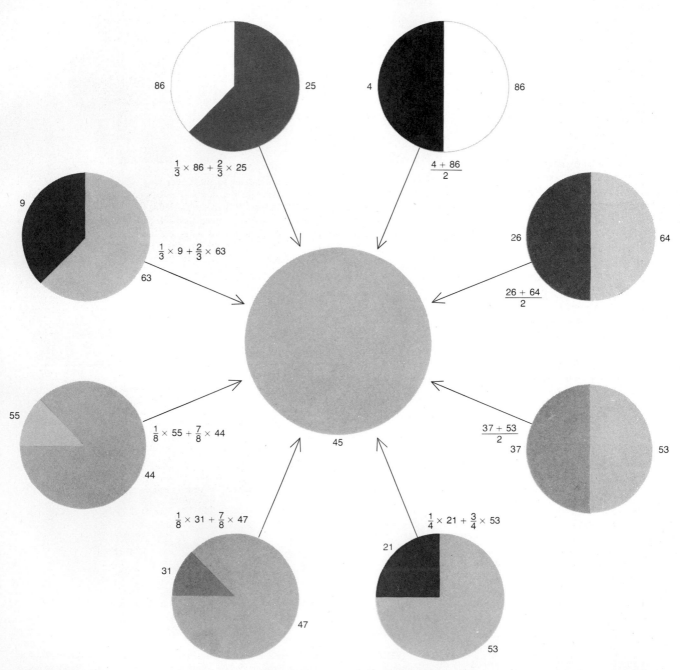

COLOR FUSION is produced when a wheel with sectors of different colors is rapidly rotated. With achromatic colors (black, gray and white) the fusion color can be calculated. For example, if the disk has two sectors of equal size, then the fusion color perceived will be the simple average of the reflectance of each sector. If the sectors are of unequal size, the fusion color is the weighted average. The reflectance figures given here are only representative. The same shade of gray (*center*) can be produced by a variety of color mixtures. Since color scission is the reverse of color fusion, it is apparent that a particular gray can split in a great variety of ways.

than the difference of reflectance of the colors in the underlying layers [*see top illustration on page 43*].

Another powerful factor in perceiving transparency (in addition to the proportion of color going to the opaque and the transparent layer) is the color of the transparent layer itself. All other conditions being equal, the darker the transparent layer, the greater its perceived transparency.

The conditions for the perception of transparency that are deduced from the algebraic formula also enable us to predict the degree of lightness of the transparent layer when the colors of the stimulus regions are varied. With our model figure it is not always easy to judge the color of the transparent layer. With a checkerboard pattern, however, such estimations are easier to make and predictions about the transparent layer are visually confirmed [*see bottom illustration on page 43*].

The color conditions for perceptual transparency discussed here are theoretically derived without any empirical correction or adaptation. They state relations for "pure" achromatic conditions. Figural conditions, as has been noted, play a role and cannot be entirely excluded, but they can be held constant. It must be stressed that the inferences drawn from the theory should be considered as describing some (but not all) necessary conditions for the perception of transparency. In other words, certain instances are described where the perception of transparency is possible and instances where it is impossible. Of

THEORY OF COLOR SCISSION explains transparency as a case of perceptual color-splitting. The achromatic colors can be defined simply by the percentage of light they reflect (*1*). When transparency is perceived, the areas P and Q split and appear to consist of two surfaces, equal in form and size but different in color. Assuming that this color scission follows the same law as color fusion, then the proportion of the stimulus color going to each of the perceived surfaces can be described by an algebraic formula (*2*). The symbols α and α' stand for the proportion of color (which can vary from zero to one) going to the opaque layers a and b respectively. The remainder of the color goes to the transparent layers t and t'. If $\alpha = \alpha'$ and $t = t'$ (*3*), then the algebraic equations can be solved for α (transparency) and for t (color of transparent layer). From the formulas certain predictions about the perceived lightness of the transparent layer can be made from the relations of the colors of the A, P, Q and B regions (*4*). The symbol $>$ here means "lighter than."

1

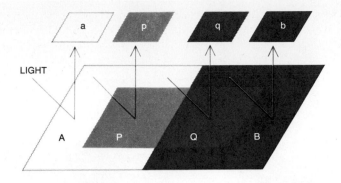

2

$$p = \alpha a + (1-\alpha)t \quad \text{OR} \quad \alpha = \frac{p-t}{a-t} \qquad q = \alpha'b + (1-\alpha')t' \quad \text{OR} \quad \alpha' = \frac{q-t'}{b-t'}$$

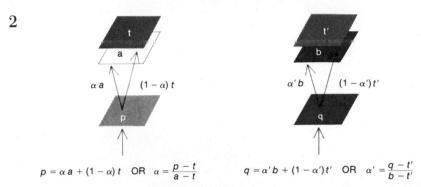

3

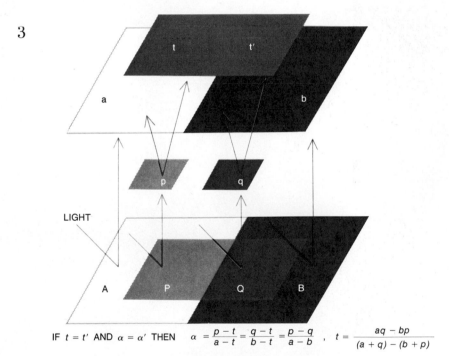

$$\text{IF } t = t' \text{ AND } \alpha = \alpha' \text{ THEN } \quad \alpha = \frac{p-t}{a-t} = \frac{q-t}{b-t} = \frac{p-q}{a-b} \quad , \quad t = \frac{aq-bp}{(a+q)-(b+p)}$$

4

LEFT HALF $\alpha = \frac{p-t}{a-t}$				RIGHT HALF $\alpha = \frac{q-t}{b-t}$		
a	> p >	t	AND	b	> q >	t
a	> p >	t	AND	t	> q >	b
t	> p >	a	AND	t	> q >	b
t	> p >	a	AND	b	> q >	t

TRIANGLE IS PERCEIVED as being transparent and on top of the black and white concentric circles even though no elements of the illustration actually are physically transparent. The triangle is a mosaic composed of individual light gray and dark gray sections.

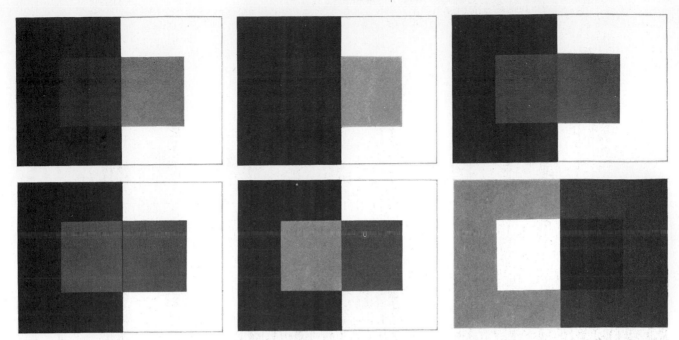

COLOR CONDITIONS necessary for the perception of transparency are demonstrated. In the model figure transparency is readily perceived (*top left*). According to the author's theoretical formula, the degree of perceived transparency increases when the difference between the dark and light gray regions is increased (*top middle*). When the gray regions are similar, perceived transparency is low (*top right*). When the grays are identical, no transparency is perceived (*bottom left*). Transparency is impossible when the darker gray is over the lighter background (*bottom middle*). If the difference between light and dark colors of the background is less than the difference between the colors of the central region, then the central region is not perceived as transparent (*bottom right*).

course, not everyone will perceive transparency when it is theoretically possible. On the other hand, when it is predicted that it is impossible for transparency to exist in a figure, no one should be able to perceive it.

There is an important limitation to the index of transparency that has been discussed: it measures the degree of transparency only if the lightness of the transparent layer is held constant. It is possible to develop a new formula in which the color of the transparent layer is variable, but this can only be done empirically, and it would not give rise to the interesting deductions possible with a theoretical formula. We have dealt here primarily with instances of balanced transparency, that is, instances where the perceived transparent layer is uniform in degree of transparency and color. There are instances of unbalanced transparency, where the perceived transparent layer varies in degree of transparency. A special case is that of partial transparency, where one part of the upper layer is perceived as being transparent and the other as being opaque. Unbalanced transparency and partial transparency, of course, require different formulas for their theoretical description. Other factors such as motion and three-dimensionality are often involved in the phenomenon of transparency. It appears, however, that the main conditions for the perception of transparency are to be found in the figural and chromatic conditions that have been described here.

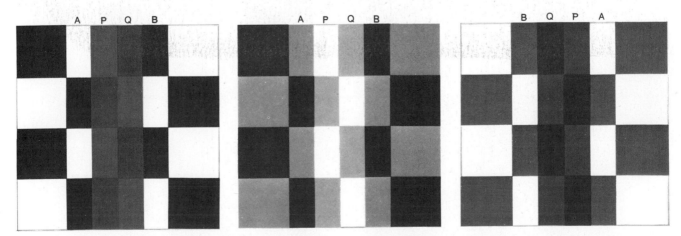

PERCEIVED LIGHTNESS OF TRANSPARENT LAYER depends on the relation of the colors in the figure and can be deduced from the author's theoretical formulas given in the illustration on page 41. According to his theory, if region A is lighter than P and region Q is lighter than B, then the perceived transparent layer appears to be darker than P and lighter than Q (*left*). If region P is lighter than A and region Q is lighter than B, then the transparent layer appears to be lighter than any of the colors (*middle*). If region A is lighter than P and region B is lighter than Q, then the transparent layer appears to be darker than any of the colors (*right*).

II

SPATIAL DIMENSIONS OF VISION

II SPATIAL DIMENSIONS OF VISION

INTRODUCTION

Discrepancies between object and image are particularly evident in the distortions of size and shape that occur when certain figures, many of them quite simple, are viewed. The many examples displayed in Gregory's article, "Visual Illusions," make this point very clear. Gregory adds the suggestion that these illusions may arise from the operation of mechanisms that, under normal conditions, act to make the world more comprehensible rather than less. He alludes to the perceptual phenomena of size constancy. This effect is displayed by the apparently unchanged size of the perceived image of an object as its distance from the observer changes. We might expect that since the retinal image reduces in size when an object moves away from the observer, the mental image would change proportionately. But it doesn't, a result which suggests the operation of a constancy mechanism that takes account of distance by discounting its effect on the apparent size of the image. By the same reasoning, two objects of the same size, but at seemingly different distances in two-dimensional figures, will appear to be of different sizes because of the constancy mechanism. Gregory conceives of this mechanism of perception as being a kind of hypothesis-generating and -testing procedure: the hypothesis which best fits the sensory information is the one adopted. Obviously, this conception is a very far cry from the notion that the percept is a copy of an object.

The third, or depth, dimension of visual space has always intrigued commentators on vision because it does not appear to be represented in the two-dimensional images on the retinas. Is it a figment of the imagination or is there some property of visual stimulation which conveys information about depth? Bela Julesz, in his article, "Texture and Visual Perception," gives us an answer. He shows that the impression that an image has depth may arise from two retinal images which, taken by themselves, convey no similar impression. The visual system performs a correlation of the texture points of the image which assesses their relative displacement across the retinas of the two eyes. This displacement, sometimes called a retinal disparity, is crucial information for the perception of depth, which, as such, is obviously not present in the information on a single retina.

Irwin Rock, in "The Perception of Disoriented Figures," shows how the orientation of a form can alter its apparent shape, and thus demonstrates still another contextual determinant of images. The orientation of a form in relation to gravity can radically alter its apparent shape. Certain intrinsic properties of a form can also mark its orientation and serve to define its uprightness independent of gravity. Nonupright forms require correction to their normal orientations before shape recognition can be accomplished. Rock concludes that perception of shape cannot be reduced to an analysis of edges but involves complex cognitive processes. Progress will, of course, be marked by advances in our understanding of these cognitive processes.

As Deregowski discusses in his article, "Pictorial Perception and Culture," the impression of depth can arise from two-dimensional pictures having either differences in size of the objects depicted, or one figure obscuring another by overlapping it. These properties of plane pictures apparently act as signs for the perception of depth—signs that appear to be learned, since they do not serve to convey an impression of depth to observers in the non-Western culture he observed. If Deregowski is correct, still another factor—learning—can affect the formation of images.

5 Visual Illusions

Richard L. Gregory
November 1968

*Why do simple figures sometimes appear distorted
or ambiguous? Perhaps because the visual system has
to make sense of a world in which everyday objects
are normally distorted by perspective*

A satisfactory theory of visual perception must explain how the fleeting patterns of light reaching the retina of the eye convey knowledge of external objects. The problem of how the brain "reads" reality from the eye's images is an acute one because objects are so very different from images, which directly represent only a few of the important characteristics of objects. At any instant the retinal image represents the color of an object and its shape from a single position, but color and shape are in themselves trivial. Color is dependent on the quality of the illumination, and on the more subtle factors of contrast and retinal fatigue. Shape, as we all know, can be strongly distorted by various illusions. Since it is obviously not in the best interests of the possessor of an eye to be tricked by visual illusions, one would like to know how the illusions occur. Can it be that illusions arise from information-processing mechanisms that under normal circumstances make the visible world easier to comprehend? This is the main proposition I shall examine here.

Illusions of various kinds can occur in any of the senses, and they can cross over between the senses. For example, small objects feel considerably heavier than larger objects of exactly the same weight. This can be easily demonstrated by filling a small can with sand and then putting enough sand in a much larger can until the two cans are in balance. The smaller can will feel up to 50 percent heavier than the larger can of precisely the same weight. Evidently weight is perceived not only according to the pressure and muscle senses but also according to the expected weight of the object, as indicated by its visually judged size. When the density is unexpected, vision produces the illusion of weight. I believe all systematic-distortion illusions are essentially similar to this size-weight illusion.

Although several visual illusions were known to the ancient Greeks, they have been studied experimentally for only a little more than a century. The first scientific description in modern times is in a letter to the Scottish physicist Sir David Brewster from a Swiss naturalist, L. A. Necker, who wrote in 1832 that a drawing of a transparent rhomboid reverses in depth: sometimes one face appears to be in front and sometimes the other. Necker noted that although changes of eye fixation could induce this change in perception, it would also occur quite spontaneously. This celebrated effect is generally illustrated with an isometric cube rather than with Necker's original figure [*see top illustration on page 50*].

Somewhat later W. J. Sinsteden reported an equally striking effect that must have long been familiar to Netherlanders. If the rotating vanes of a windmill are viewed obliquely or directly from the side, they spontaneously reverse direction if there are no strong clues to the direction of rotation. This effect can be well demonstrated by projecting on a screen the shadow, seen in perspective, of a slowly rotating vane. In the absence of all clues to the direction of rotation the vane will seem to reverse direction spontaneously and the shadow will also at times appear to expand and contract on the plane of the screen. It is important to note that these effects are not perceptual distortions of the retinal image; they are alternative interpretations of the image in terms of possible objects. It is as though the brain entertains alternative hypotheses of what object the eye's image may be representing. When sensory data are inadequate, alternative hypotheses are entertained and the brain never "makes up its mind."

The most puzzling visual illusions are systematic distortions of size or shape. These distortions occur in many quite simple figures. The distortion takes the same direction and occurs to much the same extent in virtually all human observers and probably also in many animals. To psychologists such distortions present an important challenge because they must be explained by a satisfactory theory of normal perception and because they could be important clues to basic perceptual processes.

Distortion Illusions

The simplest distortion illusion was also the first to be studied. This is the horizontal-vertical illusion, which was described by Wilhelm Wundt, assistant to Hermann von Helmholtz at Heidelberg and regarded as the father of experimental psychology. The illusion is simply that a vertical line looks longer than a horizontal line of equal length. Wundt attributed the distortion to asymmetry in the system that moves the eye. Although this explanation has been invoked many times since then, it must be ruled out because the distortions occur in afterimages on the retina and also in normal images artificially stabilized so as to remain stationary on the retina. In addition, distortions can occur in several directions at the same time, which could hardly be owing to eye movements. It is also difficult to see how curvature distortions could be related to eye movements. All the evidence suggests that the distortions originate not in the eyes but in the brain.

Interest in the illusions became general on the publication of several figures showing distortions that could produce errors in the use of optical instruments. These errors were an important concern to physicists and astronomers a centu-

ZÖLLNER ILLUSION was published in 1860 by Johann Zöllner; the first of the special distortion illusions.

ry ago, when photographic and other means of avoiding visual errors were still uncommon. The first of the special distortion figures was the illusion published by Johann Zöllner in 1860 [*see illustration above*]. The same year Johann Poggendorff published his line-displacement illusion [*see middle illustration on page 50*]. A year later Ewald Hering presented the now familiar illusion in which parallel lines appear bowed; the converse illusion was conceived in 1896 by Wundt [*see illustration on page 52*].

Perhaps the most famous of all distortion illusions is the double-headed-arrow figure devised by Franz Müller-Lyer and presented in 15 variations in 1889 [*see illustration on page 53*]. This figure is so simple and the distortion is so compelling that it was immediately accepted as a primary target for theory and experiment. All kinds of theories were advanced. Wundt again invoked his eye-movement theory. It was also proposed that the "wings" of the arrowheads drew attention away from the ends of the central line, thus making it expand or contract; that the heads induced a state of empathy in the observer, making him feel as if the central line were being either stretched or compressed; that the distortion is a special case of a supposed general principle that acute angles tend

to be overestimated and obtuse angles underestimated, although why this should be so was left unexplained.

All these theories had a common feature: they were attempts to explain the distortions in terms of the stimulus pattern, without reference to its significance in terms of the perception of objects. There was, however, one quite different suggestion. In 1896 A. Thiery proposed that the distortions are related to the way the eye and brain utilize perspective to judge distances or depths. Thiery regarded the Müller-Lyer arrows as drawings of an object such as a saw-horse, seen in three dimensions; the legs would be going away from the observer

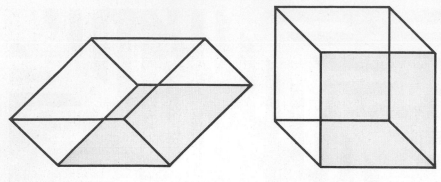

NECKER ILLUSION was devised in 1832 by L. A. Necker, a Swiss naturalist. He noticed that a transparent rhomboid (*left*) spontaneously reverses in depth. The area lightly tinted in color can appear either as an outer surface or as an inner surface of a transparent box. The illusion is now more usually presented as a transparent cube (*right*), known as a Necker cube.

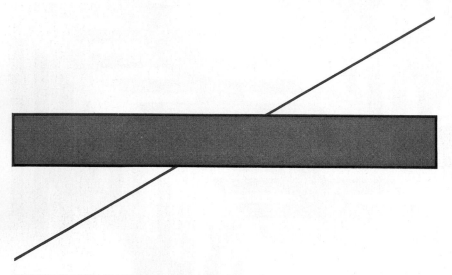

POGGENDORFF ILLUSION was proposed by Johann Poggendorff in 1860, the same year that Johann Zöllner proposed the figure shown on the preceding page. In Poggendorff's figure the two segments of the diagonal line seem to be offset.

PONZO ILLUSION, also known as the railway lines illusion, was proposed by Mario Ponzo in 1913. It is the prototype of the illusion depicted in the photograph on the opposite page.

in the acute-angled figure and toward him in the obtuse-angled figure. Except for a brief discussion of the "perspective theory" by Robert S. Woodworth in 1938, Thiery's suggestion has seldom been considered until recently.

Woodworth wrote: "In the Müller-Lyer figure the obliques readily suggest perspective and if this is followed one of the vertical lines appears farther away and therefore objectively longer than the other." This quotation brings out the immediate difficulties of developing an adequate theory along such lines. The distortion occurs even when the perspective suggestion is not followed up, because the arrows generally appear flat and yet are still distorted. Moreover, no hint is given of a mechanism responsible for the size changes. An adequate theory based on Thiery's suggestion must show how distortion occurs even though the figures appear flat. It should also indicate the kind of brain mechanisms responsible.

The notion that geometric perspective—the apparent convergence of parallel lines with distance—has a bearing on the problem is borne out by the occurrence of these distortions in photographs of actual scenes in which perspective is pronounced. Two rectangles of equal size look markedly unequal if they are superposed on a photograph of converging railroad tracks [*see illustration on facing page*]. The upper rectangle in the illustration, which would be the more distant if it were a real object lying between the tracks, looks larger than the lower (and apparently nearer) one. This corresponds to the Ponzo illusion [*see bottom illustration on this page*].

Similarly, the eye tends to expand the inside corner of a room, as it is seen in a photograph, and to shrink the outside corners of structures [*see illustration on page 58*]. The effect is just the same as the one in the Müller-Lyer figures, which in fact resemble outline drawings of corners seen in perspective. In both cases the regions indicated by perspective as being distant are expanded, whereas those indicated as being closer are shrunk. The distortions are opposite to the normal shrinking of the retinal image when the distance to an object is increased. Is this effect merely fortuitous, or is it a clue to the origin of the illusions?

Paradoxical Pictures

Before we come to grips with the problem of trying to develop an adequate theory of perspective it will be helpful to consider some curious fea-

ILLUSION INVOLVING PERSPECTIVE is remarkably constant for all human observers. The two rectangles superposed on this photograph of railroad tracks are precisely the same size, yet the top rectangle looks distinctly larger. The author regards this illusion as the prototype of visual distortions in which the perceptual mechanism, involving the brain, attempts to maintain a rough size constancy for similar objects placed at different distances. Since we know that the distant railroad ties are as large as the nearest ones, any object lying between the rails in the middle distance (the upper rectangle) is unconsciously enlarged. Indeed, if the rectangles were real objects lying between the rails, we would know immediately that the more distant was larger.

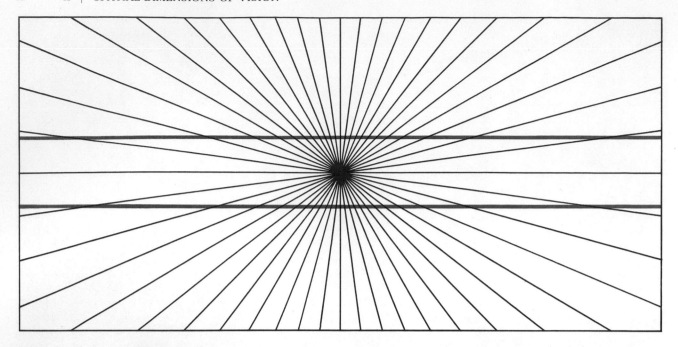

HERING ILLUSION was published in 1861 by Ewald Hering. The horizontal lines are of course straight. Physicists and astronomers of that period took a lively interest in illusions, being concerned that visual observations might sometimes prove unreliable.

tures of ordinary pictures. Pictures are the traditional material of perceptual research, but all pictures are highly artificial and present special problems to the perceiving brain. In a sense all pictures are impossible because they have a dual reality. They are seen both as patterns of lines lying on a flat background and as objects depicted in a quite different three-dimensional space. No actual object can be both two-dimensional and three-dimensional, yet pictures come close to it. Viewed as patterns they are seen as being two-dimensional; viewed as representing other objects they are seen in a quasi-three-dimensional space. Pictures therefore provide a paradoxical visual input. They are also ambiguous, because the third dimension is never precisely defined.

The Necker cube is an example of a picture in which the depth ambiguity is so great that the brain never settles for a single answer. The fact is, however, that any perspective projection could represent an infinity of three-dimensional shapes. One would think that the perceptual system has an impossible task! Fortunately for us the world of objects does not have infinite variety; there is usually a best bet, and we generally interpret our flat images more or less correctly in terms of the world of objects.

The difficulty of the problem of seeing the third dimension from the two dimensions of a picture, or from the

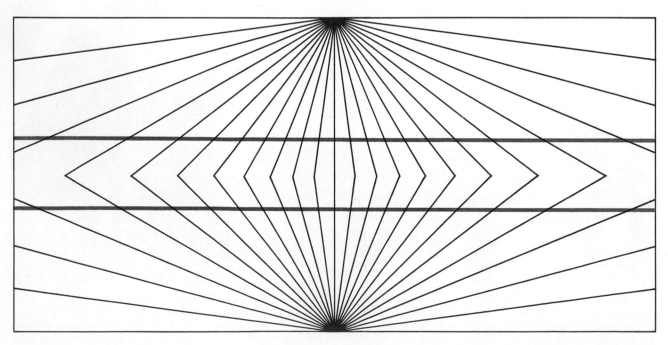

CONVERSE OF HERING ILLUSION was conceived in 1896 by Wilhelm Wundt, who introduced experimentation into psychology. Wundt earlier described the simplest of the visual illusions: that a vertical line looks longer than a horizontal line of equal length.

retinal images of normal objects, is ingeniously brought out by special "impossible pictures" and "impossible objects." They show what happens when clearly incompatible distance information is presented to the eye. The impossible triangle devised by Lionel S. Penrose and R. Penrose cannot be perceptually interpreted as an object in normal three-dimensional space [see illustration on page 54]. It is, however, perfectly possible to make actual three-dimensional objects, not mere pictures, that give rise to the same perceptual confusion—provided that they are viewed with only one eye. For example, the Penrose triangle can be built as an open three-dimensional structure [see top illustration on page 56] that looks like an impossible closed structure when it is viewed with one eye (or photographed) from exactly the right position [see bottom illustration on page 56].

Ordinary pictures are not so very different from obviously impossible pictures. All pictures showing depth are paradoxical: we see them both as being flat (which they really are) and as having a kind of artificial depth that is not quite right. We are not tempted to touch objects shown in a picture through the surface of the picture or in front of it. What happens, however, if we remove the surface? Does the depth paradox of pictures remain?

The Removal of Background

To remove the background for laboratory experiments we make the pictures luminous so that they glow in the dark. In order to deprive the brain of stereoscopic information that would reveal that the pictures are actually flat the pictures are viewed with one eye. They may be wire figures coated with luminous paint or photographic transparencies back-illuminated with an electroluminescent panel. In either case there is no visible background, so that we can discover how much the background is responsible for the depth paradox of pictures, including the illusion figures.

Under these conditions the Müller-Lyer arrows usually look like true corners according to their perspective. They may even be indistinguishable from actual luminous corners. The figures are not entirely stable: they sometimes reverse spontaneously in depth. Nonetheless, they usually appear according to their perspective and without the paradoxical depth of pictures with a background. The distortions are still present. The figure that resembles a

double-headed arrow looks like an outside corner and seems shrunk, whereas the figure with the arrowheads pointing the wrong way looks like an inside corner and is expanded. Now, however, the paradox has disappeared and the figures look like true corners. With a suitable apparatus one can point out their depth as if they were normal three-dimensional objects.

Having removed the paradox, it is possible to measure, by quite direct means, the apparent distance of any selected part of the figures. This we do by using the two eyes to serve as a range finder for indicating the apparent depth of the figure, which is visible to only one eye. The back-illuminated picture is placed behind a polarizing filter so that one eye is prevented from seeing the picture by a second polarizing filter oriented at right angles to the first. Both eyes, however, are allowed to see one or more small movable reference lights that are optically introduced into the picture by means of a half-silvered mirror set at 45 degrees to the line of sight. The distance of these lights is given by stereoscopic vision, that is, by the convergence angle of the eyes; by moving the lights so that they seem to coincide with the apparent distance of selected parts of the picture we can plot the visual space of the ob-

server in three dimensions [see top illustration on page 55].

When this plotting is done for various angles of the "fin," or arrowhead line, in the Müller-Lyer illusion figure, it becomes clear that the figures are perceived as inside and outside corners. The illusion of depth conforms closely to the results obtained when the magnitude of the illusion is independently measured by asking subjects to select comparison lines that match the apparent length of the central line between two kinds of arrowhead [see bottom illustration on page 55]. In the latter experiment the figures are drawn on a normally textured background, so that they appear flat.

The two experiments show that when the background is removed, depth very closely follows the illusion for the various fin angles. The similarity of the plotted results provides evidence of a remarkably close connection between the illusion as it occurs when depth is not seen and the depth that is seen when the background is removed. This suggests that Thiery was essentially correct: perspective can somehow create distortions. What is odd is that perspective produces the distortions according to indicated perspective depth even when depth is not consciously seen.

MÜLLER-LYER ILLUSION was devised by Franz Müller-Lyer in 1889. Many theories were subsequently invoked in an attempt to explain why reversed arrowheads (right) seem to lengthen a connecting shaft whereas normal arrowheads seem to shrink the shaft (left).

Size Constancy

The next step is to look for some perceptual mechanism that could produce this relation between perspective and apparent size. A candidate that should have been obvious many years ago is size constancy. This phenomenon was clearly described in 1637 by René Descartes in his *Dioptrics*. "It is not the absolute size of images [in the eyes] that counts," he wrote. "Clearly they are 100 times bigger [in area] when objects are very close than when they are 10 times farther away, but they do not make us see the objects 100 times bigger. On the contrary, they seem almost the same size, at any rate as we are not deceived by too great a distance."

We know from many experiments that Descartes is quite right. What happens, however, when distance information, such as perspective, is presented to the eye but two components of the scene, one of which should be shrunk by distance, are the same size? Could it be that perspective presented on a flat plane triggers the brain to compensate for the expected shrinking of the images with distance even though there is no shrinking for which to compensate? If some such thing happens, it is easy to see why figures that suggest perspective can give rise to distortions. This would provide the start of a reasonable theory of illusions. Features indicated as being distant would be expanded, which is just what we find, at least for the Müller-Lyer and the Ponzo figures.

It is likely that this approach to the problem was not developed until recently because, although size constancy was quite well known, it has always been assumed that it simply follows apparent distance in all circumstances. Moreover, it has not been sufficiently realized how very odd pictures are as visual inputs. They are highly atypical and should be studied as a special case, being both paradoxical and ambiguous.

Size constancy is traditionally identified with an effect known as Emmert's law. This effect can be explained by a simple experiment involving the apparent size of afterimages in vision. If one can obtain a good afterimage (preferably by briefly illuminating a test figure with an electronic flash lamp), one can "project" it on screens or walls located at various distances. The afterimage will appear almost twice as large with each doubling of distance, even though the size of the image from the flash remains constant. It is important to note, however, that there *is* a change in retinal stimulation for each screen or wall lying at a different distance; their images *do* vary. It is possible that the size change of the afterimage is due not so much to a brain mechanism that changes its scal as to its size on the retina with respect to the size of the screen on which it appears to lie. Before we go any further, it is essential to discover whether Emmert's law is due merely to the relation between the areas covered by the afterimage and the screen, or whether the visual information of distance changes the size of the afterimage by some kind of internal scaling. This presents us with a tricky experimental problem.

As it turns out, there is a simple solution. We can use the ambiguous depth phenomenon of the Necker cube to establish whether Emmert's law is due to a central scaling by the brain or is merely an effect of relative areas of stimulation of the retina. When we see a Necker cube that is drawn on paper reverse in depth, there is no appreciable size change. When the cube is presented on a textured background, it occupies the paradoxical depth of all pictures with visible backgrounds; it does not change in size when it reverses in pseudo-depth.

What happens, however, if we remove the cube's background? The effect is dramatic and entirely repeatable: with each reversal in depth the cube changes its apparent shape, even though there is no change in the retinal image. Whichever face appears to be more distant always appears to be the larger. The use of depth-ambiguous figures in this way makes it possible to separate what happens when the pattern of stimulation of the retina is changed. The answer is that at least part of size constancy, and of Emmert's law, is due to a central size-scaling mechanism in the brain that responds to changes in apparent distance although the retinal stimulation is unchanged.

Apparent size, then, is evidently established in two ways. It can be estab-

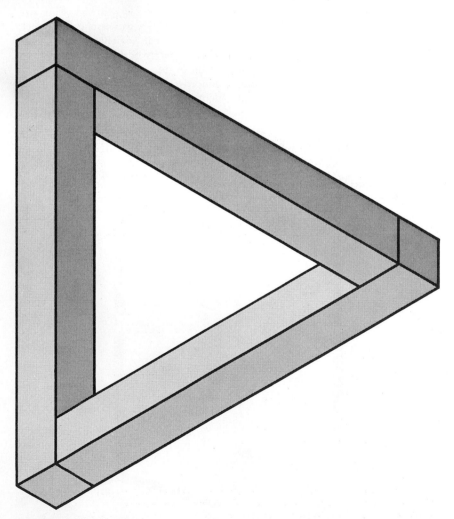

IMPOSSIBLE TRIANGLE was devised by Lionel S. Penrose and R. Penrose of University College London. It is logically consistent over restricted regions but is nonsensical overall. The author sees a certain similarity between such impossible figures and ordinary photographs, which provide the illusion of a third dimension even though they are flat.

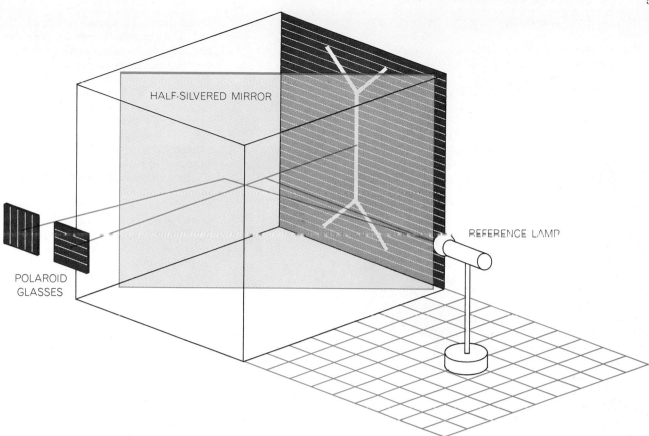

HALF-SILVERED MIRROR

POLAROID GLASSES

REFERENCE LAMP

APPARATUS FOR STUDYING ILLUSIONS was devised by the author. The objective is to present figures such as the Müller-Lyer arrows with the background removed so that the figures seem suspended in space. Under these conditions the Müller-Lyer arrows generally look like true corners. The subject can adjust a small light so that it appears to lie at the same depth as any part of the figure. The light, which the subject sees in three-dimensional space with both eyes, is superposed on the illuminated figure by means of a half-silvered mirror. A polarizing filter is placed over the figure and the subject wears polarizing glasses that allow him to see the figure with only one eye. Thus he has no way of telling whether the figure is really two-dimensional or three-dimensional.

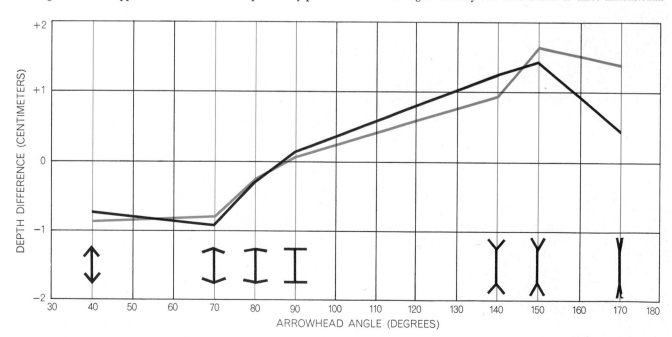

QUANTITATIVE MEASUREMENT OF ILLUSION produced the results plotted here for Müller-Lyer arrows. The black curve shows the average results for 20 subjects who were asked to select a comparison line that matched the length of a central shaft to which were attached arrowheads set at the angles indicated. When arrowheads were set at less than 90 degrees, the comparison lines were as much as one centimeter shorter. When the arrowhead was set at 150 degrees, the comparison line was more than 1.5 centimeters longer. The colored curve shows the maximum depth difference perceived for the same set of arrows when displayed, with the background removed, in the apparatus shown in the illustration at the top of the page. The two curves match quite closely except at the extreme setting of 170 degrees, when the figure no longer resembles a true corner when presented in the light box.

ACTUAL IMPOSSIBLE TRIANGLE was constructed by the author and his colleagues. The only requirement is that it be viewed with one eye (or photographed) from exactly the right position. The top photograph shows that two arms do not actually meet. When viewed in a certain way (*bottom*), they seem to come together and the illusion is complete.

lished purely by apparent distance. It can also be established directly by visual depth features, such as perspective in two-dimensional pictures, even though depth is not seen because it is countermanded by competing depth information such as a visible background. When atypical depth features are present, size scaling is established inappropriately and we have a corresponding distortion illusion.

The size scaling established directly by depth features (giving systematic distortions when it is established inappropriately) we may call "depth-cue scaling." It is remarkably consistent and independent of the observer's perceptual "set." The other system is quite different and more subtle, being only indirectly related to the prevailing retinal information. It is evidently linked to the interpretation of the retinal image in terms of what object it represents. When it appears as a different object, the scaling changes at once to suit the alternative object. If we regard the seeing of an object as a hypothesis, suggested (but never strictly proved) by the image, we may call the system "depth-hypothesis scaling," because it changes with each change of the hypothesis of what object is represented by the image. When the hypothesis is wrong, we have an illusion that may be dramatic. Such alternations in hypotheses underlie the changes in direction, and even size, that occur when one watches the shadow of a rotating vane.

Observers in Motion

The traditional distortion illusions can be attributed to errors in the setting of the depth-cue scaling system, which arise when figures or objects have misleading depth cues, particularly perspective on a flat plane. Although these illusions might occasionally bother investigators making visual measurements, they are seldom a serious hazard. The other kind of illusion—incorrect size-scaling due to an error in the prevailing perceptual hypothesis—can be serious in unfamiliar conditions or when there is little visual information available, as in space flight. It can also be important in driving a car at night or in landing an airplane under conditions of poor visibility. Illusions are most hazardous when the observer is in rapid motion, because then even a momentary error may lead to disaster.

So far little work has been done on the measurement of illusions experienced by observers who are in motion with respect to their surroundings. The experimental difficulties involved in making such measurements are severe; nevertheless, we have been tackling the problem with support from the U.S. Air Force. The equipment, which is fairly elaborate, can move the observer with controlled velocity and acceleration through various visual environments, including the blackness of space (with or without artificial stars presented optically at infinite distance).

We measure the observer's visual sense of size constancy as he is moving by having him look at a projected display that changes size as he approaches or recedes from it. As he moves away from it, the display is made to expand in size; as he approaches it, the display is made to shrink. The change in size is adjusted until, to the moving observer, the display appears fixed in size. If there were no perceptual mechanism for constancy scaling, the size of the display would have to be adjusted so that its image on the observer's retina would be the same size regardless of his distance from it. If, at the other extreme, the size-constancy effect were complete, we could leave the display unchanged and it would still appear to be the same size regardless of its actual distance from the observer. In practice some size change between these limits provides the illusion of an unchanging display, and this gives us a measure of the size-constancy effect as the observer is moved about.

We find that when the observer is in complete darkness, watching a display that is projected from the back onto a large screen, there is no measureable size constancy when the observer is moving at a fixed speed. When he is accelerated, size constancy does appear but it may be wildly wrong. In particular, if he interprets his movement incorrectly, either in direction or in amount, size constancy usually fails and can even work in reverse. This is rather similar to the reversal of size constancy with reversal of the depth of the luminous Necker cube. In the conditions of space, perception may be dominated by the prevailing hypothesis of distance and velocity. If either is wrong, as it may well be for lack of reliable visual information, the astronaut may suffer visual illusions that could be serious.

The Nonvisual in Vision

Visual perception involves "reading" from retinal images a host of characteristics of objects that are not represented directly by the images in the eyes. The image does not convey directly many important characteristics of objects:

whether they are hard or soft, heavy or light, hot or cold. Nonvisual characteristics must somehow be associated with the visual image, by individual learning or conceivably through heredity, for objects to be recognized from their images. Psychologists now believe individual perceptual learning is very important for associating the nonoptical properties of objects with their retinal images. Such learning is essential for perception; without it one would have mere stimulus-response behavior.

Perception seems to be a matter of looking up information that has been stored about objects and how they behave in various situations. The retinal image does little more than select the relevant stored data. This selection is rather like looking up entries in an encyclopedia: behavior is determined by the contents of the entry rather than by the stimulus that provoked the search. We can think of perception as being essentially the selection of the most appropriate stored hypothesis according to current sensory data.

Now, a look-up system of this kind has great advantages over a control system that responds simply to current input. If stored information is used, behavior can continue in the temporary absence of relevant information, or when there is inadequate information to provide precise control of behavior directly. This advantage has important implications for any possible perceptual system, including any future "seeing machine": a robot equipped with artificial eyes and a computer and designed to control vehicles or handle objects by means of artificial limbs. Even when enough direct sensory information is available for determining the important characteristics of surrounding objects (which is seldom the case), it would require a rate of data transmission in excess of that provided by the human nervous system (or current computers) to enable a robot to behave appropriately. Hence there are strong general design reasons for supposing that any effective seeing system—whether biological or man-made—should use current sensory

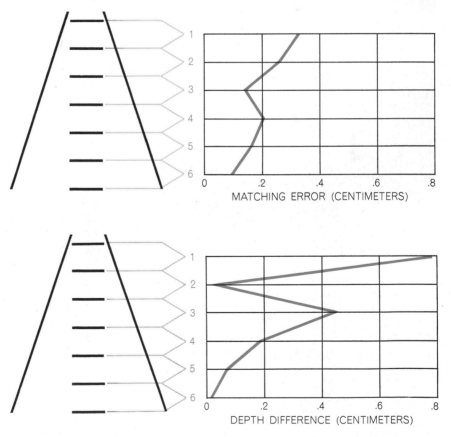

RAILWAY LINES ILLUSION can also be studied quantitatively. The methods are the same as those described in the bottom illustration on page 55. Subjects were presented with a horizontal line at one of the indicated positions and asked to select a second line that seemed to match it in length. The matching error for different pairs is plotted in the top curve. Pairs of lines were then presented in the apparatus shown at the top of page 55 and the subjects adjusted the light to match the apparent depth of each line. Under these conditions (bottom curve) the illusion of depth is much more dependent on where a given pair of lines is located with respect to the "rails," but the trend of the top curve is preserved.

information for selecting performed hypotheses, or models, representing important features of the external world of objects as opposed to controlling behavior directly from sensory inputs.

If we consider the problems of storing information about objects, it soon becomes clear that it would be most uneconomical to store an independent model of each object for every distance and orientation it might occupy in surrounding space. It would be far more economical to store only typical characteristics of objects and to use current sensory information to adjust the selected model to fit the prevailing situation.

The model must be continually scaled for distance and orientation if the owner of the perceptual system is to interact with the object.

We might guess that depth-cue scaling represents this adjustment of the selected model in the light of the available depth information. When the available information is inappropriate (as in the case of perspective features on a flat plane), it will scale the perceptual model wrongly. There will be a systematic error: a distortion illusion due to inappropriate depth-cue scaling. There will also be errors—possibly very large ones—whenever a wrong model is selected. We

see this happening in a repeatable way in the ambiguous figures, such as the luminous Necker cube, that change shape with each depth reversal even though the sensory input is unchanged.

If this general account of perception as essentially a look-up system is correct, we should expect illusions similar to our own to arise in any effective perceptual system, including future robots. Illusions are not caused by any limitation of our brain. They are the result of the imperfect solutions available to any data-handling system faced with the problem of establishing the reality of objects from ambiguous images.

THEORY OF MÜLLER-LYER ILLUSION favored by the author suggests that the eye unconsciously interprets the arrow-like figures as three-dimensional skeleton structures, resembling either an outside (*left*) or inside corner (*right*) of a physical structure. A perceptual mechanism evidently shrinks the former and enlarges the latter to compensate for distortion caused by perspective.

6

Texture and Visual Perception

Bela Julesz
February 1965

*Random–dot patterns generated by computer show
that the recognition of familiar shapes is not needed
for the discrimination of textures or even, as had been
thought, for the binocular perception of depth*

Because we are surrounded every waking minute by objects of different sizes, shapes, colors and textures we are scarcely surprised that we can tell them apart. There are so many visual clues to the distinctiveness of objects that we hardly ever make the mistake of believing that two different objects are one object unless we have been deliberately tricked.

Four years ago I became interested in studying the extent to which one can perceive differences in visual patterns when all familiar cues are removed. In this way I hoped to dissociate the primitive mechanisms of perception from the more complex ones that depend on lifelong learned habits of recognition. To obtain suitable patterns for this investigation a computer was used to generate displays that had subtly controlled statistical, topological or other properties but entirely lacked familiar features.

This method is basically different from those employed earlier by workers interested in visual perception. One method that has been widely used is to impoverish or degrade the images presented to the subject. This can be done by adding visual "noise," by presenting the stimuli for a limited time or by otherwise impairing the normal conditions of viewing. Another approach is to study human subjects whose perceptual mechanisms are known to be deficient

(such as color-blind people) or animals whose perceptual mechanisms have been altered by surgical operations. I hoped that my approach of "familiarity deprivation" might be a useful addition to these other methods.

In a broad sense I was interested in the same kind of problem that has long concerned psychologists of the *Gestalt* school. One such problem has been to explain why it is that under certain conditions an outline drawing is seen as a unified whole—as a *Gestalt*—and under other conditions is seen as having two or more parts. I undertook to reduce this problem to how one discriminated between the parts (or did not discriminate between them). In my investigations, which have been conducted at the Bell Telephone Laboratories, I have been concerned with two specific questions. First, can two unfamiliar objects connected in space be discriminated solely by differences in their surface texture? Second, can two unfamiliar objects with identical surface texture be discriminated solely on the basis of their separation in space?

To make these questions less abstract let me give examples that could arise in real life. The first question would be involved if you wanted to replace a section of wallpaper and discovered that the original pattern was no longer available. If the pattern happened to be

nonrepresentational and irregular, you might be able to find a new pattern that could not easily be discriminated from the old one when the two were placed side by side. Yet if you studied the two patterns closely, you might find that they differed substantially in detail. You would conclude that the matching must be attributable to the similarity of certain critical features in the two patterns.

The second question has its counterpart in aerial reconnaissance to detect objects that have been camouflaged. Flying at a height of several thousand feet, an observer can easily be deceived by the camouflage because normal binocular depth perception is inoperative beyond 100 feet or so. But if he photographs the ground from two points several hundred feet apart and views the resulting pictures stereoscopically, he will usually discover that even a camouflaged object will stand out vividly in three dimensions.

Of course neither of these examples provides an adequate test of the discrimination problems I hoped to examine with artificial displays. The weakness in the wallpaper analogy is that most wallpaper patterns, including irregular ones, have repetitive features and even forms that suggest familiar objects. The aerial reconnaissance example has the important defect that most camouflaged objects have contours

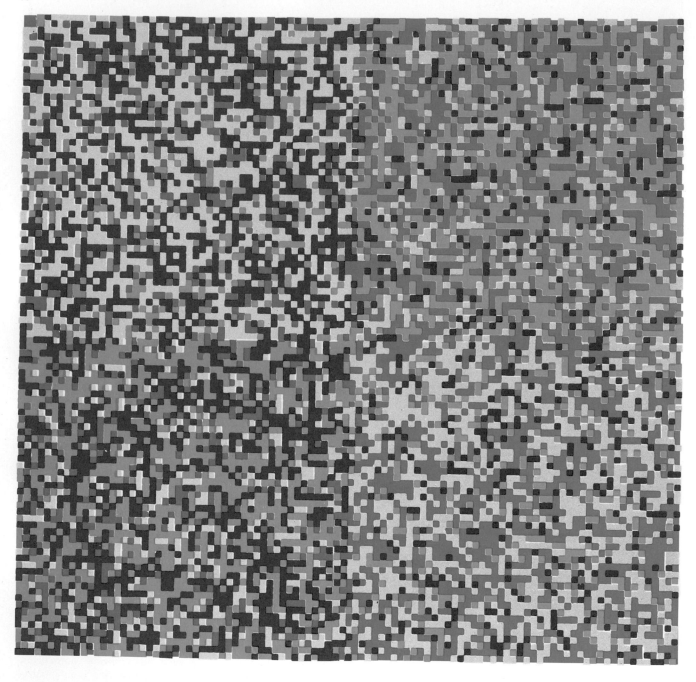

TEXTURE DISCRIMINATION in random fields of colored dots is highly dependent on the way the component colors are paired. The two patterns at the top of the opposite page are basically the same as those shown one above the other in the figure on this page. Neither version adequately reproduces the author's laboratory demonstration, in which the patterns are created by colored lights of equal subjective brightness. To simulate this condition the yellow picture elements above have been reduced in brightness by a fine-mesh overlay of black dots. They have the drawback, however, of making the yellow areas look greenish. In the version on the opposite page the black-dot overlay has been omitted, with the result that the yellow elements are much too bright. On the whole the figure above comes closer to achieving the desired effect, which is to show that a texture composed chiefly of red and yellow dots is readily discriminated from a texture composed chiefly of blue and green dots (top half of figure on this page), whereas a texture composed chiefly of red and green dots is not so readily discriminated from one composed chiefly of blue and yellow dots (bottom half of figure). These paired textures—one easily discriminable, the other less so—are respectively repeated at top left and right on the opposite page. The makeup of each top panel is shown in the four panels below it. The only difference is in the transposition of yellow and green.

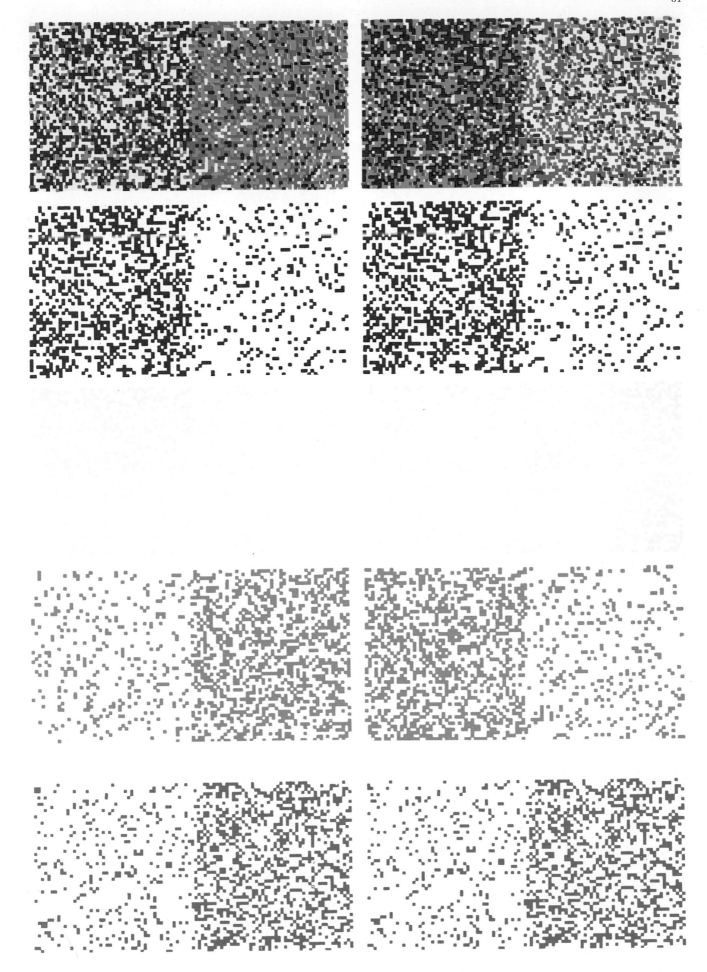

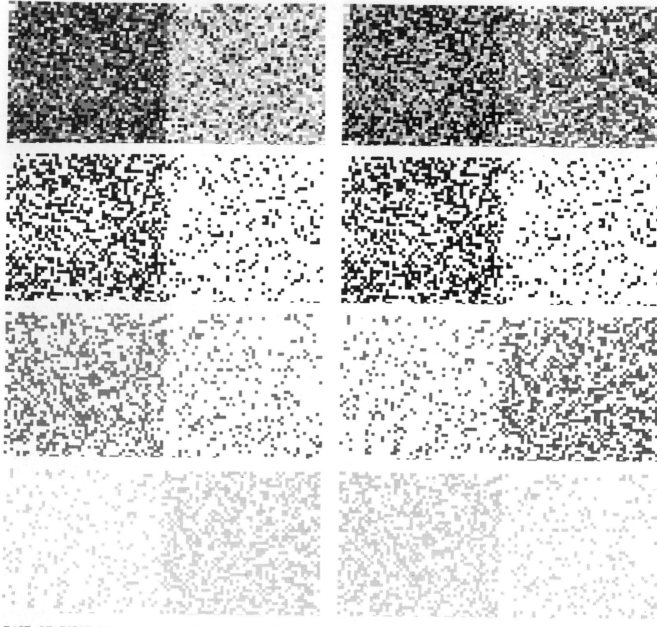

EASE OF DISCRIMINATION in random patterns of various brightness levels seems to depend on whether or not adjacent dots of different values form clusters. The pattern at top left forms two easily discriminated areas because the half field on the left contains mostly black and dark gray dots, which form dark clusters, whereas the half field on the right contains mostly light gray and white dots, which form light clusters. When the dark gray and light gray components are reversed (*top right*), the clustering does not take place and the half fields are not so readily discriminated. The composition of each top pattern is shown in the three panels below it.

SPONTANEOUS DISCRIMINATION occurs even though the smaller field has the same average tonal quality as the larger field because the granularity of the two fields is different. At a distance the granularity is less noticeable and discrimination more difficult.

```
SCIENCE SPECIFY PRECISE SUBJECT MERCURY GOVERNS   ECNEICS YFICEPS ESICERP TCEJBUS YRUCREM SNREVOG
METHODS RECORDS OXIDIZE COLUMNS CERTAIN QUICKLY   SDOHTEM SDROCER EZIDIXO SNMULOC NIATREC YLKCIUQ
DEPICTS ENGLISH CERTAIN RECORDS EXAMPLE SCIENCE   STCIPED HSILGNE NIATREC SDROCER ELPMAXE ECNEICS
SUBJECT PUNCHED GOVERNS MERCURY SPECIFY PRECISE   TCEJBUS DEHCNUP SNREVOG YRUCREM YFICEPS ESICERP
EXAMPLE QUICKLY SPECIFY METHODS COLUMNS MERCURY   ELPMAXE YLKCIUQ YFICEPS SDOHTEM SNMULOC YRUCREM
SCIENCE PRECISE EXAMPLE CERTAIN DEPICTS ENGLISH   ECNEICS ESICERP ELPMAXE NIATREC STCIPED HSILGNE
SPECIFY MERCURY PUNCHED QUICKLY METHODS EXAMPLE   YFICEPS YRUCREM DEHCNUP YLKCIUQ SDOHTEM ELPMAXE
EXAMPLE GOVERNS OXIDIZE ENGLISH SUBJECT RECORDS   ELPMAXE SNREVOG EZIDIXO HSILGNE TCEJBUS SDROCER
COLUMNS SUBJECT PRECISE MERCURY PUNCHED CERTAIN   SNMULOC TCEJBUS ESICERP YRUCREM DEHCNUP NIATREC
ENGLISH RECORDS EXAMPLE SUBJECT OXIDIZE GOVERNS   HSILGNE SDROCER ELPMAXE TCEJBUS EZIDIXO SNREVOG
CERTAIN PRECISE PUNCHED METHODS ENGLISH COLUMNS   NIATREC ESICERP DEHCNUP SDOHTEM HSILGNE SNMULOC
OXIDIZE QUICKLY SCIENCE DEPICTS SPECIFY PRECISE   EZIDIXO YLKCIUQ ECNEICS STCIPED YFICEPS ESICERP
DEPICTS EXAMPLE ENGLISH CERTAIN RECORDS SCIENCE   STCIPED ELPMAXE HSILGNE NIATREC SDROCER ECNEICS
SPECIFY MERCURY GOVERNS PRECISE QUICKLY METHODS   YFICEPS YRUCREM SNREVOG ESICERP YLKCIUQ SKOHTEM
```

NONSPONTANEOUS DISCRIMINATION is represented by two half fields that have the same apparent texture and granularity. The left half field, however, contains familiar English words, whereas the right half field contains only random sequences of seven letters.

that can be recognized monocularly as shapes of some sort; they are not, in other words, random patterns.

These and other difficulties are quite easily circumvented by using a computer to generate random-dot patterns in which all familiar cues and other unwanted factors are eliminated. For the purpose of studying the first problem—the role of texture in discrimination —random-dot patterns with different properties were generated side by side. The objective was to determine those pattern properties that make it possible to discriminate between the adjacent visual displays. I was concerned primarily with the discrimination that can be achieved immediately. Such discrimination can be regarded as a spontaneous process and thus can be ascribed to a primitive perceptual mechanism.

An example of spontaneous discrimination is given by the illustration at bottom left on the opposite page. Both fields of the pattern contain black, gray and white dots with equal first-order, or overall, probability; therefore if the pattern is viewed from a distance, both fields appear uniformly gray. When the two fields are viewed at close range, however, they exhibit a different second-order, or detailed, probability. This shows up immediately as a difference in granularity.

The illustration at bottom right on the opposite page represents a case in which there can be no spontaneous discrimination between two fields. In this case discrimination can be achieved only by someone who knows the difference between English words and random sequences of letters. Here discrimination requires a sophisticated kind of pattern recognition. This article is concerned only with discrimination of the spontaneous type.

In the case of random-dot patterns one might expect that discrimination of visual texture is fundamentally governed by variations in the statistical properties of the patterns. That is true in the most general sense, because any two different patterns must differ in some such property. It turns out, however, that simple statistical measurements of brightness distribution are not adequate to describe perceptual performance.

This is demonstrated in the illustration at upper left on this page, which consists of two patterns made up of black, gray and white dots. In one quadrant the dots are distributed with equal probability and completely at random. The surrounding area matches the quadrant in overall brightness, but it also contains small triangular units com-

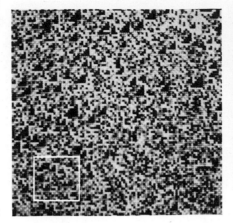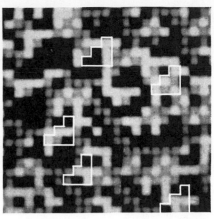

CLUSTER IDENTIFICATION in the pattern at left extends only to triangular shapes made up entirely of black dots. Other equally probable triangles containing dots of mixed brightness do not form clusters. These are marked in the enlargement at right.

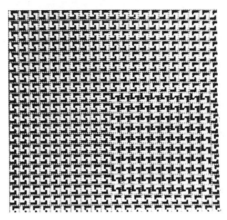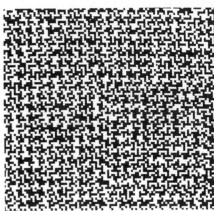

EFFECT OF "NOISE" is demonstrated in these two patterns. In the pattern at left the two subpatterns containing either black or white "S" shapes are easily discriminated. Moreover, every fifth horizontal and vertical row is gray. The pattern at right is identical except that the dots in the gray rows have been made black or white at random. By breaking up the connectivity of the pattern in this way the subpatterns are almost obliterated.

posed of black, white and gray dots in various arrangements. Although these triangular units occur with equal probability, the only ones observed are those made up entirely of black dots; the others pass unnoticed.

This indicates that discrimination of visual texture is not based on complex statistical analysis of brightness distribution but involves a kind of preprocessing. Evidently the preprocessing extracts neighboring points that have similar brightness values, which are perceived as forming clusters or lines. This process, which should not be confused with the actual spatial connection of objects, might be called connectivity detection. It is on the relatively simple statistics of these clusters and some simple description of them, such as spatial extent, that texture discrimination is really based.

The lower pair of illustrations above shows this connectivity detection even

more clearly. In the left member of the pair two textures are easily discriminated; in the right member discrimination is difficult, if not impossible. In the pattern at the left every fifth horizontal and vertical row is gray; in the pattern at the right, which is otherwise identical, every fifth row is randomly peppered black and white. The "noise" added to the pattern at the right has only a minor effect on the statistics of the two subpatterns to be discriminated, yet it breaks up the connectivity of the subpatterns enough for them to merge into one field. The black and white "S" shapes that appear so clearly in the pattern at the left are completely destroyed in the pattern at the right. If the disrupted pattern is viewed at a sharp angle, however, the line clusters reappear and discrimination is facilitated.

The importance of proximity and similarity was emphasized early in the

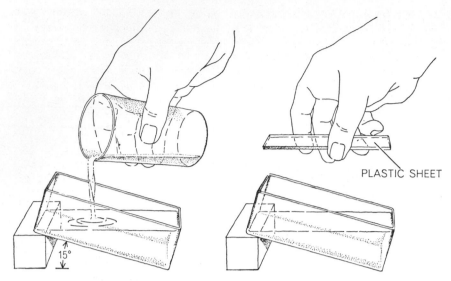

GELATIN PRISM provides a simple stereoscopic viewer. A clear plastic box for hold-ing the gelatin can be obtained at a five-and-ten-cent store. Use five parts of very hot water to one part of household gelatin and mix thoroughly. Tilt the box about 15 degrees and pour in the gelatin solution. In about 30 minutes, when the solution has gelled, dampen the surface and press a rectangular sheet of clear plastic (or glass) against it. The prism will ordinarily work without this top sheet, but images may appear fuzzy.

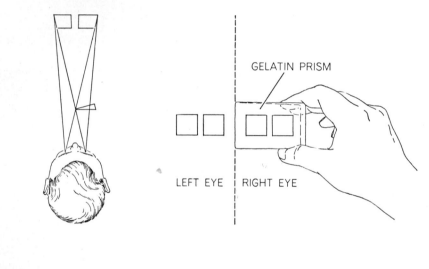

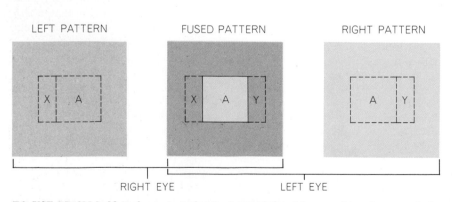

TO USE PRISM hold it about six inches in front of the right eye, thin edge toward the nose. Adjust the prism so that both stereoscopic images can be seen through it. Both images should also be visible to the left eye, as shown in the upper two diagrams. With little difficulty the images should rearrange themselves so that there appear to be only three images, of which the center one is the fused stereoscopic image. Once binocular fusion has occurred the image can be made sharper by moving the prism closer to the right eye.

work of the *Gestalt* psychologists, par-ticularly that of Kurt Koffka and Max Wertheimer. Now, with the help of the random-dot-pattern technique one can give a more precise meaning to these notions. For example, the last experi-ment, in which the disrupted pattern is viewed at an angle, shows that neigh-boring points need not touch each other to appear connected. This notion comes as no surprise. On the other hand, when one observes that neighboring points of similar brightness are perceived as clus-ters, the meaning of "similar brightness" requires further clarification. How dis-similar in brightness can adjacent points be and still be perceived as clusters? In order to examine this question two com-puter patterns were generated.

In one pattern, shown at top left on page 62, the field at the left is com-posed chiefly of black and dark grey ran-dom dots; the field at the right contains mostly white and light gray dots. As a result the field at the left forms a large dark cluster and the field at the right forms a light cluster, with a fairly sharp boundary between them. In the adja-cent pattern the light gray and dark gray dots are transposed so that the field at the left contains chiefly black and light gray dots and the field at the right contains chiefly white and dark gray dots. Here discrimination between the two fields is more difficult. These and similar results suggest that the visual system incorporates a slicer mechanism that separates adjacent brightness levels into two broad categories: dark and light. The level of slicing can be ad-justed up and down, but it is impossible to form clusters by shifting our attention to dots that are not adjacent in bright-ness.

One might argue that the eye could hardly respond otherwise when bright-ness levels are involved. It can be shown, however, that the same con-nectivity rules hold for patterns com-posed of dots of different colors adjusted to have the same subjective brightness. This is the demonstration that is shown on pages 60 and 61. Since these pat-terns are made up of colored inks that do not reflect light with equal intensity, they do not fully simulate the labora-tory demonstration, in which the dots are projected on a screen in such a way that their subjective brightness can be carefully balanced. Nonetheless, the printed demonstration, particularly the one on the cover, is reasonably effective. In the pattern on the cover what one observes is that the top half of the pat-tern is immediately discriminated into a red-yellow field on the left and a blue-green field on the right, whereas the bottom half of the pattern seems more or less uniform in texture across its entire width. This uniformity in texture is achieved simply by transposing the yellow and green random elements so that the field at the left is composed mostly of red and green dots and the field at the right is composed mostly of blue

and yellow dots. The first demonstration shows that red and yellow dots form clusters that are easily discriminated from the clusters formed by blue and green dots. The second demonstration shows that dots of nonadjacent hue, such as red and green or blue and yellow, do not form clusters.

Evidently this clustering, whether it

is of adjacent brightness levels or of adjacent hues, represents a preprocessing mechanism of great importance in the visual system. Instead of performing complex statistical analyses when presented with complex patterns, the visual system wherever possible detects clusters and evaluates only a few of their relatively simple properties. One now

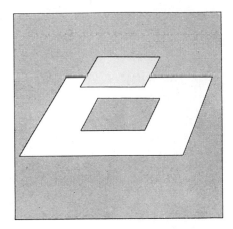

STEREOSCOPIC IMAGES investigated by the author consist of random-dot patterns generated by a computer. When these two images are viewed with a stereoscope or with a prism held in front of one eye, a center panel should be seen floating above the background, as illustrated at the far right. The principle employed in making such stereoscopic images is explained below.

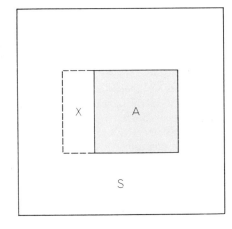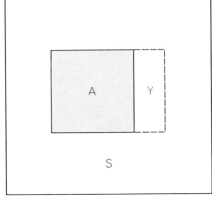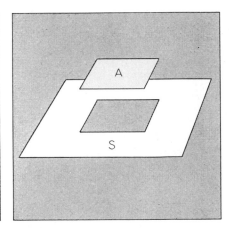

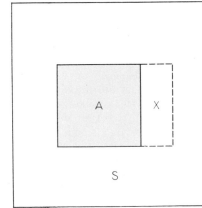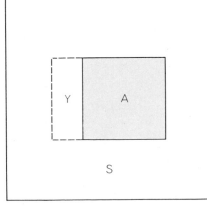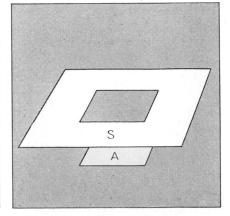

STEREOSCOPIC PRINCIPLE is simply that identical areas that appear in both fields must be shifted horizontally with respect to each other. Because these areas are themselves random-dot patterns they cannot be seen monocularly against a random-dot surround. In these diagrams A identifies the area common to both fields. In the upper pair of fields A is shifted inward, leaving two areas, X and Y, that are filled in with different random-dot patterns. When viewed stereoscopically, A seems to float above the surround. When A is shifted outward as shown in the two lower fields, A seems to lie behind the surround.

has a formula for matching wallpaper patterns. As long as the brightness value, the spatial extent, the orientation and the density of clusters are kept similar in two patterns, they will be perceived as one. Even for familiar patterns with recognizable and differ-

ent forms discrimination can be made very difficult or impossible if the simple rules that govern clustering are observed. Thus a wallpaper pattern made up of seven-letter English words arranged in columns, as in the illustration at bottom right on page 62, would

appear to be matched by a similar pattern containing nonsense sequences. The seven-letter nonwords would form clusters that could not be discriminated spontaneously from English words.

These findings answer in the affirmative the first question raised at the beginning. Objects can indeed be discriminated by differences in their surface texture alone even if they are spatially connected and cannot be recognized. The basis of this texture discrimination depends on simple properties of clusters, which are detected according to simple rules. Cluster detection seems to be a quite primitive and general process. Recent neurophysiological studies of frogs and cats have disclosed that their visual systems extract certain basic features of a scene prior to more complex processing [see the articles "Vision in Frogs," by W. R. A. Muntz; SCIENTIFIC AMERICAN, March, 1964; and "The Visual Cortex of the Brain," by David H. Hubel; SCIENTIFIC AMERICAN Offprint 168]. The "bug" detector in the frog's visual system and the slit detector in the cat's visual system are special cases of connectivity detection. It will be interesting to see if neurophysiologists can find evidence for cluster detectors of the type suggested by these perception experiments.

BLURRED IMAGE was produced by defocusing the field at left in the random-dot stereoscopic patterns on the preceding page. The field at right is unchanged. In spite of the blurring the two fields will fuse into a stereoscopic image; moreover, the image looks sharp.

REDUCED IMAGE also does not interfere seriously with the ability to obtain a good stereoscopic image. The two random-dot patterns are again those shown on the preceding page. The stereoscopic field at left, however, has been reduced about 10 percent in size.

We are now ready to consider the second question: Can two unfamiliar objects of identical texture be discriminated solely on the basis of their spatial separation? To study this question it was necessary to create patterns that were unfamiliar, that had the same surface texture and that could be perceived in depth. Again the problem was solved with the help of random-dot patterns generated by a computer. This time the computer was used to generate pairs of patterns that were identical except for a central area that was displaced in various ways. I had hoped that one would obtain a sensation of depth when the two patterns were viewed stereoscopically, and I was delighted when that turned out to be the case. This proved that one can perceive a camouflaged object in depth even when the camouflage is perfect and the hidden object cannot be discerned monocularly. In short, the answer to the second question is also yes.

A pair of these random-dot stereoscopic patterns is shown in the upper illustration on the preceding page. The two patterns are identical except for a center square that is shifted horizontally to the left by six dots in the pattern at the right. By virtue of this shift the

NOISY IMAGE (left) is produced by breaking up triplets of black dots along one diagonal and white triplets along the other diagonal wherever they occur in the left field on the preceding page. Nevertheless, the two fields will still fuse stereoscopically.

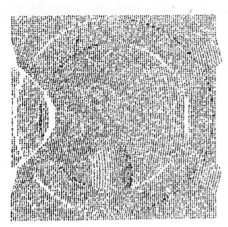
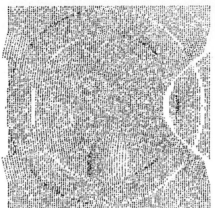
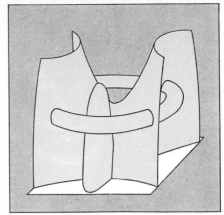

SADDLE-SHAPED FIGURE (*far right*) was transformed into left and right stereoscopic fields by a computer program devised by the author. The picture elements consist of 64 standard characters randomly selected but paired in the left and right fields.

square seems to float above the background when it is viewed stereoscopically. If the reader does not have an old-fashioned stereoscopic viewer at hand, by following the instructions on page 64 he can easily make a prism of gelatin that will serve the same purpose.

The phenomenon demonstrated by the binocular fusion of such random-dot patterns has a number of surprising implications. First of all, as the original statement of the problem requires, the stereoscopic picture is completely devoid of all familiarity and depth cues. Although the area selected for stereoscopic displacement in the first example is a simple square, it could be of any shape and it could also give the illusion of having more than one level [*see illustration above*]. The fact that the center square and its surround are horizontally shifted by different amounts in the fields at left and right corresponds to the different depth levels that are perceived. Thus spatial disconnectivity alone is enough for the center square and its surround to be perceived as two distinct objects.

The demonstration also demolishes a long-standing hypothesis of stereopsis, or binocular depth perception, in which it is assumed that the slightly different images that are simultaneously projected on the retinas of the two eyes are first monocularly recognized and then matched. The process was thought to be somewhat analogous to the operation of an optical range finder, in which the corresponding separate images are first recognized and then brought into alignment. This last step corresponds to measuring the amount of displacement between patterns and determining the amount of depth by simple trigonometry (which the range finder performs automatically).

Research in stereopsis has traditionally been devoted to the problem of relating the displacement, or disparity, of images and the perception of depth. It has become increasingly apparent that depth perception involves many cues and cannot be described by trigonometry alone. Little or no attention was paid to the more fundamental problem of how the visual system is able to identify the same object in the separate two-dimensional images formed on each retina. The studies with random-dot patterns have now shown that monocular recognition of shapes is unnecessary for depth perception.

The method of producing random-dot stereoscopic images is shown in the lower illustration on page 65. The surround (S) is composed of randomly selected but identical dot patterns in the fields at left and right. The center panel (A) is also identical in the two fields but is shifted in one field with respect to the other as if it were a solid sheet. If the shift is inward (toward the nose of the observer), the center panel seems to float in front of the surround. If the shift is in the opposite direction, the panel seems to lie behind the surround. The greater the parallax shift, the greater the perceived depth.

If one simply cut a panel out of a random-dot pattern and shifted it, say, to the left, an empty space would be exposed along the right edge of the panel. The empty region (labeled Y in the middle diagram on page 65) is simply filled in with more random dots. A similar region (labeled X) must be filled when the panel is shifted to the right. Each region is projected onto only one retina (X onto the left retina and Y onto the right) and therefore exhibits no displacement. It is curious that these regions are always perceived as being the continuation of the adjacent area that seems to be farthest away.

By further manipulation of the random-dot patterns, it is possible to produce panels whose apparent location in space is ambiguous. If the X and Y regions described above are filled in with the same random-dot pattern, which we will label B, then when the two fields are viewed stereoscopically the center panel A may seem to be raised above the surround or area B may seem to lie below the surround. The diagram on page 68 illustrates the reason for this ambiguity. If the center panel is to be wider than the parallax shift (that is, wider than B), it must contain repeating vertical stripes of ABAB and so on in one field and stripes of BABA and so on in the other. An ambiguous panel created in this way is shown in the lower pair of stereoscopic images on page 69.

All these depth phenomena can be perceived in a very short interval, provided that the two fields are presented to the observer in reasonable alignment. The presentation time is so short (a few milliseconds) that there is no time for the eye to move and thus no time for a range-finder mechanism to operate. One must therefore conclude that depth perception occurs at some point in the central nervous system after the images projected onto the left and right retinas have been fed into a common neural pathway. This was actually demonstrated as long ago as 1841 by Heinrich Wilhelm Dove of Germany, who used brief electric sparks to illuminate stereoscopic images only three years after Charles Wheatstone of England had first shown how the young art of photography could be used to produce them. Evidently the convergence movements of the eye serve mainly to bring the images on the left and right retinas into approximate register. This does not mean, however, that convergence motions do not influence the perception of depth when the presentation time is of long duration.

The processing in the nervous system that gives rise to depth perception is now more of a mystery than ever.

The German physiologist Ewald Hering believed that this processing involves the crossing or uncrossing of images that are initially perceived as double because they lie either in front of or behind the eyes' point of convergence. The extent to which this cue is utilized

could not previously be determined because double images were inherent in stereoscopic presentation. The random-dot stereoscopic images, on the other hand, do not contain recognizable images prior to their actual perception in depth; thus it is impossible to perceive double images either before or after fusion.

It could still be argued that although random-dot stereoscopic pairs do not contain recognizable shapes, some similar patterns can be perceived in the two fields and these might serve as the basis for fusion. This possibility can be tested in several ways. In the top stereoscopic pair on page 66 the field at the left has been blurred by being printed out of focus. Even when the patterns are almost obliterated in this way, stereopsis is easily obtained. What is more surprising is that the perceived image resembles the sharp one. The blurred image serves only to convey the required disparity information and is then suppressed.

The bottom stereoscopic pair on page 66 carries the disruption of patterns still further. This is achieved by breaking the diagonal connectivity in the field at the left. Along one diagonal whenever three adjacent dots were black, the middle dot was changed to white, and along the other diagonal whenever three adjacent dots were white, the middle one was changed to black. In the field at the right diagonally adjacent groups of three black or white dots were left unchanged. This procedure changes 20 percent of the picture elements in the field at the left and so removes them from the fusion process. The fact that the two fields look so different when viewed monocularly and yet can be perceived in depth when viewed stereoscopically provides additional evidence that no monocular pattern recognition is necessary and that the ultimate three-dimensional pattern emerges only after fusion has taken place.

Although the random-dot stereoscopic images lack monocular depth cues, which normally augment depth perception, they are actually easier to perceive in depth than stereoscopic images of real objects. The explanation is that each black or white dot in a random pattern contributes depth information, whereas in actual objects there are large homogeneous areas that carry no depth information. Thus random-dot stereoscope fields that differ in size by 10 percent or more can easily be perceived in depth [see middle illustration on page 66].

It is probably obvious that these find-

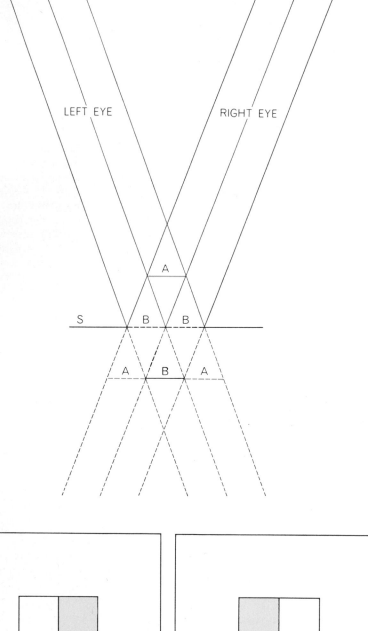

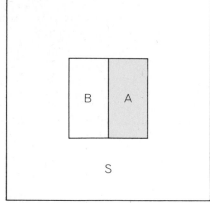
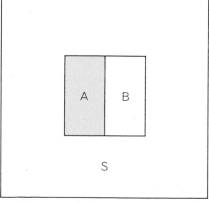

AMBIGUOUS DEPTH EFFECT can be obtained by transposing the *A* and *B* fields in the random-dot patterns. When viewed stereoscopically (*top diagram*), area *A* may seem to be raised above the surround or area *B* may seem to lie below it. In either case the nonfused area seems to be a continuation of the field that looks farthest away.

ings have important implications for *Gestalt* psychology. According to this school stereoptic perception is not a result of disparity in the images projected on the two retinas; rather each eye works up its complex of stimuli into a *Gestalt* and it is the difference between the two *Gestalten* that gives rise to the impression of depth. The fact that stereopsis can be obtained in random-dot images without any monocular cues decisively settles this question, since no *Gestalten* can be worked up.

It might still be argued that *Gestalt* factors may operate after the binocular fusion of the two fields. In this connection it is interesting to look closely at the vertical boundaries of the raised panel formed by the top stereoscopic pair on page 65. The boundaries are fuzzy. The reason is that the black-and-white picture elements along the boundary have an equal probability of being perceived as belonging either to the raised panel or to the surround. Because a square has a "good *Gestalt*" one might expect to perceive these points as forming a straight line. That they do not suggests that perception is governed by simple considerations of probability.

In presenting random-dot stereoscopic pairs for very brief intervals I have found evidence for a restricted but unmistakable kind of subliminal perception. This term refers, of course, to the idea that an individual can be influenced by a stimulus he does not consciously perceive. Efforts to demonstrate this phenomenon by other techniques have been inconclusive and controversial.

The finding was made while I was trying to measure the minimum time needed to perceive stereopsis in random-dot images. The time cannot be measured simply by presenting the images for briefer and briefer periods, for the reason that an afterimage remains on the retina for an indeterminate time. I found that it was possible to "erase" these afterimages by a new technique in which a second stereoscopic pair of random-dot images is flashed onto a screen almost immediately after the first pair.

In these short-interval experiments the first stereoscopic pair flashed onto a screen has a panel that is unmistakably either in front of the surround or behind it. This pair is followed quickly by another in which the location of the panel is ambiguous; under more leisurely viewing conditions it will seem to lie either in front of or behind the surround. Not only were the subjects un-

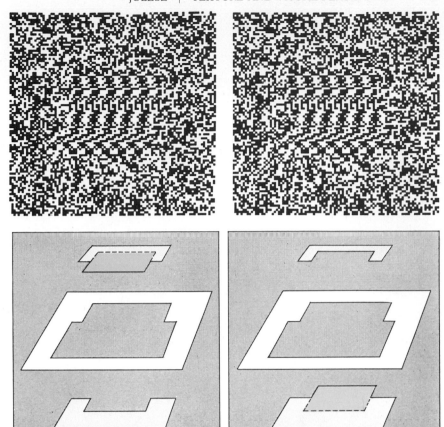

AREA OF AMBIGUOUS DEPTH appears in the middle of this periodically striped stereoscopic pattern. Sometimes it will seem to be a continuation of an elevated panel (*lower left*); at other times it will seem to be part of a depressed panel (*lower right*).

aware that the second pair was ambiguous but if the interval between the two presentations was made short enough they were also unaware that they were seeing anything but the second pair. The second pair erased all conscious knowledge of the first. The real presentation time of the first pair could therefore be established because it was governed by the time allowed to elapse before presentation of the second pair.

The main result was that the first stereoscopic pair, although not consciously perceived, can influence the way in which the second pair—the ambiguous pair—is perceived. When the presentation time of the first pair was long enough, the ambiguous panel in the second pair consistently seemed to be at the same depth as the panel in the first pair. A presentation time adequate to produce this result was about 40 milliseconds; it can be regarded as the "minimum perception time" for stereopsis. When the first pair is presented for a shorter time, or when the second pair is delayed by more than a certain interval, which I have called the "attention time," the second pair is removed from the subliminal influence of the first and is perceived ambiguous-

ly. These experiments suggest that the first pair serves as a "depth marker" and determines which of the two possible depth organizations in the second pair should be favored. All this processing must take place in the central nervous system because the times are too short for any eye motion to be initiated.

The various studies described in this article indicate that visual texture discrimination and binocular depth perception operate under simpler conditions than has been thought, since they do not require the recognition of form. This finding makes it attractive to try to design a machine that will automatically produce contour maps according to information contained in aerial stereoscopic photographs. As long as it seemed that such a task could only be done by a machine that could recognize complex and virtually unpredictable shapes, the job seemed all but hopeless. On the basis of the new findings I have helped to devise a computer program (called Automap-1) that can be used to compile a three-dimensional contour map from high-resolution stereoscopic images [*see illustration on page 70*]. This computer program not only should be useful for reducing the tedium of pro-

70

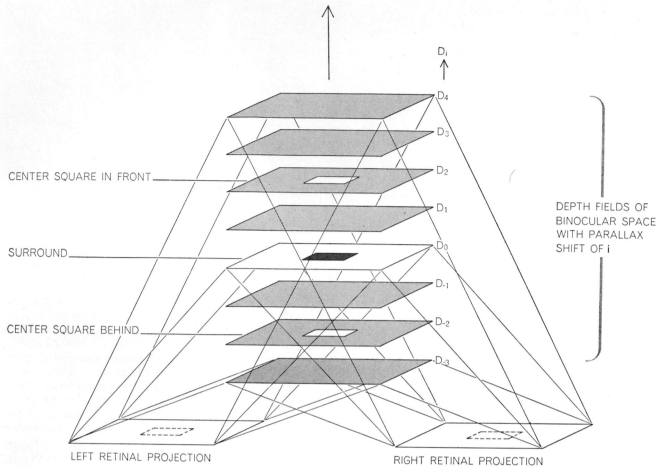

CENTER SQUARE IN FRONT

SURROUND

CENTER SQUARE BEHIND

D_i

D_4

D_3

D_2

D_1

D_0

D_{-1}

D_{-2}

D_{-3}

DEPTH FIELDS OF
BINOCULAR SPACE
WITH PARALLAX
SHIFT OF i

LEFT RETINAL PROJECTION

RIGHT RETINAL PROJECTION

AUTOMAP-1 is a computer program that compiles a three-dimensional contour map from two-dimensional stereoscopic images. The program compares left and right fields point by point and subtracts the brightness of each point from its counterpart. Where the two fields match, the difference is zero, shown above as a white area. Thus the surround (D_0) is white except where there is a shifted center panel. The program repeats the point-by-point comparison after shifting one field horizontally (both left and right) by one unit, two units and so on. This provides an ordered set of depth planes (D_i). When a shift such as D_2 or D_{-2} brings a shifted panel into alignment, the points in the panel cancel and show up as zero (white). Form recognition is not needed.

ducing such maps but since it is based on psychologically observed phenomena it is also a crude model of part of the visual system.

This article has described methods for studying visual texture discrimina-tion and depth perception in their purest form. The methods have shown that connectivity detection is basic to both visual tasks and that it is a more primitive process than form recognition. It remains to be seen if on the psychologi-cal level a simpler "explanation" can be given. I hope that the next findings in this area will come from neurophysi-ologists.

7

The Perception of Disoriented Figures

by Irvin Rock
January 1974

*Many familiar things do not look the same when their
orientation is changed. The reason appears to be that
the perception of form embodies the automatic
assignment of a top, a bottom and sides*

Many common experiences of everyday life that we take for granted present challenging scientific problems. In the field of visual perception one such problem is why things look different when they are upside down or tilted. Consider the inverted photograph on the following page. Although the face is familiar to most Americans, it is difficult to recognize when it is inverted. Even when one succeeds in identifying the face, it continues to look strange and the specific facial expression is hard to make out.

Consider also what happens when printed words and words written in longhand are turned upside down. With effort the printed words can be read, but it is all but impossible to read the longhand words [*see top illustration on page 73*]. Try it with a sample of your own handwriting. One obvious explanation of why it is hard to read inverted words is that we have acquired the habit of moving our eyes from left to right, and that when we look at inverted words our eyes tend to move in the wrong direction. This may be one source of the difficulty, but it can hardly be the major one. It is just as hard to read even a single inverted word when we look at it without moving our eyes at all. It is probable that the same factor interfering with the recognition of disoriented faces and other figures is also interfering with word recognition.

The partial rotation of even a simple figure can also prevent its recognition, provided that the observer is unaware of the rotation. A familiar figure viewed in a novel orientation no longer appears to have the same shape [*see bottom illustration on page 73*]. As Ernst Mach pointed out late in the 19th century, the appearance of a square is quite different when it is rotated 45 degrees. In fact, we call it a diamond.

Some may protest that a familiar shape looks different in a novel orientation for the simple reason that we rarely see it that way. But even a figure we have not seen before will look different in different orientations [*see top illustration on page 74*]. The fact is that orientation affects perceived shape, and that the failure to recognize a familiar figure when it is in a novel orientation is based on the change in its perceived shape.

On the other hand, a figure can be changed in various ways without any effect on its perceived shape. For example, a triangle can be altered in size, color and various other ways without any change in its perceived shape [*see middle illustration on page 74*]. Psychologists, drawing an analogy with a similar phenomenon in music, call such changes transpositions. A melody can be transposed to a new key, and although all the notes then are different, there is no change in the melody. In fact, we generally remain unaware of the transposition. Clearly the melody derives from the relation of the notes to one another, which is not altered when the melody is transposed. In much the same way a visual form is based primarily on how parts of a figure are related to one another geometrically. For example, one could describe a square as being a four-sided figure having parallel opposite sides, four right angles and four sides of equal length. These features remain unchanged when a square is transposed in size or position; that is why it continues to look like a square. We owe a debt to the Gestalt psychologists for emphasizing the importance in perception of relations rather than absolute features.

Since a transposition based on rotation also does not alter the internal geometric relations of a figure, then why does it look different in an altered orientation? At this point we should consider

the meaning of the term orientation. What changes are introduced by altering orientation? One obvious change is that rotating a figure would result in a change in the orientation of its image on the retina of the eye. Perhaps, therefore, we should ask why different retinal orientations of the same figure should give rise to different perceived shapes. That might lead us into speculations about how the brain processes information about form, and why differently oriented projections of a retinal image should lead to different percepts of form.

Before we go further in this direction we should consider another meaning of the term orientation. The inverted and rotated figures in the illustrations for this article are in different orientations with respect to the vertical and horizontal directions in their environment. That part of the figure which is normally pointed upward in relation to gravity, to the sky or to the ceiling is now pointed downward or sideways on the page. Perhaps it is this kind of orientation that is responsible for altered perception of shape when a figure is disoriented.

It is not difficult to separate the retinal and the environmental factors in an experiment. Cut out a paper square and tape it to the wall so that the bottom of the square is parallel to the floor. Compare the appearance of the square first with your head upright and then with your head tilted 45 degrees. You will see that the square continues to look like a square when your head is tilted. Yet when your head is tilted 45 degrees, the retinal image of the square is the same as the image of a diamond when the diamond is viewed with the head upright. Thus it is not the retinal image that is responsible for the altered appearance of a square when the square is rotated 45 degrees. The converse experiment points to the same conclusion. Rotate the square on the wall so that it becomes a diamond. The diamond viewed with your head tilted 45 degrees produces a retinal image of a square, but the diamond still looks like a diamond. Needless to say, in these simple demonstrations one continues to perceive correctly where the top, bottom and sides of the figures are even when one's posture changes. It is therefore the change of a figure's perceived orientation in the environment that affects its apparent shape and not the change of orientation of its retinal image.

These conclusions have been substantiated in experiments Walter I. Heimer and I and other colleagues have conducted with numerous subjects. In one series of experiments the subjects were shown unfamiliar figures. In the first part of the experiment a subject sat at a table and simply looked at several figures shown briefly in succession. Then some of the subjects were asked to tilt

their head 90 degrees by turning it to the side and resting it on the table. In this position the subject viewed a series of figures. Most of the figures were new, but among them were some figures the subject had seen earlier. These figures were shown in either of two orientations: upright with respect to the room (as they had been in the first viewing) or rotated 90 degrees so that the "top" of the figure corresponded to the top of the subject's tilted head. The subject was asked to say whether or not he had seen each figure in the first session. He did not know that the orientation of the figures seen previously might be different. Other subjects viewed the test figures while sitting upright.

When we compared the scores of subjects who tilted their head with subjects who sat upright for the test, the results were clear. Tilted-head subjects recognized the environmentally upright (but retinally tilted) figures about as well as the upright observers did. They also

failed to recognize the environmentally tilted (but retinally upright) figures about as often as the upright subjects did. In other words, the experiments confirmed that it is rotation with respect to the up-down and left-right coordinates in the environment that produces the change in the perceived shape of the figure. It is not rotation of the retinal image that produces the change, since altering the image's orientation does not adversely affect recognition and preserving it does not improve recognition.

In another experiment subjects viewed an ambiguous or reversible figure that could be perceived in one of two ways depending on its orientation. For example, when one figure that looked like a map of the U.S. was rotated 90 degrees, it looked like the profile of a bearded man. Subjects were asked to rest their head on the table when viewing the ambiguous figures. The question we asked ourselves was: Which "upright" would dominate, the retinal upright or the environmental upright? The results were decisive. About 80 percent of the subjects reported seeing only the aspect of the ambiguous figure that was environmentally upright, even though the alternative was upright on their retina [*see bottom illustration on page 75*].

Why does the orientation of a figure with respect to the directional coordinates of the environment have such a profound effect on the perceived shape of the figure? The answer I propose is that perceived shape is based on a cognitive process in which the characteristics of the figure are implicitly described by the perceptual system. For example, the colored figure at the left in the top illustration on page 74 could be described as a closed figure resting on a horizontal base with a protrusion on the figure's left side and an indentation on its right side. The colored figure to the right of it, although it is identical and only rotated 90 degrees, would be described quite differently, as being symmetrical with two bumps on the bottom and with left and right sides more or less straight and identical with each other. I am not suggesting that such a description is conscious or verbal; obviously we would be aware of the descriptive process if it were either. Furthermore, animals and infants who are nonverbal perceive shape much as we do. I am proposing that a process analogous to such a description does take place and that it is not only based on the internal geometry of a figure but also takes into account the location of the figure's top, bottom and sides. In such a description orienta-

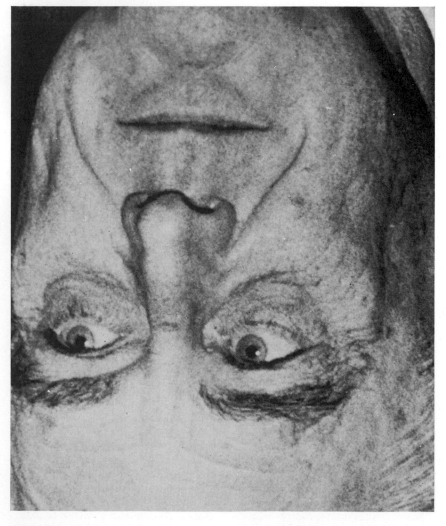

INVERTED PHOTOGRAPH of a famous American demonstrates how difficult it is to recognize a familiar face when it is presented upside down. Even after one succeeds in identifying the inverted face as that of Franklin D. Roosevelt, it continues to look strange.

tion is therefore a major factor in the shape that is finally perceived.

From experiments I have done in collaboration with Phyllis Olshansky it appears that certain shifts in orientation have a marked effect on perceived shape. In particular, creating symmetry around a vertical axis where no symmetry had existed before (or vice versa), shifting the long axis from vertical to horizontal (or vice versa) and changing the bottom of a figure from a broad horizontal base to a pointed angle (or vice versa) seemed to have a strong effect on perceived shape. Such changes of shape can result from only a moderate angular change of orientation, say 45 or 90 degrees. Interestingly enough, inversions or rotations of 180 degrees often have only a slight effect on perceived shape, perhaps because such changes will usually not alter perceived symmetry or the perceived orientation of the long axis of the figure.

There is one kind of orientation change that has virtually no effect on perceived shape: a mirror-image reversal. This is particularly true for the novel figures we used in our experiments. How can this be explained? It seems that although the "sides" of visual space are essentially interchangeable, the up-and-down directions in the environment are not. "Up" and "down" are distinctly different directions in the world we live in. Thus a figure can be said to have three main perceptual boundaries: top, bottom and sides. As a result the description of a figure will not be much affected by whether a certain feature is on the left side or the right. Young children and animals have great difficulty learning to discriminate between a figure and its mirror image, but they can easily distinguish between a figure and its inverted counterpart.

Related to this analysis is a fact observed by Mach and tested by Erich Goldmeier: A figure that is symmetrical around one axis will generally appear to be symmetrical only if that axis is vertical. Robin Leaman and I have demonstrated that it is the perceived vertical axis of the figure and not the vertical axis of the figure's retinal image that produces this effect. An observer who tilts his head will continue to perceive a figure as being symmetrical if that figure is symmetrical around an environmental vertical axis. This suggests that perceived symmetry results only when the two equivalent halves of a figure are located on the two equivalent sides of perceptual space.

If, as I have suggested, the description of a figure is based on the location of its top, bottom and sides, the question arises: How are these directions assigned in a figure? One might suppose that the top of a figure is ordinarily the area uppermost in relation to the ceiling, the sky or the top of a page. In a dark room an observer may have to rely on his sense of gravity to inform him which way is up.

Numerous experiments by psychologists have confirmed that there are indeed two major sources of information for perceiving the vertical and the horizontal: gravity (as it is sensed by the vestibular apparatus in the inner ear, by the pressure of the ground on the body and by feedback from the muscles)

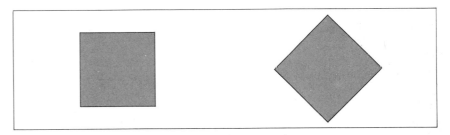

INVERTED WORDS are difficult to read when they are set in type, and words written in longhand are virtually impossible to decipher. The difficulty applies to one's own inverted handwriting in spite of a lifetime of experience reading it in the normal upright orientation.

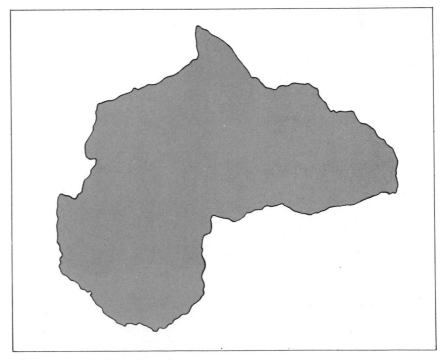

SQUARE AND DIAMOND are two familiar shapes. The two figures shown here are identical; their appearance is so different, however, that we call one a square and the other a diamond. With the diamond the angles do not spontaneously appear as right angles.

"UNFAMILIAR" SHAPE shown here becomes a familiar shape when it is rotated clockwise 90 degrees. In a classroom experiment, when the rotated figure was drawn on the blackboard, it was not recognized as an outline of the continent of Africa until the teacher told the class at the end of the lecture that the figure was rotated out of its customary orientation.

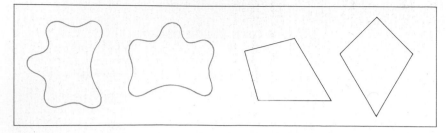

NOVEL OR UNFAMILIAR FIGURES look different in different orientations, provided that we view them naïvely and do not mentally rotate them. The reason may be the way in which a figure is "described" by the perceptual system. The colored figure at left could be described as a closed shape resting on a horizontal base with a protrusion on its left side and an indentation on its right side. The colored figure adjacent to it, although identical, would be described as a symmetrical shape resting on a curved base with a protrusion at the top. The first black figure could be described as a quadrilateral resting on a side. The black figure at right would be described as a diamondlike shape standing on end.

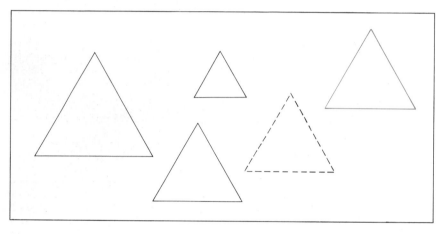

ALTERATION IN SIZE, color or type of contour does not change the perceived shape of a triangle. Even varying the location of the triangle's retinal image (by looking out of the corner of your eyes or fixating on different points) does not change perceived shape.

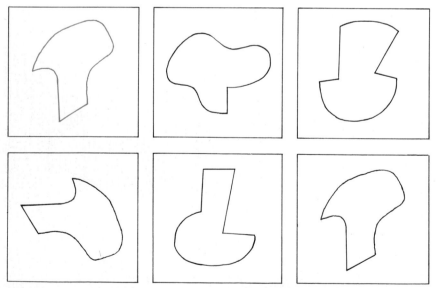

ROTATION OF RETINAL IMAGE by tilting the head 90 degrees does not appreciably affect recognition of a novel figure (*color*). Subjects first viewed several novel targets while sitting upright. Then they were shown a series of test figures (*black*) and were asked to identify those they had seen before. Some subjects tilted their head 90 degrees; others viewed the test figures with their head upright. Tilted-head subjects failed to recognize figures that were retinally "upright" (for example figure at bottom left) about as much as upright viewers did (to whom such figures were not retinally upright). Tilted-head subjects recognized environmentally upright figures (*bottom right*) as often as upright viewers did.

and information from the scene itself. We have been able to demonstrate that either can affect the perceived shape of a figure. A luminous figure in a dark room will not be recognized readily when it is rotated to a new orientation even if the observer is tilted by exactly the same amount. Here the only source of information about directions in space is gravity. In a lighted room an observer will often fail to recognize a figure when he and the figure are upright but the room is tilted. The tilted room creates a strong impression of where the up-down axis should be, and this leads to an incorrect attribution of the top and bottom of the figure [see "The Perception of the Upright," by Herman A. Witkin; SCIENTIFIC AMERICAN Offprint 410].

Merely informing an observer that a figure is tilted will often enable him to perceive the figure correctly. This may explain why some readers will not perceive certain of the rotated figures shown here as being strange or different. The converse situation, misinforming an observer about the figures, produces impressive results. If a subject is told that the top of a figure he is about to see is somewhere other than in the region uppermost in the environment, he is likely not to recognize the figure when it is presented with the orientation in which he first saw it. The figure is not disoriented and the observer incorrectly assigns the directions top, bottom and sides on the basis of instructions.

Since such knowledge about orientation will enable the observer to shift the directions he assigns to a figure, and since it is this assignment that affects the perception of shape, it is absolutely essential to employ naïve subjects in perception experiments involving orientation. That is, the subject must not realize that the experiment is concerned with figural orientation, so that he does not examine the figures with the intent of finding the regions that had been top, bottom and sides in previous viewings of it. There are, however, some figures that seem to have intrinsic orientation in that regardless of how they are presented a certain region will be perceived as the top [see top illustration on facing page]. It is therefore difficult or impossible to adversely affect the recognition of such figures by disorienting them.

In the absence of other clues a subject will assign top-bottom coordinates according to his subjective or egocentric reference system. Consider a figure drawn on a circular sheet of paper that is lying on the ground. Neither gravity nor visual clues indicate where the top and bottom are. Nevertheless, an observer will assign a top to that region of the figure which is uppermost with respect to his egocentric coordinate reference system. The vertical axis of the figure is seen as being aligned with the long axis of the observer's head and body. The upward direction corresponds to the position of his head. We have been able to demonstrate that such assignment of direction has the same effect on the recognition that other bases of assigning direction do. A figure first seen in one orientation on the circular sheet will generally not be recognized if its egocentric orientation is altered.

Now we come to an observation that seems to be at variance with much of what I have described. When a person lies on his side in bed to read, he does not hold the book upright (in the environmental sense) but tilts it. If the book is not tilted, the retinal image is disoriented and reading is quite difficult. Similarly, if a reader views printed matter or photographs of faces that are environmentally upright with his head between his legs, they will be just as difficult to recognize as they are when they are upside down and the viewer's head is upright. The upright pictures, however, are still perceived as being upright even when the viewer's head is inverted. Conversely, if the pictures are upside down in the environment and are viewed with the head inverted between the legs, there is no difficulty in recognizing them. Yet the observer perceives the pictures as being inverted. Therefore in these cases it is the orientation of the retinal image and not the environmental assignment of direction that seems to be responsible for recognition or failure of recognition.

Experiments with ambiguous figures conducted by Robert Thouless, G. Kanizsa and G. Tampieri support the notion that retinal orientation plays a role in recognition of a figure [see illustration on page 78]. Moreover, as George Steinfeld and I have demonstrated, the recognition of upright words and faces falls off in direct proportion to the degree of body tilt [see illustration on following page]. With such visual material recognition is an inverse function of the degree of disorientation of the retinal image. As we have seen, the relation between degree of disorientation and recognizability does not hold in cases where the assignment of direction has been altered. In such cases the greatest effect is not with a 180-degree change but with a 45- or 90-degree change.

The results of all these experiments

FIGURES WITH INTRINSIC ORIENTATION appear to have a natural vertical axis regardless of their physical orientation. A region at one end of the axis is perceived as top.

IMPRESSION OF SYMMETRY is spontaneous only when a figure is symmetrical around a vertical axis. Subjects were asked to indicate which of two figures (middle and right) was most like the target figure (left). The figure at right was selected most frequently, presumably because it is symmetrical around its vertical axis. If the page is tilted 90 degrees, the figure in the middle will now be selected as being more similar to the target figure. Now if the page is held vertically and the figures are viewed with the head tilted 90 degrees, the figure at right is likely to be seen as being the most similar. This suggests that it is not the symmetry around the egocentric vertical axis on the retina but rather the symmetry around the environmental axis of the figure that determines perceived symmetry.

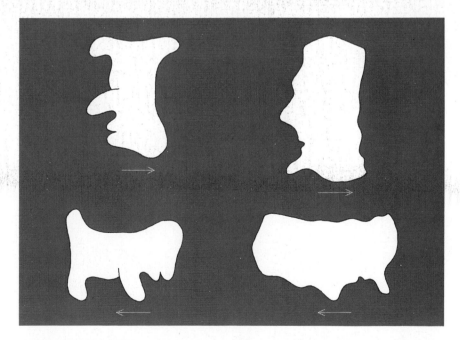

AMBIGUOUS FIGURES can be perceived in different ways depending on the orientation assigned to them. Figure at left can look like the profile of a man's head with a chef's hat (top left) or, when rotated 90 degrees, like a dog (bottom left). Figure at right can look like the profile of a bearded man's head (top right) or like a map of the U.S. (bottom right). When subjects with their head tilted 90 degrees to one side viewed these ambiguous figures (direction of subject's head is shown by arrow), they preferentially recognized the figure that was upright in the environment instead of the figure that was upright on the retina.

have led me to conclude that there are two distinct factors involved in the perception of disoriented figures: an assignment-of-direction factor and a retinal factor. I believe that when we view a figure with our head tilted, we automatically compensate for the tilt in much the same way that we compensate for the size of distant objects. An object at a moderate distance from us does not appear small in spite of the fact that its retinal image is much smaller than it is when the object is close by. This effect usually is explained by saying that the information supplied by the retinal image is somehow corrected by allowing for the distance of the object from us. Similarly, when a vertical luminous line in a dark room is viewed by a tilted observer, it will still look vertical or almost vertical in spite of the fact that the retinal image in the observer's eye is tilted. Thus the tilt of the body must be taken into account by the perceptual system. The tilted retinal image is then corrected, with the result that the line is perceived as being vertical. Just as the correction for size at a distance is called size constancy, so can correction for the vertical be called orientation constancy.

When we view an upright figure with our head tilted, before we have made any correction, we begin with the information provided by an image of the figure in a particular retinal orientation. The first thing that must happen is that the perceptual system processes the retinal image on the basis of an egocentrically assigned top, bottom and sides, perhaps because of a primitive sense of orientation derived from retinal orientation. For example, when we view an upright square with our head tilted, which yields a diamondlike retinal image, we may perceive a diamond for a fleeting moment before the correction goes into operation. Head orientation is then automatically taken into account to correct the perception. Thus the true top of the figure is seen to be one of the sides of the square rather than a corner. The figure is then "described" correctly as one whose sides are horizontal and vertical in the environment, in short as a "square." This correction is made quickly and usually without effort. In order to describe a figure the viewer probably must visualize or imagine it in terms of its true top, bottom and sides rather than in terms of its retinal top, bottom and sides.

If the figure is relatively simple, the correction is not too difficult to achieve. If we view an upright letter with our head tilted, we recognize it easily; it is of interest, however, that there is still something strange about it. I believe the dual aspect of the perception of orientation is responsible for this strangeness. There is an uncorrected perception of the letter based on its retinal-egocentric orientation and a corrected perception of it based on its environmental orientation. The first perception produces an unfamiliar shape, which accounts for the strange appearance of the letter in spite of its subsequent recognition. In our experiments many of the figures we employed were structurally speaking equivalent to letters, and in some cases we actually used letters from unfamiliar alphabets.

With a more complex figure, such as an inverted word or an upright word

RECOGNITION OF CERTAIN KINDS OF VISUAL MATERIAL decreases almost in direct proportion to the degree of head tilt of the observer. In a series of experiments the number of correct recognitions of faces (*colored bars*), written words (*gray*) and fragmented figures (*black*) were recorded for various degrees of head tilt. Subject saw several examples of each type of test material in each of the head positions. For this visual material recognition is an inverse function of the degree of disorientation of the retinal image.

viewed by an inverted observer, the corrective mechanism may be entirely overtaxed. Each letter of the word must be corrected separately, and the corrective mechanism apparently cannot cope simultaneously with multiple components. It is true that if an observer is given enough time, an inverted word can be deciphered, but it will never look the same as it does when it is upright. While one letter is being corrected the others continue to be perceived in their uncorrected form. There is a further difficulty: letter order is crucial for word recognition, and inverting a word reverses the normal left-to-right order.

The recognition of inverted longhand writing is even more difficult. When such writing is turned upside down, many of the inverted "units" strongly resemble normal upright longhand letters. Moreover, since the letters are connected, it is difficult to tell where one letter ends and another begins. Separating the letters of the inverted word makes recognition easier. Even so, it is all too easy to confuse a *u* and an *n*. This type of confusion is also encountered with certain printed letters, namely, *b* and *q*, *d* and *p* and *n* and *u*, although not as frequently. In other words, if a figure is recognized on the basis of its upright retinal-egocentric orientation, this may tend to stabilize the perception and block the correction process. The dominance of the retinally upright faces in the illustration on the following page probably is an effect of just this kind.

There may be a similar overtaxing of the corrective mechanism when we view an inverted face. It may be that the face contains a number of features each of which must be properly perceived if the whole is to be recognized [see "The Recognition of Faces," by Leon D. Harmon, beginning on page 101]. While attention is focused on correcting one feature, say the mouth, other features remain uncorrected and continue to be perceived on the basis of the image they form on the retina. Of course, the relation of features is also important in the recognition of a face, but here too there are a great number of such relations and the corrective mechanism may again be overtaxed.

Charles C. Bebber, Douglas Blewett and I conducted an experiment to test the hypothesis that it is the presence of multiple components that creates the difficulty of correcting figures. Subjects were briefly shown a quadrilateral figure and asked to study it. They viewed the target figure with their head upright. Then they were shown a series of test

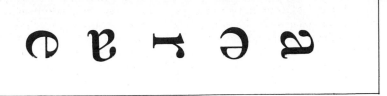

SINGLE LETTER that is tilted can be easily identified once it is realized how it is oriented. A strangeness in its appearance, however, remains because the percept arising from the uncorrected retinal image continues to exist simultaneously with the corrected percept.

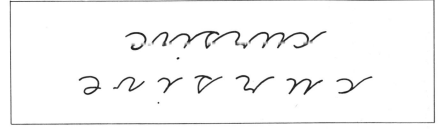

INVERTED LONGHAND WRITING is difficult to decipher because many inverted units resemble written upright letters. For example, an inverted *u* will look like an *n* and an inverted *c* like an *s*. Moreover, the connection between letters leads to uncertainty about where a letter begins and ends. Several inverted units can be grouped together and misperceived as an upright letter. Separating the inverted letters makes them easier to decipher.

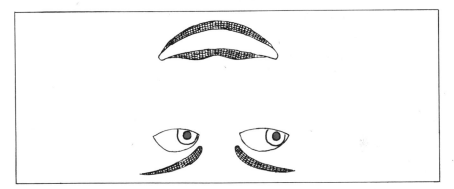

INVERTED FACIAL FEATURES are difficult to interpret because while attention is focused on correcting one feature other features remain uncorrected. For example, one might succeed in correcting the eyes shown here so that they are perceived as gazing downward and leftward, but at that very moment the mouth is uncorrected and expresses sorrow rather than pleasure. Conversely, one might correct the mouth and misperceive the eyes.

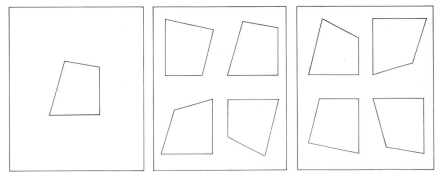

MULTIPLE ITEMS were found to have an adverse effect on recognition of even simple figures. Subjects sitting upright viewed the target (*left*). Then they were briefly shown test cards, some of which contained the target figure (*middle*) and some of which did not (*right*). The subjects were to indicate when they saw a figure that was identical with the target figure. Half of the test cards were viewed with the head upright and half with the head inverted. Recognition was poor when inverted subjects viewed the test cards. In other experiments with a single test figure head inversion did not significantly affect recognition.

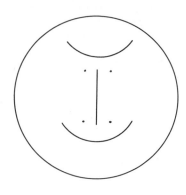

AMBIGUOUS FACES are perceived differently when their images on the retina of the observer are inverted. If you hold the illustration upright and view it from between your legs with your head inverted, the alternative faces will be perceived even though they are upside down in terms of the environment. The same effect occurs when the illustration is inverted and viewed from an upright position. Such tests provide evidence that figures such as faces are recognized on the basis of their upright retinal orientation.

cards each of which had four quadrilateral figures. The test cards were viewed for one second, and the subjects were required to indicate if the target figure was on the card.

The subjects understood that they were to respond affirmatively only when they saw a figure that was identical with the target figure both in shape and in orientation. (Some of the test figures were similar to the target figure but were rotated by 180 degrees.) Half of the test cards were seen with the subject's head upright and half with the subject's head inverted. It was assumed that the subject would not be able to correct all four test figures in the brief time that was allowed him while he was viewing them with his head down. He had to perceive just as many units in the same brief time while he was viewing them with his head upright, but he did not have to correct any of the units. We expected that target figures would often not be recognized and that incorrect figures would be mistakenly identified as the target when the subjects viewed the test cards with their head inverted.

The results bore out our prediction. When multiple components have to be corrected, retinal disorientation has an adverse effect on recognition. The observer responded to twice as many test cards correctly when he was upright than he did when he was inverted.

As I have noted, when we look at figures that are difficult to recognize when they are retinally disoriented, the difficulty increases as the degree of disorientation increases. Why this happens may also be related to the nature of the correction process. I suggested that the observer must suppress the retinally (egocentrically) upright percept and substitute a corrected percept. To do this, however, he must visualize or imagine how the figure would look if it were rotated until it was upright with respect to himself or, what amounts to the same thing, how it would look if he rotated himself into alignment with the figure. The process of mental rotation requires visualizing the entire sequence of angular change, and therefore the greater the angular change, the greater the difficulty.

As every parent knows, children between the ages of two and five seem to be quite indifferent to how a picture is oriented. They often hold a book upside down and seem not at all disturbed by it. On the basis of such observations and the results of some early experiments, many psychologists concluded that the orientation of a figure did not enter into its recognition by young children. More recent laboratory experiments, however, do not confirm the fact that children recognize figures equally well in any orientation. They have as much difficulty as, or more difficulty than, adults in recognizing previously seen figures when the figure is shown in a new orientation. Why then do young children often spontaneously look at pictures upside down in everyday situations? Perhaps they have not yet learned to pay attention to orientation, and do not realize that their recognition would improve if they did so. When children learn to read after the age of six, they are forced to pay attention to orientation because certain letters differ only in their orientation.

In summary, the central fact we have learned about orientation is that the perceived shape of a figure is not simply a function of its internal geometry. The perceived shape is also very much a function of the up, down and side directions we assign to the figure. If there is a change in the assigned directions, the figure will take on a different perceptual shape. I have speculated that the change in perceived shape is based on a new "description" of the figure by the perceptual system. The directions assigned are based on information of various kinds about where the top, bottom and sides of a figure are and usually do not depend on the retinal orientation of the image of the figure. When the image is not retinally upright, a process of correction is necessary in order to arrive at the correct description, and this correction is difficult or impossible to achieve in the case of visual material that has multiple components.

All of this implies that form perception in general is based to a much greater extent on cognitive processes than any current theory maintains. A prevailing view among psychologists and sensory physiologists is that form perception can be reduced to the perception of contours and that contour perception in turn can be reduced to abrupt differences in light intensity that cause certain neural units in the retina and brain to fire. If this is true, then perceiving form results from the specific concatenation of perceived contours. Although the work I have described does not deny the possible importance of contour detection as a basis of form perception, it does suggest that such an explanation is far from sufficient, and that the perception of form depends on certain mental processes such as description and correction. These processes in turn are necessary to account for the further step of recognition of a figure. A physically unchanged retinal image often will not lead to recognition if there has been a shift in the assigned directions. Conversely, if there has been no shift in the assigned directions, even a very different retinal image will still allow recognition.

Pictorial Perception and Culture

by Jan B. Deregowski
November 1972

*Do people of one culture perceive a picture differently
from people of another? Experiments in Africa show
that such differences exist, and that the perception
of pictures calls for some form of learning*

A picture is a pattern of lines and shaded areas on a flat surface that depicts some aspect of the real world. The ability to recognize objects in pictures is so common in most cultures that it is often taken for granted that such recognition is universal in man. Although children do not learn to read until they are about six years old, they are able to recognize objects in pictures long before that; indeed, it has been shown that a 19-month-old child is capable of such recognition. If pictorial recognition is universal, do pictures offer us a lingua franca for intercultural communication? There is evidence that they do not: cross-cultural studies have shown that there are persistent differences in the way pictorial information is interpreted by people of various cultures. These differences merit investigation not only because improvement in communication may be achieved by a fuller understanding of them but also because they may provide us with a better insight into the nature of human perceptual mechanisms.

Reports of difficulty in pictorial perception by members of remote, illiterate tribes have periodically been made by missionaries, explorers and anthropologists. Robert Laws, a Scottish missionary active in Nyasaland (now Malawi) at the end of the 19th century, reported: "Take a picture in black and white and the natives cannot see it. You may tell the natives, 'This is a picture of an ox and a dog,' and the people will look at it and look at you and that look says that they consider you a liar. Perhaps you say again, 'Yes, this is a picture of an ox and a dog.' Well, perhaps they will tell you what they think this time. If there are a few boys about, you say: 'This is really a picture of an ox and a dog. Look at the horn of the ox, and there is his

tail!' And the boy will say: 'Oh! yes and there is the dog's nose and eyes and ears!' Then the old people will look again and clap their hands and say, 'Oh! yes, it is a dog.' When a man has seen a picture for the first time, his book education has begun."

Mrs. Donald Fraser, who taught health care to Africans in the 1920's, had similar experiences. This is her description of an African woman slowly discovering that a picture she was looking at portrayed a human head in profile: "She discovered in turn the nose, the mouth, the eye, but where was the other eye? I tried by turning my profile to explain why she could only see one eye but she hopped round to my other side to point out that I possessed a second eye which the other lacked."

There were also, however, reports of vivid and instant responses to pictures: "When all the people were quickly seated, the first picture flashed on the sheet was that of an elephant. The wildest excitement immediately prevailed, many of the people jumping up and shouting, fearing the beast must be alive, while those nearest to the sheet sprang up and fled. The chief himself crept stealthily forward and peeped behind the sheet to see if the animal had a body, and when he discovered that the animal's body was only the thickness of the sheet, a great roar broke the stillness of the night."

Thus the evidence gleaned from the insightful but unsystematic observations quoted is ambiguous. The laborious way some of these Africans pieced together a picture suggests that some form of learning is required to recognize pictures. Inability to perceive that a pattern of lines and shaded areas on a flat surface represents a real object would

render all pictorial material incomprehensible. All drawings would be perceived as being meaningless, abstract patterns until the viewer had learned to interpret and organize the symbolic elements. On the other hand, one could also argue that pictorial recognition is largely independent of learning, and that even people from cultures where pictorial materials are uncommon will recognize items in pictures, provided that the pictures show familiar objects. It has been shown that an unsophisticated adult African from a remote village is unlikely to choose the wrong toy animal when asked to match the toy to a picture of, say, a lion. Given a photograph of a kangaroo, however, he is likely to choose at random from the array of toys. Yet one can argue that this sample was not as culturally remote as those described above. It is therefore probably safer to assume that utter incomprehension of pictorial material may be observed only in extremely isolated human populations.

Conventions for depicting the spatial arrangement of three-dimensional objects in a flat picture can also give rise to difficulties in perception. These conventions give the observer depth cues that tell him the objects are not all the same distance from him. Inability to interpret such cues is bound to lead to misunderstanding of the meaning of the picture as a whole. William Hudson, who was then working at the National Institute for Personnel Research in Johannesburg, stumbled on such a difficulty in testing South African Bantu workers. His discovery led him to construct a pictorial perception test and to carry out much of the pioneering work in cross-cultural studies of perception.

Hudson's test consists of a series of pictures in which there are various com-

binations of three pictorial depth cues. The first cue is familiar size, which calls for the larger of two known objects to be drawn considerably smaller to indicate that it is farther away. The second cue is overlap, in which portions of nearer objects overlap and obscure portions of objects that are farther away; a hill is partly obscured by another hill that is closer to the viewer. The third cue is perspective, the convergence of lines known to be parallel to suggest distance; lines representing the edges of a road converge in the distance. In all but one of his tests Hudson omitted an entire group of powerful depth cues: density gradients. Density gradients are provided by any elements of uniform size: bricks in a wall or pebbles on a beach. The elements are drawn larger or smaller depending on whether they are nearer to the viewer or farther away from him.

Hudson's test has been applied in many parts of Africa with subjects drawn from a variety of tribal and linguistic groups. The subjects were shown one picture at a time and asked to name all the objects in the picture in order to determine whether or not the elements were correctly recognized. Then they were asked about the relation between the objects. (What is the man doing? What is closer to the man?) If the subject takes note of the depth cues and makes the "correct" interpretations, he is classified as having three-dimensional perception. If the depth cues are not taken into account by the subject, he is said to have two-dimensional perception [see illustration on opposite page]. The results from African tribal subjects were unequivocal: both children and adults found it difficult to perceive depth in the pictorial material. The difficulty varied in extent but appeared to persist

PICTORIAL DEPTH PERCEPTION is tested by showing subjects a picture such as the top illustration on the opposite page. A correct interpretation is that the hunter is trying to spear the antelope, which is nearer to him than the elephant. An incorrect interpretation is that the elephant is nearer and is about to be speared. The picture contains two depth cues: overlapping objects and known size of objects. The bottom illustration depicts the man, elephant and antelope in true size ratios when all are the same distance from the observer.

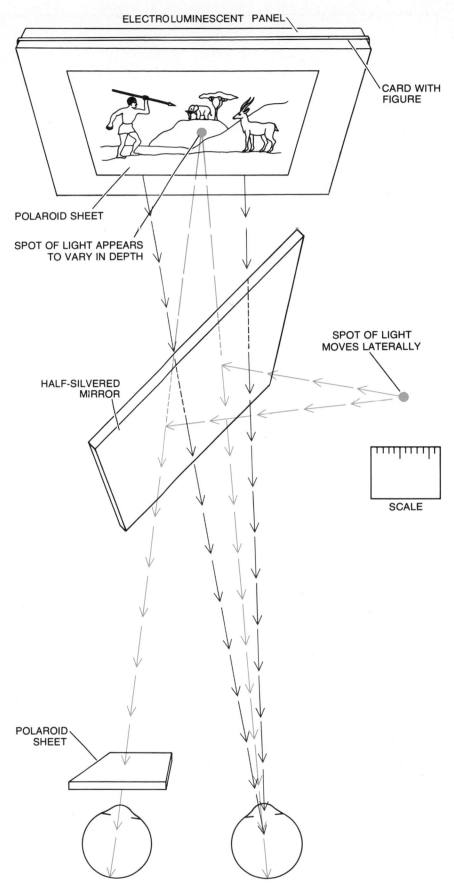

APPARATUS FOR STUDYING PERCEIVED DEPTH enables the subject to adjust a spot of light so that it appears to lie at the same depth as an object in the picture. The light is seen stereoscopically with both eyes but the picture is seen with only one eye. Africans unfamiliar with pictorial depth cues set the light at the same depth on all parts of the picture.

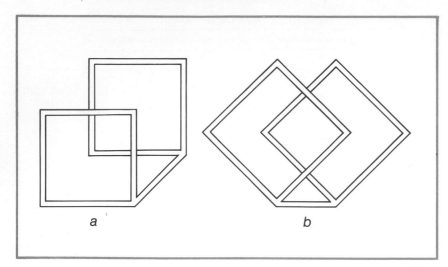

CONSTRUCTION-TASK FIGURES consist of two squares connected by a single rod. Most subjects from Western cultures see the figure *a* as a three-dimensional object, but when the figure is rotated 45 degrees (*right*), they see it as being flat. Subjects from African cultures are more likely to see both figures as being flat, with the two squares in the same plane.

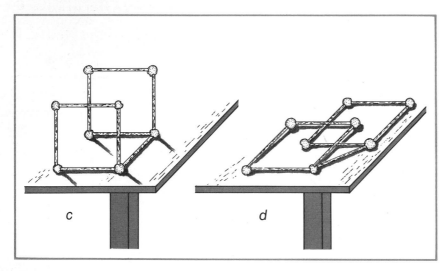

STICK-AND-CLAY MODELS of the figure *a* in the top illustration were made by test subjects. Almost all the three-dimensional perceivers built a three-dimensional object (*left*). Subjects who did not readily perceive depth in pictures tended to build a flat model (*right*).

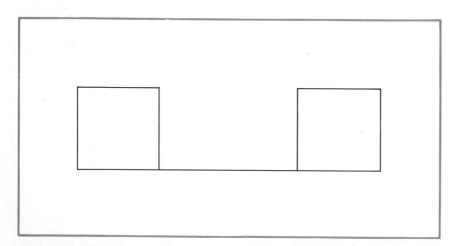

"SPLIT" DRAWING was preferred by two-dimensional perceivers when shown a model like figure *c* and given a choice between the split drawing and figure *a* in top illustration.

through most educational and social levels.

Further experimentation revealed that the phenomenon was not simply the result of the pictorial material used in the test. Subjects were shown a drawing of two squares, one behind the other and connected by a single rod [*see top illustration at left*]. They were also given sticks and modeling clay and asked to build a model of what they saw. If Hudson's test is valid, people designated as two-dimensional perceivers should build flat models when they are shown the drawing, whereas those designated as three-dimensional perceivers should build a cubelike object. When primary-school boys and unskilled workers in Zambia were given Hudson's test and then asked to build models, a few of the subjects who had been classified as three-dimensional responders by the test made flat models. A substantial number of the subjects classified as two-dimensional perceivers built three-dimensional models. Thus Hudson's test, although it is more severe than the construction task, appears to measure the same variable.

The finding was checked in another experiment. A group of Zambian primary-school children were classified into three-dimensional and two-dimensional perceivers on the basis of the model-building test. They were then asked to copy a "two-pronged trident," a tantalizing drawing that confuses many people. The confusion is a direct result of attempting to interpret the drawing as a three-dimensional object [*see top illustration on facing page*]. One would expect that those who are confused by the trident would find it difficult to recall and draw. The students actually made copies of two tridents: the ambiguous one and a control figure that had three simple prongs. To view the figure the student had to lift a flap, which actuated a timer that measured how long the flap was held up. The student could view the figure for as long as he wanted to, but he could not copy it while the flap was open. After the flap was closed the student had to wait 10 seconds before he began to draw. The delay was introduced to increase the difficulty of copying the figure. The results confirmed that the students who were three-dimensional perceivers spent more time looking at the ambiguous trident than at the control trident, whereas the two-dimensional perceivers did not differ significantly in the time spent viewing each of the two tridents.

Do people who perceive pictorial

depth really see depth in the picture or are they merely interpreting symbolic depth cues in the same way that we learn to interpret the set of symbols in "horse" to mean a certain quadruped? An ingenious apparatus for studying perceived depth helped us to obtain an answer. This is how the apparatus is described by its designer, Richard L. Gregory of the University of Bristol:

"The figure is presented back-illuminated, to avoid texture, and it is viewed through a sheet of Polaroid. A second sheet of Polaroid is placed over one eye crossed with the first so that no light from the figure reaches this eye. Between the eyes and the figure is a half-silvered mirror through which the figure is seen but which also reflects one or more small light sources mounted on an optical bench. These appear to lie in the figure; indeed, optically they *do* lie in the figure provided the path length of the lights to the eyes is the same as that of the figure to the eyes. But the small light sources are seen with both eyes while the figure is seen with only *one* eye because of the crossed Polaroids. By moving the lights along their optical bench, they may be placed so as to lie at the same distance as any selected part of the figure."

A Hudson-test picture that embodied both familiar-size and overlap depth cues was presented in the apparatus to a group of unskilled African workers, who for the most part do not show perception of pictorial depth in the Hudson test and in the construction test [*see illustration on page 81*]. The test picture showed a hunter and an antelope in the foreground and an elephant in the distance. The subjects set the movable light at the same apparent depth regardless of whether they were asked to place it above the hunter, the antelope or the elephant. In contrast, when three-dimensional perceivers were tested, they set the light farther away from themselves when placing it on the elephant than when setting it on the figures in the foreground. The result shows that they were not simply interpreting symbolic depth cues but were actually seeing depth in the picture.

When only familiar size was used as the depth cue, neither group of subjects placed the movable light farther back for the elephant. The result should not be surprising, since other studies have shown that familiar-size cues alone do not enable people even in Western cultures to see actual depth in a picture, even though they may interpret the pic-

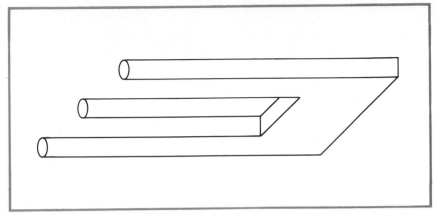

AMBIGUOUS TRIDENT is confusing to observers who attempt to see it as a three-dimensional object. Two-dimensional perceivers see the pattern as being flat and are not confused.

ture three-dimensionally.

The fact that depth was seen in the picture only in the presence of overlap cues is of theoretical interest because it had been postulated that a perceptual mechanism for seeing depth cues where none are intended is responsible for certain geometric illusions, for example overestimating the length of the vertical limb of the letter *L*. If the mechanism is the same as the one for the perception of pictorial depth in Hudson's tests, then one would expect a decrease in the perception of geometric illusions in people who have low three-dimensional scores.

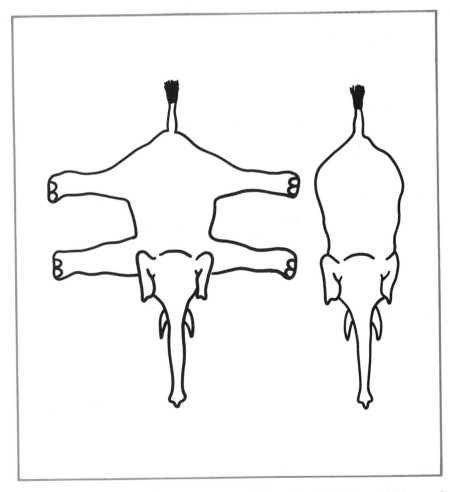

SPLIT-ELEPHANT DRAWING (*left*) was generally preferred by African children and adults to the top-view perspective drawing (*right*). One person, however, did not like the split drawing because he thought the elephant was jumping around in a dangerous manner.

Do people who find pictures of the perspective type difficult to interpret tend to prefer pictures that depict the essential characteristics of an object even if all those characteristics cannot be seen from a single viewpoint? Here again the first systematic cross-cultural observations were carried out by Hudson. He showed African children and adults pictures of an elephant. One view was like a photograph of an elephant seen from above; the other was a top view of an elephant with its legs unnaturally split to the sides. With only one exception all the subjects preferred the drawing of the split elephant [*see bottom illustration on preceding page*]. The one person who did not prefer the draw-

ing said that it was because the elephant was jumping about dangerously.

Other studies have shown that preference for drawings of the split type is not confined to meaningful pictures but also applies to geometric representations. Unskilled Zambian workers were shown a wire model and were asked to make a drawing of it. Only an insignificant proportion of them drew a figure that had pictorial depth; most drew a flat figure of the split type [*see bottom illustration on page 82*]. They also preferred the split drawing when they were shown the model and were asked to choose between it and a perspective drawing. Then the process was reversed, and the subjects were asked to choose

the appropriate wire model after looking at a drawing. Only a few chose the three-dimensional model after looking at the split drawing; instead they chose a flat wire model that resembled the drawing. Paradoxically the split drawing had proved to be less efficient than the less preferred perspective drawing when an actual object had to be identified.

Although preference for drawings of the split type has only recently been studied systematically, indications of such a preference have long been apparent in the artistic styles of certain cultures, for example the Indians of the northwestern coast of North America. Other instances of the split style in art are rock paintings in the caves of the Sahara and primitive art found in Siberia and New Zealand. What art historians often fail to note is that the style is universal. It can be found in the drawings of children in all cultures, even in those cultures where the style is considered manifestly wrong by adults.

Perspective drawings and drawings of the split type are not equally easy to interpret. Even industrial draftsmen with a great deal of experience in interpreting engineering drawings, which are essentially of the split type, find it more difficult to assemble simple models from engineering drawings than from perspective drawings.

One theory of the origin of the split style was put forward by the anthropologist Franz Boas. His hypothesis postulated the following sequence of events. Solid sculpture was gradually adapted to the ornamentation of objects such as boxes or bracelets. In order to make a box or a bracelet the artist had to reduce the sculpture to a surface pattern and include an opening in the solid form, so that when the sculptured object was flattened out, it became a picture of the split type. It is possible that this development led to the beginnings of split drawings and that the natural preference of the style ensured its acceptance. There is no historical evidence that this evolution actually took place, however, and it does seem that the hypothesis is unnecessarily complicated.

The anthropologist Claude Lévi-Strauss has proposed a theory in which the split style has social origins. According to him, split representation can be explored as a function of a sociological theory of split personality. This trait is common in "mask cultures," where privileges, emblems and degrees of prestige are displayed by means of elaborate masks. The use of these mask symbols

STYLIZED BEAR rendered by the Tsimshian Indians on the Pacific coast of British Columbia is an example of split drawing developed to a high artistic level. According to anthropologist Franz Boas, the drawings are ornamental and not intended to convey what an object looks like. The symbolic elements represent specific characteristics of the object.

apparently generates a great deal of personality stress. Personalities are torn asunder, and this finds its reflection in split-style art.

Both Boas' and Lévi-Strauss's hypotheses ignore the universality of the phenomenon. If one accepts the existence of a fundamental identity of perceptual processes in all human beings and extrapolates from the data I have described, one is led to postulate the following. In all societies children have an aesthetic preference for drawings of the split type. In most societies this preference is suppressed because the drawings do not convey information about the depicted objects as accurately as perspective drawings do. Therefore aesthetic preference is sacrificed on the altar of efficiency in communication.

Some societies, however, have developed the split drawing to a high artistic level. This development occurs if the drawings are not regarded as a means of communication about objects or if the drawings incorporate cues that compensate for the loss of communication value due to the adoption of the split style. Both of these provisions are found in the art of the Indians of the Pacific Northwest. These pictures were intended to serve primarily as ornaments. They also incorporate symbolic elements that enable the viewer to interpret the artist's intention. Every such code, however, carries the penalty that communication is confined to people familiar with the code. Highly stylized art is not likely to be easily understood outside of its specific culture. Thus whereas the same psychological processes under the influence of different cultural forces may lead to widely different artistic styles, the styles arrived at are not equally efficient in conveying the correct description of objects and evoking the perception of pictorial depth.

What are the forces responsible for the lack of perception of pictorial depth in pictures drawn in accordance with the efficacious conventions of the West? At present we can only speculate. Perhaps the basic difficulty lies in the observers' inability to integrate the pictorial elements. They see individual symbols and cues but are incapable of linking all the elements into a consolidated whole. To the purely pragmatic question "Do drawings offer us a universal lingua franca?" a more precise answer is available. The answer is no. There are significant differences in the way pictures can be interpreted. The task of mapping out these differences in various cultures is only beginning.

III

FORM ANALYSIS

FORM ANALYSIS

INTRODUCTION

Nowhere is the working of the perceptual system so evident as in our perception of ambiguous figures (discussed by Attneave in his article "Multistability in Perception"). When shapes appear to change without any detectable change in stimulation, we must attribute these alterations to the operation of our own brains. The apparent capriciousness of the brain's action is limited by the fact that the alternative percepts are few and each has its own meaning, whether that be a familiar one or a simple alternative configuration. This limited amount of ambiguity seems a small price to pay for the enormous flexibility of the perceptual system. In this regard, visual ambiguity resembles the ambiguities inherent in our use of language. The alternative meanings of the sentence "The mayor discouraged shooting policemen," result from alternative parsings based, in turn, upon linguistic structure.

Our understanding of the structure and rules of operation of the system for analyzing form is at a primitive stage. Harmon's article, "The Recognition of Faces," presents some intriguingly simple illustrations of the analysing power of the perceiver. But despite their simplicity these examples and their interpretation are based upon highly sophisticated technical knowledge. The notion of spatial frequence—the number of repetitions of a simple wave form in a given distance—has become a much used and useful description of properties of visual displays. However, as Harmon shows, it provides only a beginning in the search for methods of defining the crucial features used for the recognition of an object by the visual system. The difficulty of computer-aided recognition of faces by machines points up the complexity of the problem.

Noton and Stark, in their article, "Eye Movements and Visual Perception," make a bold effort to deal with the problem of recognition by linking it to eye movements. They postulate that sequential movements of the eye serve to scan the features appropriate for recognizing familiar patterns. Such scanning may be part of the process of recognition but, as they mention, it cannot be a necessary factor since recognition may and often does occur without overt scanning: the possibility that an internal scanner exists remains purely hypothetical.

If we understood more of how the *eidetiker* does what he does, then we might have important information on how visual scenes are "parsed" and the pieces stored by the nervous system. Nevertheless, the feats of imagery discussed in the article "Eidetic Images" by Haber are enough to pose challenges to current thinking in the field of perception. Perhaps the most puzzling aspect of these remembered perceptions is how they are represented in the visual systems of their possessors. We might think that such literal copies of previously seen objects would have to be recorded at very early stages of the visual system: perhaps at the retina. But then how can we conceive of such an image being freely scanned by the very eye on whose retina it is projected?

9

Multistability in Perception

by Fred Attneave
December 1971

Some kinds of pictures and geometric forms spontaneously shift in their principal aspect when they are looked at steadily. The reason probably lies in the physical organization of the perceptual system

Pictures and geometric figures that spontaneously change in appearance have a peculiar fascination. A classic example is the line drawing of a transparent cube on this page. When you first look at the cube, one of its faces seems to be at the front and the other at the back. Then if you look steadily at the drawing for a while, it will suddenly reverse in depth and what was the back face now is the front one. The two orientations will alternate spontaneously; sometimes one is seen, sometimes the other, but never both at once.

When we look steadily at a picture or a geometric figure, the information received by the retina of the eye is relatively constant and what the brain perceives usually does not change. If the figure we are viewing happens to be an ambiguous figure, what the brain perceives may change swiftly without any change in the message it is receiving from the eye. The psychologist is interested in these perceptual alternations not as a curiosity but for what they can tell us about the nature of the perceptual system.

It is the business of the brain to represent the outside world. Perceiving is not just sensing but rather an effect of sensory input on the representational system. An ambiguous figure provides the viewer with an input for which there are two or more possible representations

that are quite different and about equally good, by whatever criteria the perceptual system employs. When alternative representations or descriptions of the input are equally good, the perceptual system will sometimes adopt one and sometimes another. In other words, the perception is multistable. There are a number of physical systems that have the same kind of multistable characteristics, and a comparison of multistability in physical and perceptual situations may yield some significant clues to the basic processes of perception. First, however, let us consider several kinds of situations that produce perceptual multistability.

Figure-ground reversal has long been used in puzzle pictures. It is often illustrated by a drawing that can be seen as either a goblet or a pair of faces [*see top illustration on next page*]. This figure was introduced by the Danish psychologist Edgar Rubin. Many of the drawings and etchings of the Dutch artist Maurits C. Escher are particularly elegant examples of figure-ground reversal [*see bottom illustration on next page*]. These examples are somewhat misleading because they suggest that the components of a figure-ground reversal must be familiar objects. Actually you can make a perfectly good reversing figure by scribbling a meaningless line down the middle of a circle. The line will be seen as a contour or a boundary, and its appearance is quite different depending on which side of the contour is seen as the inside and which as the outside [*see top illustration on page 93*]. The difference is so fundamental that if a person first sees one side of the contour as the object or figure, the probability of his recognizing the same contour when it is shown as part of the other half of the field is little better than if he had never seen it at all; this was demonstrated by Rubin in a

classic study of the figure-ground dichotomy.

Note that it is quite impossible to see both sides of the contour as figures at the same time. Trying to think of the halves as two pieces of a jigsaw puzzle that fit together does not help; the pieces are still seen alternately and not simultaneously. What seems to be involved here is an attribution of surface properties to some parts of a field but not to others. This kind of distinction is of central importance in the problem of scene analysis that Marvin Lee Minsky of the Massachusetts Institute of Technology and other investigators of computer simulation have been grappling with lately. The figure made by drawing a line through a circle is actually tristable rather than bistable; the third possibility is being able to see the line as a thing in itself, as a twisted wire rather than the boundary of a figure.

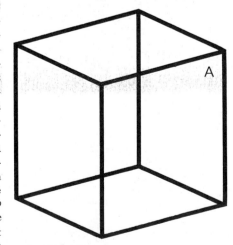

NECKER CUBE, a classic example of perspective reversal, is named after Louis Albert Necker, who in 1832 reported that line drawings of crystals appeared to reverse in depth spontaneously. Corner *A* alternates from front to back when gazed at steadily.

REVERSIBLE GOBLET was introduced by Edgar Rubin in 1915 and is still a favorite demonstration of figure-ground reversal. Either a goblet or a pair of silhouetted faces is seen.

WOODCUT by Maurits C. Escher titled "Circle Limit IV (Heaven and Hell)" is a striking example of both figure-ground reversal and competition between rival-object schemata. Devils and angels alternate repeatedly but neither seems to be able to overpower the other.

The point of basic interest in figure-ground reversal is that one line can have two shapes. Since an artist's line drawing is readily identifiable with the object it is supposed to portray, and since a shape has much the same appearance whether it is white on black, black on white or otherwise colored, many workers have suggested that the visual system represents or encodes objects primarily in terms of their contours. As we have seen, however, a contour can be part of two shapes. The perceptual representation of a contour is specific to which side is regarded as the figure and which as the ground. Shape may be invariant over a black-white reversal, but it is not invariant over an inside-outside reversal.

Under natural conditions many factors cooperate to determine the figure-ground relationship, and ambiguity is rare. For example, if one area encloses another, the enclosed area is likely to be seen as the figure. If a figure is divided into two areas, the smaller of the areas is favored as the figure [see middle illustration on opposite page].

The visual field usually consists of many objects that overlap and occlude one another. The perceptual system has an impressive ability to segregate and sort such objects from one another. Along with distinguishing figure from ground, the system must group the fragments of visual information it receives into separate sets that correspond to real objects. Elements that are close to one another or alike or homogeneous in certain respects tend to be grouped together. When alternative groupings are about equally good, ambiguity results.

For example, if a set of dots are aligned, the perceptual system tends to group them on the basis of this regularity. When the dots are in regular rows and columns, they will be seen as rows if the vertical distance between the dots is greater than the horizontal distance, and they will seem to be in columns if the horizontal distance is greater than the vertical distance. When the spacing both ways is the same, the two groupings—rows and columns—tend to alternate. What is interesting and rather puzzling about the situation is that vertical and horizontal groupings are competitive at all. Geometrically the dots form both rows and columns; why, then, does seeing them in rows preclude seeing them in columns at the same moment? Whatever the reason is in terms of perceptual mechanisms, the principle involved appears to be a general one: When elements are grouped perceptually, they are partitioned; they are not simultaneously cross-classified.

A related case of multistability involves apparent movement. Four lights are arranged in a square so that the diagonally opposite pairs of lights flash simultaneously. If the two diagonal pairs of lights are flashed alternately, it will appear to an observer as if the lights are moving. The apparent motion can take either of two forms: the observer will see motion along the vertical sides of the square, with two pairs of lights, one on the left and the other on the right, moving in opposite directions up and down, or he will see two sets of lights moving back and forth horizontally in opposite directions. If he continues to watch for a while, the motion will switch from vertical to horizontal and vice versa. When one apparent motion gives way to the other, the two perceptions are subjectively so different that the unsuspecting observer is likely to believe there has been some physical change. Apparent movement involves the grouping of events that are separated in both space and time, but the events so grouped are represented as having a common identity; specifically it appears that the same light has moved to a new place. The rivalry between the horizontal and the vertical movement is thus easier to comprehend than the rivalry between rows and columns of dots: if the representational system reflects the laws of the world it represents, the same object cannot traverse two different paths simultaneously or occupy two different places at once.

Ambiguities of grouping are also evident in fields of repetitive elements such as a floor with hexagonal tiles or even a matrix of squares drawn on paper [see top illustration on page 97]. If one stares at the matrix for a while, certain subsets of the squares will spontaneously organize themselves into simple figures. With voluntary effort one can attain fairly stable perceptions of rather complex figures. The most readily seen figures, however, tend to be simple, compact and symmetrical.

Some of the most striking and amusing ambiguous figures are pictures (which may or may not involve figure-ground reversal) that can be seen as either of two familiar objects, for example a duck or a rabbit, a young girl or an old woman, and a man or a girl [see illustrations on next two pages]. What is meant by "familiar" in this context is that the visual inputs can be matched to some acquired or learned schemata of classes of objects. Just what such class

REVERSING FIGURE can be made by scribbling a line through a circle. The shape of the contour formed depends on which side of the line is regarded as part of the figure.

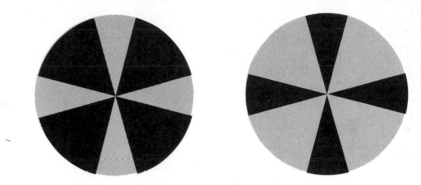

LARGER AREA of a figure is more likely to be seen as the background. Either the large crosses or the small ones may be seen as the figure, but the small crosses have the advantage.

REVERSAL AND ROTATION occur simultaneously in this ingenious design. When the stylized maple-leaf pattern alternates between black and white, it also rotates 90 degrees.

RABBIT-DUCK FIGURE was used in 1900 by psychologist Joseph Jastrow as an example of rival-schemata ambiguity. When it is a rabbit, the face looks to the right; when it is a duck, the face looks to the left. It is difficult to see both duck and rabbit at the same time.

YOUNG GIRL–OLD WOMAN was brought to the attention of psychologists by Edwin G. Boring in 1930. Created by cartoonist W. E. Hill, it was originally published in *Puck* in 1915 as "My Wife and My Mother-in-law." The young woman's chin is the old woman's nose.

schemata consist of—whether they are like composite photographs or like lists of properties—remains a matter of controversy. In any case the process of identification must involve some kind of matching between the visual input and a stored schema. If two schemata match the visual input about equally well, they compete for its perceptual interpretation; sometimes one of the objects is seen and sometimes the other. Therefore one reason ambiguity exists is that a single input can be matched to different schemata.

In certain ambiguous figures we can clearly see the nature of the positive feedback loop that accounts for the "locking in," or stabilization, of one or another aspect of the figure at any given time. For example, if in the young girl–old woman figure a certain line is tentatively identified as a nose, then a line below it must be the mouth and the shapes above it must be the eyes. These partial identifications mutually support one another to form a stable perception of an old woman. If, however, the line we started with is seen as a chin instead of as a nose, then the perception formed is that of a young woman. The identification of wholes and of parts will likewise be reciprocally supportive, contributing further to the locking-in process.

Why one aspect of an ambiguous figure, once it is locked in, should ever give way to the other is a fundamental question. Indeed, a person can look for quite a long time at an ambiguous figure and see only one aspect of it. Robert Leeper of the University of Oregon showed that if a subject was first exposed to a version of the figure that was biased in favor of one of the interpretations, he would almost always see only that aspect in the ambiguous version. Not until the other aspect was pointed out would the figure spontaneously alternate. It is only after the input has made contact with both schemata that they become competitive. Making the initial contact and the associated organization must entail a type of learning.

Ambiguities of depth characterize a large class of multistable figures, of which the cube on page 91 is the most familiar. In 1832 a Swiss geologist, Louis Albert Necker, pointed out that a drawing of a transparent rhomboid crystal could be seen in either of two different ways, that the viewer often experiences "a sudden and involuntary change in the apparent position of a crystal or solid represented by an engraved figure." Necker concluded that the aspect seen depends entirely on the point of

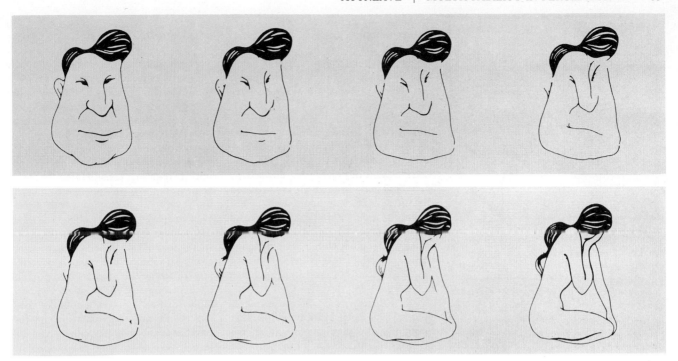

MAN-GIRL FIGURES are part of a series of progressively modi- fied drawings devised by Gerald Fisher in 1967. He found that the last drawing in the top row has equal probability of being seen as a man or as a girl. Perception of middle pictures can be biased toward the man by viewing series in sequence beginning from top left and can be biased toward the girl by starting from bottom right.

fixation, "the point of distinct vision" being perceived as the closer. Although the fixation point is indeed important, it has been shown that depth reversal will readily occur without eye movement.

If we want to understand how depth relationships can be multistable, we must first consider the more general question of how the perceptual system can derive a three-dimensional repre- sentation from a two-dimensional draw- ing. A straight line in the outside world casts a straight line on the retina. A given straight line on the retina, how- ever, could be the image of any one of an infinite number of external lines, and not necessarily straight lines, that lie in

a common plane with one another and the eye. The image on a single retina is always two-dimensional, exactly as a photograph is. We should not be sur- prised, therefore, that depth is some- times ambiguous; it is far more remark- able that the perceptual system is able to select a particular orientation for a line segment (or at worst to vacillate be- tween two or three orientations) out of the infinite number of legitimate possi- bilities that exist.

On what basis does the system per- form this feat? According to the Gestalt psychologists the answer is to be found in a principle of *Prägnanz:* one perceives the "best" figure that is consistent with

a given image. For most practical pur- poses "best" may be taken to mean "sim- plest." The advantage of this interpreta- tion is that it is easier to find objective standards for complexity than for such qualities as being "best." One observes a particular configuration of lines on pa- per, such as the Necker cube, and as- signs a three-dimensional orientation to the lines such that the whole becomes a cube (although an infinite number of noncubical forms could project the same form) because a cube is the simplest of the possibilities. In a cube the lines (edges) are all the same length; they take only three directions, and the an- gles they form are all equal and right

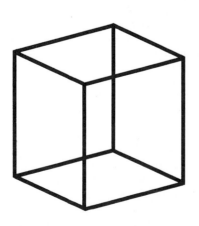
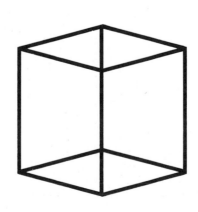
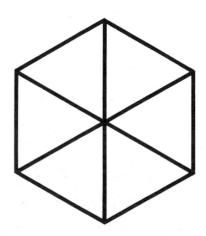

PROJECTIONS OF A CUBE onto a two-dimensional surface are nearly always seen in depth when they resemble the Necker cube (*left*). As the projection becomes simpler and more regular it is more likely to be seen as a flat figure, such as a hexagon (*right*).

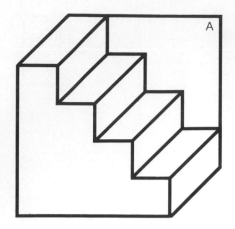

SCHRÖDER STAIRS line drawing is another classic example of perspective reversal. Corner *A* is part of the rear wall when the staircase goes up to the left; when reversal occurs, corner *A* becomes part of the front wall and the bottom of the stairway is seen.

angles. No other interpretation of the figure, including the two-dimensional aspect itself, is as simple and regular. In cases of reversible perspective two maximally simple tridimensional constructions are permissible, each being symmetrical with the other in depth.

If this reasoning is correct, simple projections of a given solid should be perceived as being flat more often than complex projections of the same solid. Julian Hochberg and his colleagues at Cornell University studied various two-dimensional projections of a cube and other regular solids [*see bottom illustra-tion on preceding page*]. Relatively complex projections are nearly always perceived in depth. A figure such as a regular hexagon divided into equilateral triangles, which is simple and regular in two dimensions, stays two-dimensional because seeing it as a cube does not make it any simpler. Intermediate figures become tristable; they are sometimes seen as being flat and sometimes as being one or another aspect of a cube. The measure of complexity devised by Hochberg and Virginia Brooks involved the number of continuous lines in the figure, the number of interior angles and the number of different angles. This measure predicted with considerable accuracy the proportion of the time that a figure was seen in depth rather than as being flat.

I have been emphasizing the importance of simplicity, but it is obvious that familiarity also plays an important role in instances of ambiguous depth. The two factors are hard to disentangle. Simple structures are experienced with great frequency, particularly in man-made environments. As Alvin G. Goldstein of the University of Missouri has shown by experiment, within limits a nonsense shape is judged to be simpler the more often it is experienced. In my view familiarity and simplicity become functionally equivalent in the perceptual system when a given input corresponds closely to a schema that is already well established by experience and can therefore be encoded or described (in the language of the nervous system) most simply in terms of that schema.

Depth reversal does not occur only with two-dimensional pictures. As the Austrian physicist and philosopher Ernst Mach pointed out, the perspective of many real objects will reverse when the object is viewed steadily with one eye. A transparent glass half-filled with water is a particularly dramatic example, but it requires considerable effort to achieve the reversal and the stability of the reversal is precarious. Mach discovered an easier reversal that is actually more instructive. Take a white card or a small piece of stiff paper and fold it once along its longitudinal axis [*see bottom illustration on this page*]. Place the folded card or paper in front of you on a table so that it makes a rooflike structure. Close one eye and view the card steadily for a while from directly above. It will reverse (or you can make it reverse) so that it appears as if the fold is at the bottom instead of the top. Now view the card with one eye from above at about a 45-degree angle so that the front of the folded card can be seen. After a few seconds the card will reverse and stand up on end like an open book with the inside toward you. If the card is asymmetrically illuminated and is seen in correct perspective, it will appear to be more or less white all over, as it is in reality, in spite of the fact that the illuminated plane reflects more light than the shadowed one. When the reversal occurs, the shadowed plane looks gray instead of white and the illuminated plane may appear luminous. In the perspective reversal the perceptual mechanism that preserves the constancy of reflectance is fooled; in order to maintain the relation between light source and the surfaces the perceptual system makes corrections that are erroneous because they are based on incorrect information.

Another remarkable phenomenon involving the folded card seems to have escaped Mach's notice. Recently Murray Eden of the Massachusetts Institute of Technology found that if after you make the folded card reverse you move your head slowly from side to side, the card will appear to rock back and forth quite as convincingly as if it were physically in motion. The explanation, very roughly, is that the mechanism that makes allowance for head movements, so that still objects appear still even though the head moves, is operating properly but on erroneous premises when the perspective is reversed. The perceived rocking of the card is exactly what would

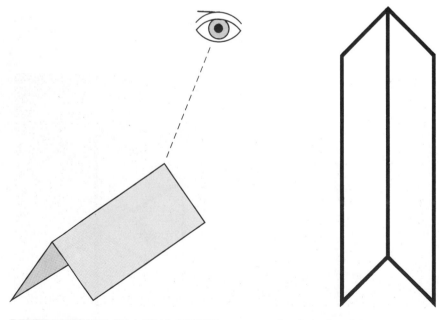

DEPTH REVERSAL OF A REAL OBJECT can occur when it is viewed from above with one eye, an effect discovered by Ernst Mach. When a folded card is viewed from above and the front, it will appear to stand on end like an open book when it reverses. The same kind of depth reversal occurs with a simple line drawing of a folded card (*above right*).

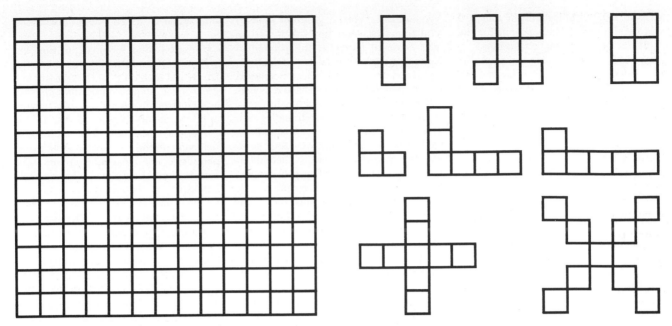

FIGURAL GROUPINGS occur when one stares at a matrix of squares. The simple figures organize themselves spontaneously and with effort more complex figures can be perceived. Some figures, however, are so complex that they are difficult to maintain.

ALIGNED DOTS fall into a regular pattern when viewed. Depending on the spacing, dots can be seen as columns (*left*) or as rows (*middle*). When vertical and horizontal spacing are equal, dots can be seen as rows or columns but not as both at the same time.

EQUILATERAL TRIANGLES appear in one of three orientations depending on the dominant axis of symmetry (*left*). Usually all point in the same direction at one time, although the direction can change spontaneously. The scalene triangles (*middle*) fluctuate in orientation even though they are asymmetrical because they can also appear as isosceles or right triangles that point down or up. The same shape can be seen as either diamonds or tilted squares (*right*) depending on the orientation of the local reference system.

have to happen objectively if the card were really reversed to account for the sequence of retinal images accompanying head movement. What is remarkable about this is not that the mechanism can be wrong but rather that it can function so efficiently as a "lightning calculator" of complex problems in projective geometry and compensate so completely to maintain the perceived orientation. It seems to me that this capacity is a good argument for the existence of some kind of working model of three-dimensional space within the nervous system that solves problems of this type by analogue operations. Indeed, the basic concept of *Prägnanz,* of a system that finds its way to stable states that are simple by tridimensional criteria, is difficult to explain without also postulating a neural analogue model of three-dimensional space. We have no good theory at present of the nature of the neural organization that might subserve such a model.

A few years ago I stumbled on a principle of ambiguity that is different from any we have been considering. While planning an experiment on perceptual grouping I drew a number of equilateral triangles. After looking at them for a time I noticed that they kept changing in their orientation, sometimes pointing one way, sometimes another and sometimes a third way [*see bottom illustration on preceding page*]. The basis for this tristable ambiguity seems to be that the perceptual system can represent symmetry about only one axis at a time, even though an equilateral triangle is objectively symmetrical about three axes. In other words, an equilateral triangle is always perceived as being merely an isosceles triangle in some particular orientation. Compare any two sides or any two angles of an equilateral triangle and you will find that the triangle immediately points in the direction around which the sides and angles are

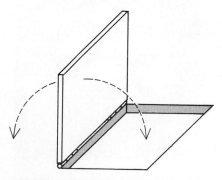

PHYSICAL SYSTEM that exhibits a simple form of multistability is a trapdoor that is stable only when it is either open or shut.

symmetrical. When a group of equilateral triangles points upward, the triangles cease to fluctuate; the perceptual system strongly prefers the vertical axis of symmetry. Indeed, any perceived axis of symmetry seems to have the character of a locally rotated vertical.

When scalene triangles (triangles with three unequal sides) are grouped together with their corresponding sides parallel, they also appear to fluctuate in orientation after a brief inspection [*see bottom illustration on preceding page*]. This is at first puzzling since they have no axes of symmetry at all. The answer to the puzzle involves the third dimension: When the triangles are seen to point in a given direction, they simultaneously go into depth in such a way that they look like isosceles triangles seen at an angle. Perspective reversal doubles the possibilities, so that there are six ways the scalene triangles can be seen as isosceles. The same triangles may also be seen as right triangles in depth, with the obtuse angles most easily becoming the right angles.

These observations begin to make sense if we suppose the perceptual system employs something quite like a Cartesian coordinate system to locate and describe things in space. (To call the system Cartesian is really putting the issue backward, since Descartes clearly took the primary perceptual directions of up-down, left-right and front-back as his reference axes.) The multistable states of triangles thus appear to involve simple relations between the figure and the reference system. The reference system may be tilted or rotated locally by the perceptual system and produce the apparent depth or orientation of the triangles.

In the same way we can explain how the same shape can appear to be so different when it is seen as a square or as a diamond. The square is perceived as having horizontal and vertical axes along its sides; the diamond is perceived as being symmetrical about a vertical axis running through opposite corners. Yet in certain kinds of grouping the perceptual axes can be locally rotated and the diamond can look like a tilted square [*see bottom illustration on preceding page*].

It should be evident by now that some principle of *Prägnanz,* or minimum complexity, runs as a common thread through most of the cases. It seems likely that the perceptual machinery is a teleological system that is "motivated" to represent the outside world as economically as possible, within the constraints of the input received and the

limitations of its encoding capabilities.

A good reason for invoking the concept of multistability to characterize figural ambiguity is that we know a great deal about multistable physical and electronic systems and may hope to apply some of this knowledge to the perceptual processes. The multistable behavior of the perceptual system displays two notable characteristics. The first is that at any one moment only one aspect of the ambiguous figure can be seen; mixtures or intermediate states occur fleetingly if at all. The second is that the different percepts alternate periodically. What accounts for this spontaneous alternation? Once the perceptual system locks into one aspect of the figure, why does it not remain in that state? An analogous physical system is a trapdoor that is stable only when it is either open or closed.

As Necker pointed out, changing the point of visual fixation may cause perspective to reverse. In the instances where the input is being matched against more than one schema visual fixation on a feature that is more critical to one representation than the other may lock perception into only one aspect of the ambiguous figure. Since the percepts can alternate without a change in the point of fixation, however, some additional explanation is needed. The most likely is that the alternative aspects of the figure are represented by activity in different neural structures, and that when one such structure becomes "fatigued," or satiated or adapted, it gives way to another that is fresher and more excitable. Several investigators have noted that a reversing figure alternates more rapidly the longer it is looked at, presumably because both alternative neural structures build up some kind of fatigue. In some respects the neural structures behave like a multistable electronic circuit. A common example of multistability in electronic circuitry is the multivibrator flip-flop circuit, which can incorporate either vacuum tubes or transistors. In the vacuum tube version [*see illustration on opposite page*] when one tube is conducting a current, the other tube is prevented from conducting by the low voltage on its grid. The plates and the grids of the two tubes are cross-coupled through capacitors, and one tube continues to conduct until the charge leaks from the coupling capacitor sufficiently for the other tube to start conducting. Once this tube begins to conduct, the positive feedback loop quickly makes it fully conducting and the other tube is cut off and becomes nonconducting. The process reverses and the system flip-flops between one state and the other.

What is "fatigued" in the multivibrator is the suppressive linkage. In other words, the inhibition of the nonconducting tube slowly weakens until it is no longer strong enough to prevent conduction. The possibility of an analogous neural process, in which the inhibition of the alternative neural structure progressively weakens, is worth considering.

Brain lesions may affect the perception of ambiguous figures. The finding most generally reported is that in people who have suffered brain damage the rate of alternation is lower, more or less independently of the locus of the lesion. On the other hand, a study of a group of brain-damaged war veterans conducted by Leonard Cohen at New York University indicated that damage to both frontal lobes increases the rate of alternation of a reversible figure, whereas damage to only one frontal lobe decreases the rate. The theoretical implications of these neurological findings are quite obscure and will doubtless remain so until we have some fundamental picture of the way the nervous system represents form and space.

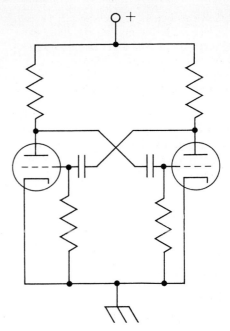

MULTIVIBRATOR CIRCUIT spontaneously alternates between two states. When one vacuum tube is conducting, the other is inhibited. A charge leaking from the coupling capacitor eventually starts the inhibited tube conducting. The positive feedback loop quickly makes it fully conducting and cuts off conduction in the first tube. The entire process is repeated in reverse, and the circuit flops from one state to the other.

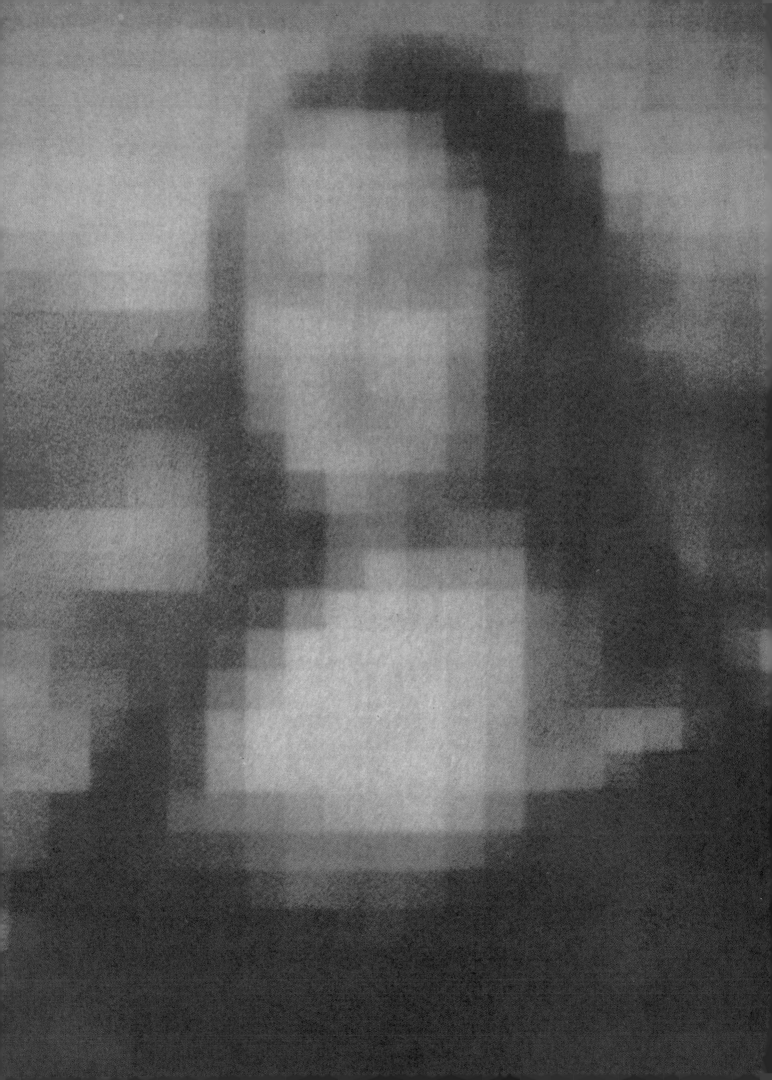

The Recognition of Faces

by Leon D. Harmon
November 1973

*One of the subtler tasks of perception can be
investigated experimentally by asking how much
information is required for recognition and what
information is the most important*

Faces, like fingerprints and snow-flakes, come in virtually infinite variety. There is little chance of encountering two so similar they cannot be distinguished, even on casual inspection. Unlike fingerprints and snowflakes, however, faces can be recognized as well as discriminated. It is possible not only to tell one from another but also to pick one from a large population and absolutely identify it, to perceive it as something previously known, just as in reading one not only can tell that an *A* is different from a *B* but also can identify and name each letter.

Why are faces so readily recognized? In seeking the answer to this question my colleagues and I posed several related but more modest questions that we believed would be more amenable to experimental investigation: How can a face be formally described? Given a verbal description, how well can a particular face be identified? To what extent is recognition impaired when the image of a face is blurred or otherwise degraded? What kinds of image degradation most seriously affect recognition? Can faces be classified and sorted as numerical data?

This inquiry was inspired by yet another question: How can a computer be made to recognize a human face? This question remains unanswered, because pattern recognition by computer is still too crude to achieve automatic identification of objects as complex as faces. Machines can recognize print and script, craters and clouds, fingerprints and

pieces of jigsaw puzzles; the recognition of human faces, however, is a much subtler task.

Even though machine recognition of faces has not been attained, the investigation of how it might be done has led to a number of related issues that in themselves are worthwhile (and tractable) areas of research. Several new approaches to problems in the manipulation of visual data have emerged. I shall recount here four series of experiments that were directed to an understanding of recognition. The first is concerned with how artists reconstruct faces from descriptions and how closely the resulting portraits resemble the person described. Next I shall comment on a set of experiments in which faces were identified from pictures that had limited information content. The third approach examines the recognition of faces from formal numerical descriptions. Finally, I shall describe a system in which man and computer interact to identify faces more efficiently than either could alone.

If one could devise an objective formulation of the criteria used by an artist in drawing a portrait, a set of properties useful for automatic recognition might emerge. One kind of art that we thought might provide useful information is the sketches drawn by police artists (called face-reconstruction artists) from descriptions provided by witnesses. (Another promising possibility is the caricature, but we have not yet studied it.)

Verbal descriptions are rarely used in

the drawing of police sketches. Few observers, unless they are specially trained, can give satisfactory clues to appearance in words. Most can point to features similar to those they remember, however, and that is how the reconstruction artist usually begins. Our initial experiments were intended to test the effectiveness of this procedure and to gain some preliminary notions of what features are considered important in describing or recognizing a face.

Frontal-view photographs were shown to an experienced artist, who compiled a written description of each face; the description included references to facial features in a catalogue of faces made up of photographs of various head shapes, eye spacings, lip thicknesses and so on, organized by feature type. Thus a large part of the description consisted of "pointing to" similar features on other portraits. The completed description was given to another artist, whose task was to reconstruct the face from the written description [*see illustration on next page*].

The first attempt, although obviously resembling the original photograph, differed from it in the depiction of important features and proportions. When limited feedback was allowed, however, there was rapid improvement. The describing artist, with the initial sketch in hand, provided simple verbal corrections, such as "The hair should be bushier at the temples"; with this information the reconstructing artist was able to draw a much more accurate likeness. Finally, to find the limit of improvement, that is, to discover just how faithful a portrait could be drawn, the reconstructing artist was given the photograph to work from. Under those conditions he was able to produce a strikingly realistic representation. Some sketches, in fact, were judged to look more like the per-

LEONARDO'S "MONA LISA," rendered as a "block portrait," consists of 560 squares, each of which is roughly uniform in color and brightness throughout its area. The degraded image was produced by an optical process from a photographic copy of the painting. In spite of its low resolution the picture can be easily identified. Recognition is enhanced by squinting at the image, by rapidly jiggling it, or by viewing it from a distance of 10 to 15 feet

son than the photograph did. Presumably the artist enhanced recognition by in some way emphasizing significant detail.

All the sketches were shown to test subjects who, as fellow employees, had seen the "suspect" often. Almost half of the sketches drawn from descriptions were correctly identified and about 93 percent of the drawings made directly from photographs were recognized.

Our work with face-reconstruction artists was a pilot experiment we hoped would lead, through informal observation, to a better understanding of the problems confronted in the recognition of faces and to the formulation of further experiments. Some of the incidental information derived from the study was indeed interesting. For example, we found that several of the faces were outstandingly easy to recognize in the

sketches. Presumably those subjects were more easily described than the others, or perhaps they possessed certain features that are conspicuous or rare. Several subjects remarked that the nose and eyes in one sketch were important to identification, yet for the same face other subjects observed that although the nose, mouth and hair were well drawn, the eyes were not and did not aid recognition.

Another way to study recognition is to ask how little information, in the informal sense of "bits," or binary digits, is required to pictorially represent a face so that it can be recognized out of a finite ensemble of faces. We explored this "threshold" of recognition with portraits that had been precisely blurred.

The type of blurring commonly encountered in photographs is caused by

an improperly focused optical system; it reduces the information content of the picture, but it proved unsuitable as a technique in our investigations because the degree of blurring cannot be precisely specified or controlled. A more measurable method degrades the image in quantifiable steps through a relatively simple computer process.

In our experiments a 35-millimeter transparency of a conventional portrait photograph is scanned by a beam of light moving in a raster pattern of 1,024 lines. The variations in the intensity of the beam caused by the varying transparency of the film are detected by a photomultiplier tube. The analogue signals produced by the photomultiplier are converted into digital form by sampling each line in the raster at 1,024 points and assigning a brightness value to each point, so that the completed image consists of $1,024^2$ (or 2^{20}) discrete points, about four times the resolution of the commercial television image. Each of the points may have 1,024 brightness values, or tones of gray. The dissected image is stored in the magnetic-tape memory of a digital computer.

To create the degraded image the computer divides the picture into $n \times n$ squares of uniform size and averages the brightness values of all the points within each square. For example, if a photograph is to be made into an array of 16×16 squares, each square will contain 64×64, or 4,096, points; the brightness to be assigned to the entire square will be found by averaging the values of these points. In a final step the number of brightness values is reduced to eight or 16 by assigning to each square the gray tone closest to its original averaged value.

The computer stores the digital information comprising the picture on magnetic tape and the tape controls a cathode-ray-tube monitor, which then displays the completed portrait. A photograph of this display constitutes the finished product. Alternatively, the magnetic tape can be used to control a facsimile printer that produces a print of the processed image without the intermediary cathode ray tube [see bottom illustration on opposite page].

Viewed from close up, these "block portraits" appear to be merely an assemblage of squares. Viewed remotely, from a distance of 30 to 40 picture diameters, faces are perceived and recognized.

Preliminary experiments were made to select the coarsest image that might be expected to yield about 50 percent accuracy of recognition. For some kinds of picture, resolution of only a few thou-

SKETCHES FROM DESCRIPTIONS were made by a "face-reconstruction artist" skilled in drawing portraits from information provided by witnesses. At top left is the photograph from which the three sketches are derived. For the first drawing (top right) a written description of the face, including references to illustrations in a catalogue of facial features, was presented to the artist. A better likeness was produced (bottom left) when simple verbal corrections were provided. For the final version (bottom right) the artist was given the photograph; the resulting portrait represents the limit of accuracy of the process.

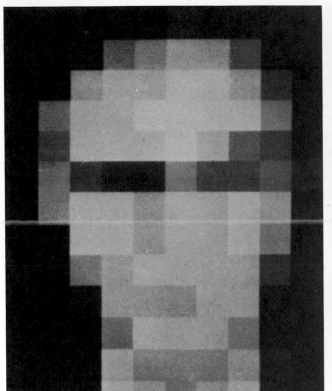
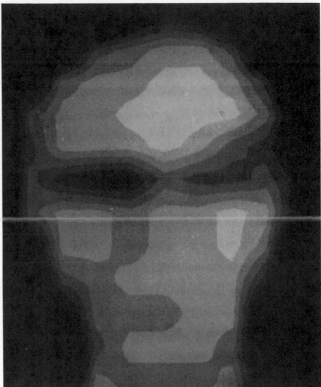

REDUCED-INFORMATION-CONTENT PORTRAITS were generated by a computer. The picture at left is a block portrait; it is an array of 16 × 16 squares, each one of which can assume any one of 16 levels of gray. Not all the 256 squares are required to represent the face. The contoured representation at right was produced by filtering the block portrait to remove high frequencies.

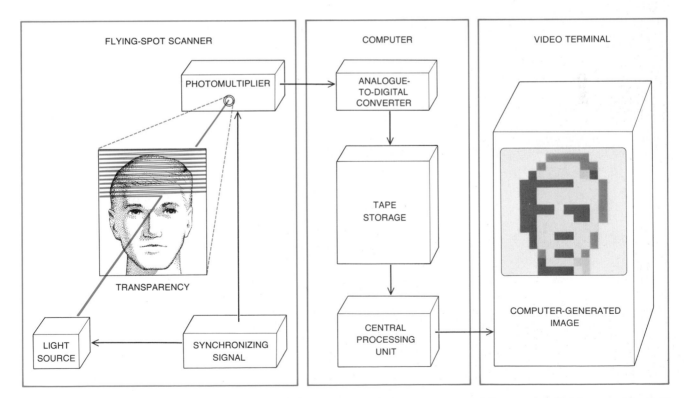

SYSTEM FOR MAKING BLOCK PORTRAITS uses a flying-spot scanner, a device similar to a television camera. The image, usually in the form of a 35-millimeter photographic transparency, is scanned in a raster pattern of 1,024 lines. In the analogue-to-digital converter each line is sampled at 1,024 points and the brightness of each point is assigned one of 1,024 values. Using this information stored on magnetic tape, the central processing unit divides the image into $n \times n$ squares and averages the brightness values of all the points within each square. The number of permissible brightness values is then reduced to eight or 16. The resulting image is displayed on a video terminal (a television screen) and photographed. The computer can also be made to operate a facsimile printer, which produces a finished picture directly. Most of the portraits used in these experiments were made by the latter process.

sand elements provides acceptable quality; the limits of recognition for photographs of faces, however, have not been reported. Our informal investigation revealed that a spatial resolution of 16×16 squares was very close to the minimum resolution that allows identification.

Tests were also made to determine the useful limits of gray-scale representation. The relation between gray-scale and spatial resolution is an interesting one: either factor can serve as a limit to recognition. It was not the object of our experiments to document this relation, however, and so only a few gray-scale tests were made once the 16×16 spatial pattern was decided on. For 16×16

portraits gray scales of either eight or 16 levels yielded eminently recognizable portraits; consequently our experiments used those levels exclusively. (The allowed gray levels can be expressed in terms of bits. A gray scale of eight levels requires three bits of information; a scale of 16 levels calls for four bits.)

Fourteen of the block portraits were shown to 28 subjects. Each subject was given a list of 28 names, including the names of the 14 persons depicted. The experiment was intended to investigate the effects of changing the gray scale from a three-bit to a four-bit one, as well as to test identification performance.

Overall recognition accuracy was found to be 48 percent. (Random guess-

ing would produce such a result only four times in a million trials.) The result was essentially indifferent to the resolution of the gray scale. Thus the number of bits required for approximately 50 percent accuracy of recognition was no more than 16×16 squares times three bits, or 768 bits. None of the portraits, however, filled all the squares in the 16×16 grid; therefore fewer than 256 squares made up each face. An average of 108 squares was needed.

Recognition of particular faces ranged from 10 percent to 96 percent. In these experiments too some faces were always easy to identify, although, as will be seen, the reasons are peculiar to the conditions of the experiment. Two portraits received outstanding recognition and four were rarely identified correctly.

Two possible explanations of these disparities were suggested. First, some faces, because of the peculiar arrangement of their features, respond notably well or particularly poorly to coarse spatial presentation. Second, the grid, arbitrarily positioned over a given face by the scanning process, may land luckily or unluckily for adequate representation. For example, a square might just bracket an eye, or it might land half on and half off. The latter possibility was judged to be the more likely. I hypothesized that those pictures that were recognized well probably had a fortuitously placed grid.

To test the hypothesis each portrait was reprocessed by shifting the 16×16 matrix with respect to the original block portrait. Three new pictures were made: one shifted a half-square to the right, one a half-square down and a third a half-square to the right and down [see *illustration at left*].

Recognition of the sets of four shifted pictures was tested. The subjects were given the identity of each photograph; their task was to rank the four portraits in each set in order of pictorial accuracy. My hypothesis predicted that in these tests those pictures that were readily identified in the earlier experiment would be ranked first in their set and that those scoring worst initially would be ranked near the bottom. So it turned out; both correlations were confirmed.

This result led us to believe that if the best grid positions had been found and used in the earlier experiments, the average accuracy of recognition might have been closer to 100 percent than to 50 percent. A new experiment confirmed this: performance rose to 95 percent.

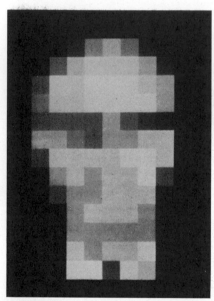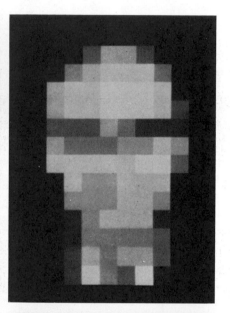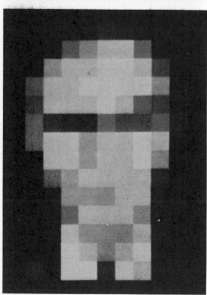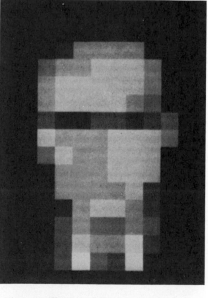

EFFECTS OF GRID PLACEMENT on recognition are illustrated by four block portraits of the same face. The original is at top left. Alternative versions were made by shifting the grid placement one half-block to the right (*top right*), one half-block down (*bottom left*) and one half-block right and down (*bottom right*). When portraits made with optimum placement replaced those made with random placement, recognition accuracy doubled.

An interesting and provocative characteristic of block portraits is that once recognition is achieved more apparent

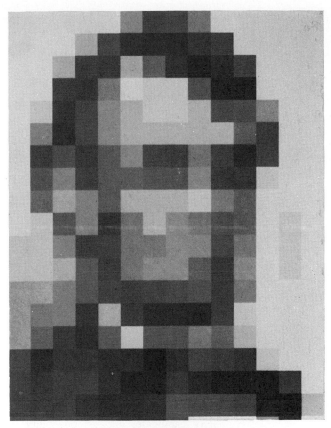

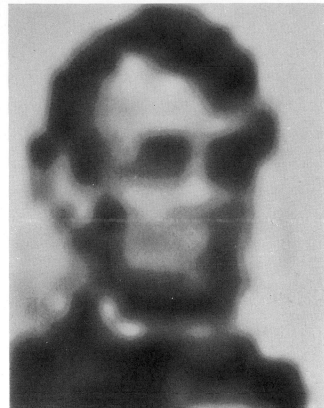

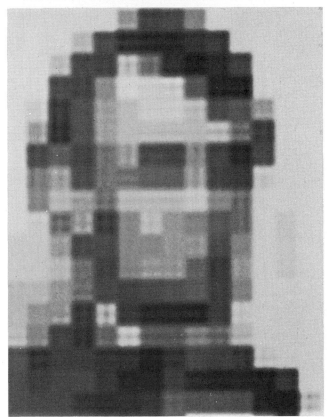

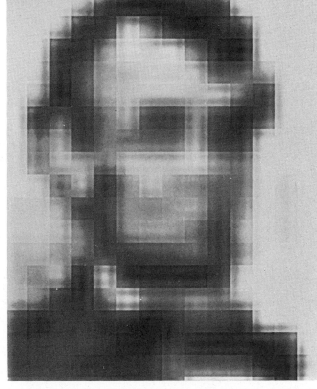

SELECTIVE FREQUENCY FILTERING influences the ease with which block portraits are recognized. The original block portrait of Abraham Lincoln is at top left. It consists of the photographic "signal," whose highest spatial frequency is 10 cycles per picture height, and noise frequencies extending above 10 cycles. As was anticipated, filtering out all spatial frequencies above 10 cycles (*top right*) greatly enhances recognition. Selective removal of only part of the noise spectrum, however, reveals which frequencies most effectively mask the image. At bottom left all frequencies above 40 cycles have been removed; even though the sharp edges of the squares are eliminated, perception is improved only slightly. When the two-octave band from 10 to 40 cycles is removed (*bottom right*), the face is more readily recognized. The phenomenon apparently responsible for this effect is critical-band masking.

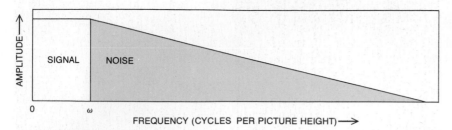

BLOCK-PORTRAIT SPECTRUM consists of a signal that extends to some finite spatial frequency **ω**, corresponding to the block-sampling frequency and noise of frequencies above **ω**. The amplitude of the noise typically decreases with increasing spatial frequency.

detail is noticed. It is as though the mind's eye superposes additional detail on the coarse optical image. Moreover, once a face is perceived it becomes difficult not to see it, as if some kind of perceptual hysteresis prevented the image from once again dissolving into an abstract pattern of squares. The observation that is most intriguing, however, is that recognition can be enhanced by viewing the picture from a distance, by squinting at it, by jiggling it or by moving the head while looking at it. The effect of all these actions is to blur the already degraded image.

Why should recognition be improved by blurring? The explanation almost certainly lies in the "noise" that tends to obscure the image.

A picture, like a sound, can be described as the sum of simple component frequencies. In acoustical signals pressure varies with time; in the optical signals discussed here the frequencies are spatial and consist of variations of "density" (or darkness) with distance. Just as a musical note consists of a fundamental frequency and its harmonics, so an optical image consists of combinations of single frequencies, which make up its spatial spectrum. The spectral representation exists in two dimensions. This spectrum refers only to spatial frequencies; the color spectrum describes another aspect of the image.

When pictures are considered combinations of spatial frequencies, they can be manipulated in the same ways as other frequency-dependent signals are. For example, Fourier analysis can be used to determine the component frequencies of an image, or low-pass filtering can be used to remove the high frequencies that represent fine detail. Signal-frequency bands, the signal and noise spectrum and other terms usually associated with discussions of acoustical phenomena can be applied to the processing of visual images.

The description of a two-dimensional image as a signal of various spatial frequencies leads to a possible explanation of the enhancement of block portraits with blurring. Whenever a signal with a spectrum running from zero to some frequency designated ω is reduced by sampling to discrete frequency components, noise artifacts whose spectrum extends above ω are introduced. The noise is a product of the sampling procedure. In two-dimensional signals it appears as patterns not present in the original image.

Because the noise in these pictures is ordinarily of higher frequency than the signal it can be readily eliminated by a low-pass filter, that is, a filter that preserves only the low frequencies, eliminating the high frequencies that represent fine detail. This operation too is performed by the computer; all spectral components above ω are removed while the desired signal is retained [*see top illustration on this page*].

In block portraits the most obvious noise is that introduced by the sharp edges of the squares. Although Fourier analysis shows that the energy content of these high frequencies is relatively small, one might speculate that because the eye is particularly sensitive to straight lines and regular geometric shapes such square-patterned noise masks particularly well. That is, such image-correlated noise might mask more effectively than randomly distributed noise of equal energy. If so, low-pass filtering should enhance perception. This explanation would seem to be confirmed by the fact that recognition is improved by progressive defocusing or distant viewing, since the effect of both of these actions is to filter out high frequencies.

This hypothesis, however, is not the only candidate; another possibility is called critical-band masking. In both hearing and vision the spectral proximity of noise to a signal drastically influences the detection threshold of the signal. For example, the threshold for detecting a single sinusoidal wave anywhere in the spectrum is elevated when a noise signal is introduced if the noise lies within about two octaves of the signal. If the noise lies outside this "critical band," masking does not occur [*see bottom illustration on this page*].

This phenomenon has been tested and confirmed by others for relatively simple visual presentations such as sine-wave and square-wave gratings in a single dimension. My colleague Bela Julesz and I reasoned that similar masking might occur in more complicated two-dimensional patterns.

If critical-band masking is the mechanism that hinders the recognition of block portraits, then those components of the noise that fall within about two octaves of the sampling frequency ω would be primarily responsible. The rest of the noise spectrum, including the high-frequency signals contributing to the sharp edges of the blocks, should cause little or no masking.

To resolve this question we prepared a series of block portraits that were spectrally manipulated by the computer. The original image was transformed to obtain its Fourier spectrum, filtered to specification, then transformed back and

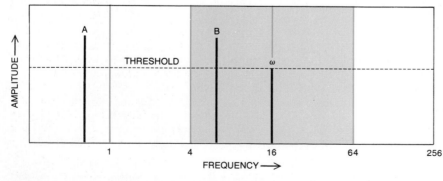

CRITICAL-BAND MASKING is known to occur in presentations of simple visual or audio signals, such as single sinusoidal waves. The test signal **ω**, at the threshold of perception, would be masked by signal *B*, within the band, but not by signal *A*. The critical band (*colored area*) extends for about two octaves above and below the test frequency. The author's investigations indicate the critical-band masking also affects two-dimensional signals.

printed out. This technique provides precise control of spatial frequencies. We were able to remove all signals above a specified frequency, or to remove only a band of frequencies adjacent to ω.

In our first attempt to evaluate the relative importance of high-frequency and critical-band noise masking we prepared a series of filtered block portraits [see illustration on page 105]. The result looked promising: removal of the very high frequencies did little to change the block aspect, and some effort was still required to perceive the face. Removal of only the frequencies adjacent to the signal produced pictures that were much closer in appearance to the original photographs. That is, the very high frequencies did not seem to be the most important in masking.

Although the results of this experiment suggest that noise spectrally adjacent to the signal is most effective in masking recognition, the point is not proved. There are three reasons why the experiment is not conclusive. First, the noise generated by the block-sampling process is spatially periodic, at the block frequency and at higher harmonics. Second, the noise amplitudes are correlated with picture information: the magnitude of the noise in any block depends on the density of the image in that block. Finally, the energy of the noise spectrum is greatest at the block-sampling frequency, and it decreases with increasing frequency. Hence the adjacent band noise may mask more effectively simply because its amplitude is higher, not because of the critical-band effect.

There is a straightforward way to avoid these difficulties. We can simply add random noise of the proper frequency to a picture that is smoothly blurred rather than block-sampled. We added random noise of constant spectral energy to a portrait that had been low-pass filtered to the same bandwidth as that used in the first recognition studies. When such a picture containing adjacent-frequency noise is compared with one masked by remote-frequency noise, the result is unequivocal: critical-band masking is responsible for the suppression of recognition [see illustration on this page].

The discovery that critical-band masking affects complex pictures as well as simple sinusoidal presentations raises additional questions. How effective in masking are noises of equal energy and bandwidth but of various spectral shapes? When noise is added to a signal, is the shape of the noise signal or its location in the spectrum more important?

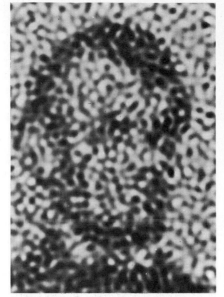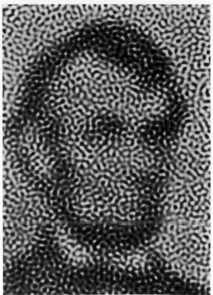

RANDOMLY DISTRIBUTED NOISE of uniform amplitude is added to smoothly blurred portraits of Lincoln. When the noise is in the band adjacent to the signal frequencies (left), it obscures the picture more effectively than when it is at least two octaves removed from the picture frequencies (right), confirming that critical-band masking is the most important mechanism limiting the recognition of degraded or blurred images such as block portraits.

What are the relative effects of spatial disposition and spectral disposition? That is, if equal amounts of noise energy are added to visual scenes, is the placement with respect to position or with respect to frequency more important for masking? These and related questions remain for future investigation. Their answers will provide new insights into the psychophysics of vision.

A more conventional means of blurring pictures is continuous smearing. In optical systems one can simply project the image out of focus; as I have noted, however, this operation cannot be precisely controlled. The analogous operation performed by a digital computer is intrinsically discrete, but by using sufficiently numerous sample points to represent an image, blurring can be made arbitrarily smooth and extremely precise.

Pictures made up of 256 × 256 elements (about one-fourth the resolution of television) produce fairly sharp portraits. Such pictures can be blurred by selecting for each point a brightness value computed by averaging the brightness of the points surrounding it. An "averaging window" of $n \times n$ points is used to compute a new value for each point in the 256 × 256 array; after a new point is written the window is moved over one element and a new average is made.

Through this process the computer can rapidly and accurately blur a picture to a specified degree. The size and shape of the averaging window and the relative weight given to each element in the array can be selected at will. For example, the average could be uniformly weighted or computed on a Gaussian, or bell-shaped, curve. In our experiments we used a square window of varying size with uniform weighting; each element contributed equally to the average value assigned the new point.

We have used portraits made in this way to study the limits of face recognition. Fourteen portraits were shown to subjects who were given a list of 28 names, including the names of the 14 "target" individuals. All 28 persons were known to the test subjects. Several degrees of blurring were tested [see illustration on next page]. Some subjects were shown the most blurred pictures first, some the least blurred, and so on, in order to simultaneously test for the effects of learning. The experiments were conducted by Ann B. Lesk, John Levinson and me.

Contrary to what we had expected, recognition scores were quite good. For photographs blurred by a 27 × 27-point averaging window the recognition was 84 percent. As the degree of blurring increased, the scores declined to about 65 percent for those portraits made with a 43 × 43-point window, which represents severe blurring. (The expected score for random guessing is 3.5 percent.)

Even more surprising were the results

of trials with photographs blurred with a 51×51-point window. Here the width of the window is 20 percent of the picture's width, and blurring is so extreme that facial features are entirely washed out. Nevertheless, the accuracy was almost 60 percent. (This level of recognition cannot continue with much more extensive blurring. When the averaging window includes all the picture elements, the field will be smeared to a uniform gray and pictures will differ only in the level of that gray.)

Recognition of the most strongly blurred of these portraits cannot depend on the identification of features. The high-frequency information required to represent the eyes, the ears and the mouth is lost. Although some intermediate frequencies remain, their representa-

tion of the chin, the cheeks and the hair is not clear. The low-frequency information that relates to head shape, neck-and-shoulder geometry and gross hairline is all that remains unimpaired, yet this alone seems to be adequate for rather good recognition among individuals in a restricted population.

Again, some faces were consistently well recognized. This time the responsible cues were easy to see. One portrait, for example, was distinguished by a round, bald head, and the picture was consistently recognized, even when it was badly blurred.

Some learning apparently took place in these experiments; it would appear that practice at struggling with the task improved performance.

Determining exactly how one recog-

nizes a face is probably an intractable problem for the present. It is possible, however, to determine how well and with what cues identification can be achieved. Similarly, although machine recognition is not yet possible, search for and retrieval of faces by machine is a problem suitable for research. My colleagues and I approached these matters by investigating how effectively one can identify an individual face from a group of faces by using verbal descriptions.

It should be noted that successful identification of faces by feature descriptions does not suggest that the normal processes of recognition regularly detect and assess such features. All we can determine from experiments of this kind is how effectively people can perform a certain recognition task on the basis of certain assigned measures.

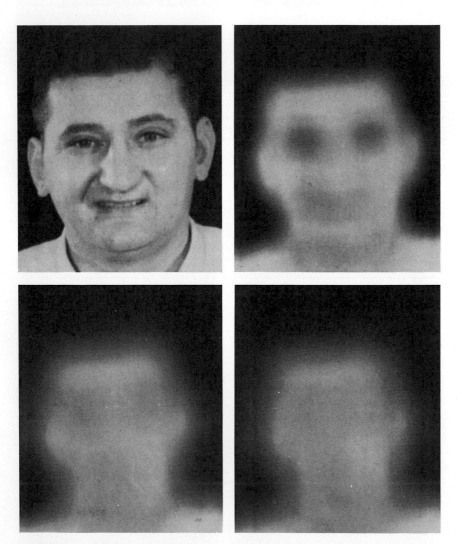

PRECISELY BLURRED PORTRAITS were constructed by a computer using an "averaging window." At top left is the original picture; it is not a continuous-tone photograph but an array of 256×256 dots. The averaging window determines a new value for each of the dots by averaging the values of those that surround it in some $n \times n$ field. When the window is set at 27×27 points (*top right*), basic facial features are still discernible. A 43×43-point window (*bottom left*) produces severe blurring and a 51×51-point window (*bottom right*) eliminates almost all information except gross forms. Accuracy of identification declined as blurring increased but even with the worst pictures approached 60 percent.

The problems of the automatic analysis of faces have received little attention. The work begun by W. W. Bledsoe and his colleagues is one of the few attempts I know of to automate the recognition of faces; the method uses a hybrid man-machine system in which a computer sorts and classifies faces on the basis of fiducial marks entered manually on photographs. The technique is called the Bertillon method, after Alphonse Bertillon, a French criminologist, and is better known for its application to fingerprint classification. A similar method has been developed by Makoto Nagao and his colleagues in Japan in an attempt to devise an automated system that would produce simple numerical descriptions of faces.

I was led to this line of inquiry by wondering if one could play a "20 questions" game with faces. (In games of this kind one player thinks of a person and the other asks him up to 20 questions, which must be answered yes or no, until the subject is guessed.) An informal, preliminary experiment began with 22 portraits; they were shown to subjects who were asked to list features they thought striking or extreme in order of decreasing extremeness. If a face displayed very wide-set eyes, for example, that statement was put at the top of the list. Or if the chin jutted extremely, that fact was listed first. A consensus list was compiled for each of the 22 faces, then new experimental subjects were selected.

Each subject was given the pile of pictures and a list of features, derived from the earlier work, describing one of the faces. He was asked to do a binary sorting, one feature at a time, starting with the most extreme and working down the list. The first sorting, therefore, produced a pile of pictures that the subject believed satisfied the first statement on the list and a pile of rejected pictures. The "accept" pile was then sorted for the second feature and for additional features until the pile was reduced to one portrait.

Two interesting questions arose: How often is the remaining portrait the correct one? How many sortings are required to reduce the population to a single member?

In this preliminary study the remaining portrait was always the correct one, and the average number of sortings required for the isolation was 4.5. We were led to wonder how the accuracy would decline as the population size increased and how rapidly the number of sortings required would grow. If the number of sortings increased linearly with population size, the process would soon become too cumbersome to be effective. (It is difficult to enumerate more than a few tens of features.) If the number of feature sortings grew, say, logarithmically, however, the process could remain useful for quite large populations.

A theoretical model devised by A. Jay Goldstein, Ann Lesk and me indicated that the feature set could indeed be expected to grow logarithmically. Under the experimental conditions we planned to employ, the feature set would grow to 5.4 for a population of 256 faces, to about 6.5 for 1,000 faces and to about a dozen features for a population of a million faces. We decided to test this model in a series of experiments using a population of 256 faces.

To make these studies it was necessary to find a pool of features that could be judged quantitatively and reliably. It was also necessary that these features be independent of one another, so that each one carried useful information.

Portraits were made of 256 faces. Each consisted of three views: frontal, three-quarter and profile. The population was deliberately made homogeneous in order to make the subsequent tasks more difficult. All the subjects were white males between 20 and 50 years

FACES WERE CLASSIFIED in the author's system by numerical judgments of 21 selected features. The population of 256 portraits was examined by a panel of 10 observers, who rated each face according to the 21 criteria shown in the chart at right. The judgments of the panel became the "official" values used as standards in later experiments.

	1	2	3	4	5
HAIR					
COVERAGE	FULL		RECEDING		BALD
LENGTH	SHORT		AVERAGE		LONG
TEXTURE	STRAIGHT		WAVY		CURLY
SHADE	DARK	MEDIUM	LIGHT	GRAY	WHITE
FOREHEAD	RECEDING		VERTICAL		BULGING
EYEBROWS					
WEIGHT	THIN		MEDIUM		BUSHY
SEPARATION	SEPARATED		MEETING		
EYES					
OPENING	NARROW		MEDIUM		WIDE
SEPARATION	CLOSE		MEDIUM		WIDE
SHADE	LIGHT		MEDIUM		DARK
EARS					
LENGTH	SHORT		MEDIUM		LONG
PROTRUSION	SLIGHT		MEDIUM		LARGE
CHEEKS	SUNKEN		AVERAGE		FULL
NOSE					
LENGTH	SHORT		MEDIUM		LONG
TIP	UPWARD		HORIZONTAL		DOWNWARD
PROFILE	CONCAVE		STRAIGHT		HOOKED
MOUTH					
LIP THICKNESS (UPPER)	THIN		MEDIUM		THICK
LIP THICKNESS (LOWER)	THIN		MEDIUM		THICK
LIP OVERLAP	UPPER	NEITHER	LOWER		
WIDTH	SMALL		MEDIUM		LARGE
CHIN					
PROFILE	RECEDING		STRAIGHT		JUTTING
	1	2	3	4	5

old, wearing no glasses, having no beards and displaying no unusual facial marks or scars.

Starting with a tentative set of 35 features, a panel of 10 trained observers filled out questionnaires describing the 256 faces. Each feature was assigned a numerical measure, usually on a scale of from 1 to 5. After a week of tedious labor the resulting data were analyzed statistically for reliability and independence. Twenty-one features were found to be the most useful and were preserved for all further experiments [*see illustration on preceding page*]. The "official" value of each feature was taken as the average of the values assigned by the 10 observers.

With these measures of features it is possible to program a computer to sort a population of faces. If the value of each feature is considered a coordinate in 21-dimensional space, each face will represent a point in that space, the collection of features providing its 21 coordinates. The distinction between any pair of faces can be calculated simply as the Euclidean distance between the points [*see illustration below*].

With this technique one can produce listings of, say, the 100 most similar pairs of faces or the 100 least similar pairs. When the computer was instructed to name the face whose feature values were closest to the average values of those in the population, "Mr. Average" was identified through a procedure that required the nontrivial comparison of 32,640 pairs of 21-dimensional items.

While seeking the most similar faces, we discovered that the Euclidean distance separating one pair was extremely small, much smaller than the distance between the faces chosen as the authentic closest pair. When we checked the photographs, we found that the same person was shown in both. One of our colleagues had visited the studio twice,

and none of the subjects examining the photographs had discovered the duplication until the computer analysis revealed it. For all subsequent study the population was reduced to 255.

Once the feature judgments were classified in the computer memory a number of simulation experiments were conducted in which the computer modeled human performance in sorting the portraits. Given a description, the computer sorted through the population, starting with the most extreme feature. It decided for each feature whether to accept or reject a given portrait on the basis of several different judgment thresholds. For the criteria and conditions that seem most reasonably to replicate human judgments the computer required about six sortings to isolate a photograph.

When human subjects were given the same task, 7.3 sortings were needed; the remaining portrait was the correct one in 53 percent of the trials. If one does not insist on absolute identification but asks only for a reduction of the population, the performance was fairly good. The population was reduced to no more than 5 percent in three-fourths of the trials. That is, 75 percent of the time the "target" face was included in a reduced group of no more than 13 faces.

One of the factors that limits the reliability and accuracy of this procedure is a characteristic of the binary sorting process itself: a mistake made in any decision can lead to the irretrievable loss of the target photograph. Once a portrait has been rejected it can no longer even be considered in later decisions.

A more forgiving process is rank ordering. If at each step the photograph is ranked according to how well it fits the description but is never discarded entirely, then any reasonably accurate description can be expected to place the correct portrait high in the resulting rank-ordered list. Again, even if the accuracy of the individual judgments is not extremely high, and even if a few judgments are clearly wrong, we can expect the procedure to focus attention on a small subset of the population that has a high probability of containing the target. (Population-reduction techniques of this kind are useful in many sorting tasks, such as handwriting recognition and document retrieval.)

The rank-ordered sorting leads to the fourth study to be discussed here: a system in which man and machine interact to identify faces by feature descriptions.

A subject at a computer terminal was given frontal, three-quarter and profile

THREE-DIMENSIONAL ANALOGUE of the 21-dimensional face-classification system makes each face a point inside or on the surface of a cube. For this simplified illustration three features are judged so that the assigned values become the coordinates of the point representing the face. Face *A*, for example, has a hair length of 4, eye separation of 3 and chin profile of 3. The distinction between any two faces can be measured simply as the Euclidean distance between the points. Thus the distinction between face *A* and face *B* in the drawing is $(2^2 + 2^2 + 1^2)^{1/2}$, or 3. In the 21-dimensional model each point is described by 21 coordinates and the equation for the distance between two points has 21 terms.

photographs of one member of the population. He was instructed to describe this target face to the computer, using the numerical feature values. After each description is entered on the keyboard the computer assigns a goodness-of-fit measure, called a "weight," to each member of the population. The weight represents the similarity of the subject's description to the official description. The population is ranked by weight and the list is revised each time a new feature is described. No portraits are rejected, but the target face is expected to climb through the ranks and eventually, if the process is effective, to be listed in first place.

The questions of interest are the same as those in the manual studies: How many feature steps are required and after a specified number of steps how often is the top-ranking face the correct one?

In addition to rank ordering we introduced another procedure to improve performance. In the earlier experiments the subject had chosen features to describe in descending order of extremeness. This technique takes advantage of the human ability to detect and describe conspicuous features, a process beyond the capabilities of machines. Eventually, however, and usually after finding only three or four extreme features, the observer is unable to identify more; few faces have more than four features that could be described as extreme. At this point the machine can contribute to identification in a way that would be difficult for a man.

Rather than the subject's being asked to choose features at random after he has exhausted his judgments of extreme features, he is instructed to invoke "automatic feature selection." The subject possesses exhaustive knowledge of the face he is describing, yet he knows very little about the characteristics of the population stored in the machine. The computer, on the other hand, does not know who the target is but does have the official descriptions of all the faces and their goodness-of-fit to the description that has been given so far. Automatic feature selection enables the computer to ask for a description of the feature that will be most discriminating at any stage of the identification process.

For example, if all members of the population have close-set ears, a description of that feature would not discriminate between faces. The most discriminating feature is the one that has the most uniform distribution of judged values over the permitted range. The

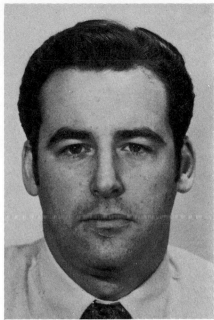

MOST SIMILAR PAIR of faces was found by comparing the 21 judged values of the features of the 32,640 possible combinations. The operation was performed by a computer.

computer, having knowledge of these statistics, can select the sequence of features that will most efficiently separate the members of the population.

After a few feature-description steps, directed by the human subject, the probability is high that the target face has risen in the rank-ordered list. The computer can therefore confine its search for discriminating features to some subset of the population that the portrait thus far describes well. This has the effect of enhancing discrimination of the target.

In our experiments subjects were told to describe conspicuous features until no more were apparent and then to invoke automatic feature selection. The procedure was terminated after 10 steps, since theory and previous experience predicted that this should be sufficient for good accuracy.

Performance was excellent. The subjects' votes and the official values were in good agreement. In spite of the vaga-

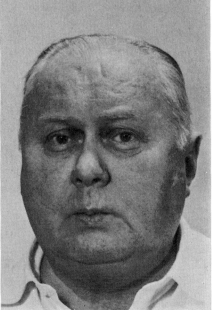

LEAST SIMILAR PAIR of faces was determined by the same procedure. The population was deliberately made homogeneous: all members were white males from 20 to 50 years old.

ries of subjective judgment the difference between the experimental and the official values, in a scale typically ranging from 1 to 5, was less than one in more than 95 percent of the trials. Accuracy of identification was also impressive. The population was reduced to less than 4 percent 99 percent of the time, that is, the correct face was in 10th place or better in 99 of every 100 trials. By the 10th sorting the target was in first place in 70 percent of all trials.

In control experiments features were selected by the human operator only and by the computer only; in both cases performance was poorer than when both man and machine participated.

This last exercise has more general applications than the identification of faces. It is a technique for the retrieval of any multidimensional vectors by information obtained from imprecise descriptions. Such probabilistic file searches are important in answering telephone-directory assistance inquiries, in medical diagnosis and in law-enforcement information retrieval.

Our studies have touched on a host of questions about human perception, automatic pattern recognition and procedures for information retrieval. Although the ultimate question of how a face is recognized remains unanswered, a few promising lines of inquiry have emerged. It has once again been clearly shown that the human viewer is a fantastically competent information processor. In some recognition tasks a synergy of man and machine is effective, but in further explorations of the identification of complex images both by men and by machines there is much to learn.

```
DESCRIBE NEXT PICTURE.


FEATURE
       EYEBRØW WT.                          ******EYE ØPENING
THIN        MEDIUM      BUSHY               NARRØW      MEDIUM      WIDE
     1    2    3    4    5                       1    2    3    4    5
=1                                         =2
    93  244  183  223  159                     76   72  226   26  191
1.00 1.00 1.00 1.00 0.82                    1.00 0.51 0.40 0.38 0.36


FEATURE
     EAR LENGTH                             ******UPPER LIP
SHØRT       MEDIUM      LØNG                THIN        MEDIUM      THICK
     1    2    3    4    5                       1    2    3    4    5
=1                                         =3
    72  244  175   93   43                     76  191   72  221   52
1.00 1.00 0.82 0.67 0.66                    1.00 0.33 0.28 0.23 0.21


FEATURE
       LIP ØVERLAP                          ******HAIR SHADE
UPPER       NEITHER    LØWER                DARK MED. LT.   GRAY WHT.
     1         2         3                       1    2    3    4    5
=1                                         =2
    72  226  114  122   76                     76  221   72  226  191
1.00 0.73 0.66 0.61 0.60                    1.00 0.34 0.34 0.33 0.25


FEATURE
     HAIR TEXTURE                           ******LØWER LIP
STRAIGHT  WAVY         CURLY                THIN        MEDIUM      THICK
     1    2    3    4    5                       1    2    3    4    5
=4                                         =1
    76  122   32  244   52                     76   72  221   84  191
1.00 0.74 0.56 0.55 0.50                    1.00 0.19 0.13 0.12 0.11


FEATURE                                     PLEASE TYPE TARGET NUMBER.
                                           =76
     AUTØMATIC FEATURE SELECTIØN
******EYE SHADE
LIGHT       MEDIUM     DARK                 ØRDER FEATURE      DESCRIPTIØN    RANK
     1    2    3    4    5                                     YØU   AVG.  NØ.   %
=3                                              1  EYEBRØW WT.   1    2.2   27  10.2
    76   52   72  221  191                      2  EAR LENGTH    1    2.3    8   2.7
1.00 0.56 0.45 0.38 0.36                        3  LIP ØVERLAP   1    1.2    5   1.6
                                               4  HAIR TEXTURE  4    3.0    1   0.

                                               5  EYE SHADE     3    2.7    1   0.
******EYEBRØW SEP.                             6  EYEBRØW SEP.  2    1.3    1   0.
SEPARATE    MEDIUM     MEETING                  7  EYE ØPENING   2    2.6    1   0.
     1         2         3                      8  UPPER LIP     3    2.9    1   0.
=2                                             9  HAIR SHADE    2    1.5    1   0.
    76  147   52   84   72                     10  LØWER LIP     1    2.3    1   0.
1.00 0.50 0.42 0.37 0.34
```

DIALOGUE WITH A COMPUTER records a search for a "target" face. The computer "speaks" first and requests a description; the subject replies by announcing that he will describe eyebrow weight. The computer then prints the range of allowable values. The subject selects "1" for "thin" and the computer ranks each member of the population according to how well it fits this value. The five members that best fit the description are printed in the next line, followed by their relative "weights." The first four faces here are tied with weights of 1.00. The target face in this trial was No. 76; by the third step it was in fifth place and by the fourth step in first place. After the fourth feature description the subject called for "automatic feature selection," which enables the computer to request descriptions of those features that would be most discriminating. After the 10th step No. 76 had a weight of 1.00 and its nearest neighbor a weight of .19. The correct face was clearly identified even though the first two descriptions were in error. Following the dialogue is a summary comparing the subject's judgments with the "official" values (AVG.) and showing the rank of the target at each step and the percent of the population with a higher rank. The procedure was stopped after 10 steps; 21 steps were possible.

11

Eye Movements
and Visual Perception

by David Noton and Lawrence Stark
June 1971

Recordings of the points inspected in the scanning of a picture and of the path the eyes follow in the inspection provide clues to the process whereby the brain perceives and recognizes objects

The eyes are the most active of all human sense organs. Other sensory receptors, such as the ears, accept rather passively whatever signals come their way, but the eyes are continually moving as they scan and inspect the details of the visual world. The movements of the eyes play an important role in visual perception, and analyzing them can reveal a great deal about the process of perception.

We have recently been recording the eye movements of human subjects as they first inspected unfamiliar objects and then later recognized them. In essence we found that every person has a characteristic way of looking at an object that is familiar to him. For each object he has a preferred path that his eyes tend to follow when he inspects or recognizes the object. Our results suggest a new hypothesis about visual learning and recognition. Before describing and explaining our experiments more fully we shall set the stage by outlining some earlier experiments that have aided the interpretation of our results.

Eye movements are necessary for a physiological reason: detailed visual information can be obtained only through the fovea, the small central area of the retina that has the highest concentration of photoreceptors. Therefore the eyes must move in order to provide information about objects that are to be inspected in any detail (except when the object is quite small in terms of the angle it subtends in the visual field). The eye-movement muscles, under the control of the brain, aim the eyes at points of interest [see "Control Mechanisms of the Eye," by Derek H. Fender, SCIENTIFIC AMERICAN, July, 1964, and "Movements of the Eye," by E. Llewellyn Thomas, SCIENTIFIC AMERICAN Offprint 516].

During normal viewing of stationary objects the eyes alternate between fixations, when they are aimed at a fixed point in the visual field, and rapid movements called saccades. Each saccade leads to a new fixation on a different point in the visual field. Typically there are two or three saccades per second. The movements are so fast that they occupy only about 10 percent of the viewing time.

Visual learning and recognition involve storing and retrieving memories. By way of the lens, the retina and the optic nerve, nerve cells in the visual cortex of the brain are activated and an image of the object being viewed is formed there. (The image is of course in the form of neural activity and is quite unlike the retinal image of the object.) The memory system of the brain must contain an internal representation of every object that is to be recognized. Learning or becoming familiar with an object is the process of constructing this representation. Recognition of an object when it is encountered again is the process of matching it with its internal representation in the memory system.

A certain amount of controversy surrounds the question of whether visual recognition is a parallel, one-step process or a serial, step-by-step one. Psychologists of the Gestalt school have maintained that objects are recognized as wholes, without any need for analysis into component parts. This argument implies that the internal representation of each object is a unitary whole that is matched with the object in a single operation. More recently other psychologists have proposed that the internal representation is a piecemeal affair—an assemblage of parts or features. During recognition the features are matched serially with the features of the object step by step. Successful matching of all the features completes recognition.

The serial-recognition hypothesis is supported mainly by the results of experiments that measure the time taken by a subject to recognize different objects. Typically the subject scans an array of objects (usually abstract figures) looking for a previously memorized "target" object. The time he spends considering each object (either recognizing it as a target object or rejecting it as being different) is measured. That time is normally quite short, but it can be measured in various ways with adequate accuracy. Each object is small enough to be recognized with a single fixation, so that eye movements do not contribute to the time spent on recognition.

Experiments of this kind yield two general results. First, it is found that on the average the subject takes longer to recognize a target object than he does to reject a nontarget object. That is the result to be expected if objects are recognized serially, feature by feature. When an object is compared mentally with the internal representation of the target object, a nontarget object will fail to match some feature of the internal representation and will be rejected without further checking of features, whereas target objects will be checked on all features. The result seems inconsistent with the Gestalt hypothesis of a holistic internal representation matched with the object in a single operation. Presumably in such an operation the subject would take no longer to recognize an object than he would to reject it.

A second result is obtained by varying the complexity of the memorized target object. It is found that the subject takes longer to recognize complex target objects than to recognize simple ones. This result too is consistent with the serial-recognition hypothesis, since more features must be checked in the more complex object. By the same token the result

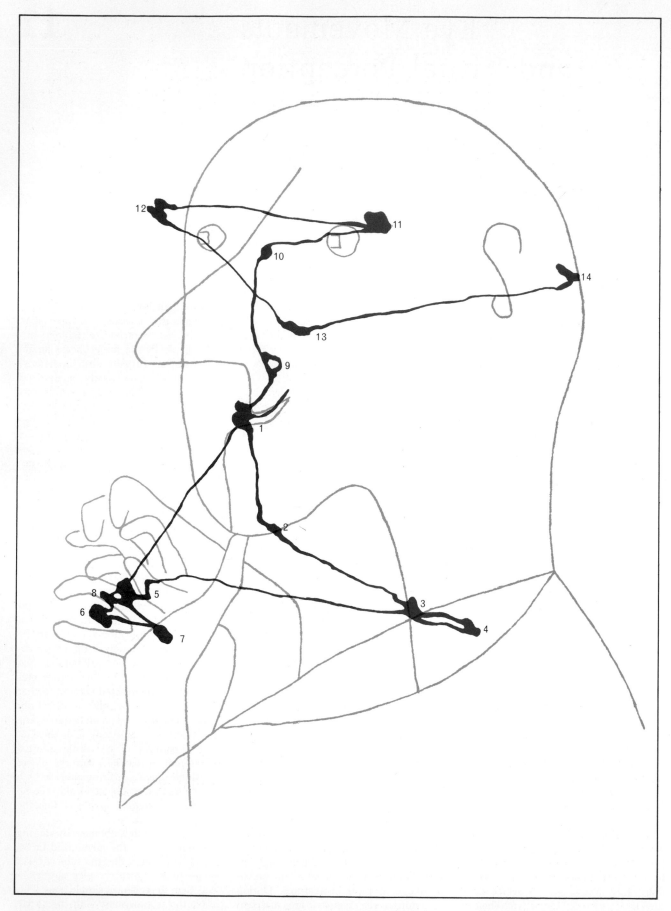

EYE MOVEMENTS made by a subject viewing for the first time a drawing adapted from Paul Klee's "Old Man Figuring" appear in black. Numbers show the order of the subject's visual fixations on the picture during part of a 20-second viewing. Lines between them represent saccades, or rapid movements of eyes from one fixation to the next. Saccades occupy about 10 percent of viewing time.

also appears to be inconsistent with the Gestalt hypothesis.

It would be incorrect to give the impression that the serial nature of object recognition is firmly established to the exclusion of the unitary concept advanced by Gestalt psychologists. They have shown convincingly that there is indeed some "primitive unity" to an object, so that the object can often be singled out as a separate entity even before true recognition begins. Moreover, some of the recognition-time experiments described above provide evidence, at least with very simple objects, that as an object becomes well known its internal representation becomes more holistic and the recognition process correspondingly becomes more parallel. Nonetheless, the weight of evidence seems to support the serial hypothesis, at least for objects that are not notably simple and familiar.

If the internal representation of an object in memory is an assemblage of features, two questions naturally suggest themselves. First, what are these features, that is, what components of an object does the brain select as the key items for identifying the object? Second, how are such features integrated and related to one another to form the complete internal representation of the object? The study of eye movements during visual perception yields considerable evidence on these two points.

In experiments relating to the first question the general approach is to present to a subject a picture or another object that is sufficiently large and close to the eyes so that it cannot all be registered on the foveas in one fixation. For example, a picture 35 centimeters wide and 100 centimeters from the eyes subtends a horizontal angle of 20 degrees at each eye—roughly the angle subtended by a page of this magazine held at arm's length. This is far wider than the one to two degrees of visual field that are brought to focus on the fovea.

Under these conditions the subject must move his eyes and look around the picture, fixating each part he wants to see clearly. The assumption is that he looks mainly at the parts of the picture he regards as being its features; they are the parts that hold for him the most information about the picture. Features are tentatively located by peripheral vision and then fixated directly for detailed inspection. (It is important to note that in these experiments and in the others we shall describe the subject is given only general instructions, such as "Just look at the pictures," or even no instruc-

tions at all. More specific instructions, requiring him to inspect and describe some specific aspect of the picture, usually result in appropriately directed fixations, as might be expected.)

When subjects freely view simple pictures, such as line drawings, under these conditions, it is found that their fixations tend to cluster around the angles of the picture. For example, Leonard Zusne and Kenneth M. Michels performed an experiment of this type at Purdue University, using as pictures line drawings of simple polygons [see illustration on

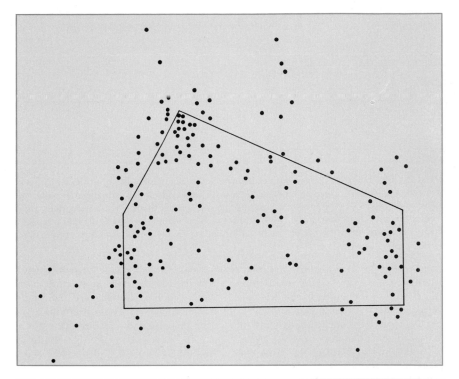

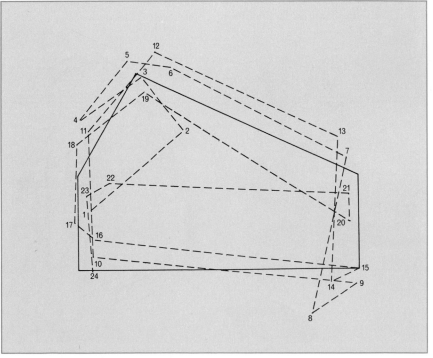

IMPORTANCE OF ANGLES as features that the brain employs in memorizing and recognizing an object was apparent in experiments by Leonard Zusne and Kenneth M. Michels at Purdue University. They recorded fixations while subjects looked at drawings of polygons for eight seconds. At top is one of the polygons; the dots indicate the fixations of seven subjects. Sequence of fixations by one subject in an eight-second viewing appears at bottom.

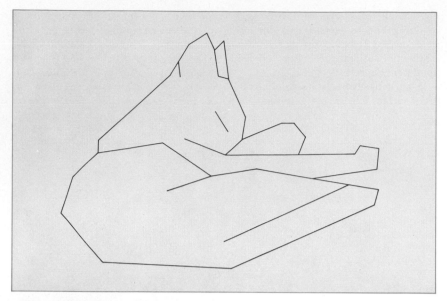

SHARP CURVES are also important as features for visual identification, as shown by Fred Attneave III of the University of Oregon in a picture made by selecting the 38 points of greatest curvature in a picture of a sleeping cat and joining them with straight lines, thus eliminating all other curves. The result is still easily recognizable, suggesting that points of sharp curvature provide highly useful information to the brain in visual perception.

page 115]. From the fixations made by their subjects in viewing such figures it is clear that the angles of the drawings attracted the eyes most strongly.

Our tentative conclusion is that, at least with such line drawings, the angles are the principal features the brain employs to store and recognize the drawing. Certainly angles would be an efficient choice for features. In 1954 Fred

Attneave III of the University of Oregon pointed out that the most informative parts of a line drawing are the angles and sharp curves. To illustrate his argument he presented a picture that was obtained by selecting the 38 points of greatest curvature in a picture of a sleeping cat and joining the points with straight lines [*see illustration above*]. The result is clearly recognizable.

Additional evidence that angles and sharp curves are features has come from electrophysiologists who have investigated the activity of individual brain cells. For example, in the late 1950's Jerome Y. Lettvin, H. R. Maturana, W. S. McCulloch and W. H. Pitts of the Massachusetts Institute of Technology found angle-detecting neurons in the frog's retina. More recently David H. Hubel and Torsten N. Wiesel of the Harvard Medical School have extended this result to cats and monkeys (whose angle-detecting cells are in the visual cortex rather than the retina). And recordings obtained from the human visual cortex by Elwin Marg of the University of California at Berkeley give preliminary indications that these results can be extended to man.

Somewhat analogous results have been obtained with pictures more complex than simple line drawings. It is not surprising that in such cases the features are also more complex. As a result no formal description of them has been achieved. Again, however, high information content seems to be the criterion. Norman H. Mackworth and A. J. Morandi made a series of recordings at Harvard University of fixations by subjects viewing two complex photographs. They concluded that the fixations were concentrated on unpredictable or unusual details, in particular on unpredictable contours. An unpredictable contour is one that changes direction rapidly and irregularly and therefore has a high information content.

We conclude, then, that angles and other informative details are the features selected by the brain for remembering and recognizing an object. The next question concerns how these features are integrated by the brain into a whole—the internal representation—so that one sees the object as a whole, as an object rather than an unconnected sequence of features. Once again useful evidence comes from recordings of eye movements. Just as study of the locations of fixations indicated the probable nature of the features, so analysis of the order of fixations suggests a format for the interconnection of features into the overall internal representation.

The illustration at left shows the fixations made by a subject while viewing a photograph of a bust of the Egyptian queen Nefertiti. It is one of a series of recordings made by Alfred L. Yarbus of the Institute for Problems of Information Transmission of the Academy of Sciences of the U.S.S.R. The illustration

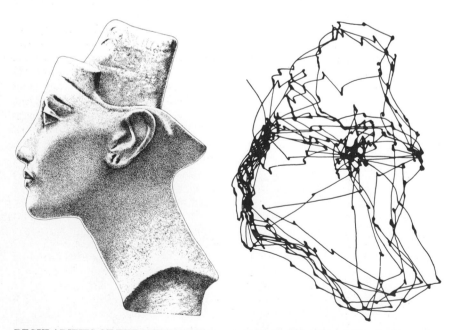

REGULARITIES OF EYE MOVEMENT appear in a recording of a subject viewing a photograph of a bust of Queen Nefertiti. At left is a drawing of what the subject saw; at right are his eye movements as recorded by Alfred L. Yarbus of the Institute for Problems of Information Transmission in Moscow. The eyes seem to visit the features of the head cyclically, following fairly regular pathways, rather than crisscrossing the picture at random.

shows clearly an important aspect of eye movement during visual perception, namely that the order of the fixations is by no means random. The lines representing the saccades form broad bands from point to point and do not crisscross the picture at random as would be expected if the eyes visited the different features repetitively in a random order. It appears that fixation on any one feature, such as Nefertiti's eye, is usually followed by fixation on the same next feature, such as her mouth. The overall record seems to indicate a series of cycles; in each cycle the eyes visit the main features of the picture, following rather regular pathways from feature to feature.

Recently at the University of California at Berkeley we have developed a hypothesis about visual perception that predicts and explains this apparent regularity of eye movement. Essentially we propose that in the internal representation or memory of the picture the features are linked together in sequence by the memory of the eye movement required to look from one feature to the next. Thus the eyes would tend to move from feature to feature in a fixed order, scanning the picture.

Most of Yarbus' recordings are summaries of many fixations and do not contain complete information on the ordering of the fixations. Thus the regularities of eye movements predicted by our hypothesis could not be definitely confirmed from his data. To eliminate this constraint and to subject our hypothesis to a more specific test we recently made a new series of recordings of eye movements during visual perception.

Our subjects viewed line drawings of simple objects and abstract symbols as we measured their eye movements (using photocells to determine the movements of the "white" of the eye) and recorded them on magnetic tape [see illustration above]. We thereby obtained a permanent record of the order of fixations made by the subjects and could play it back later at a lower speed, analyzing it at length for cycles and other regularities of movement. As in the earlier experiments, the drawings were fairly large and close to the subject's eyes, a typical drawing subtending about 20 degrees at the eye. In addition we drew the pictures with quite thin lines and displayed them with an underpowered slide projector, throwing a dim image on a screen that was fully exposed to the ordinary light in the laboratory. In this way we produced an image of

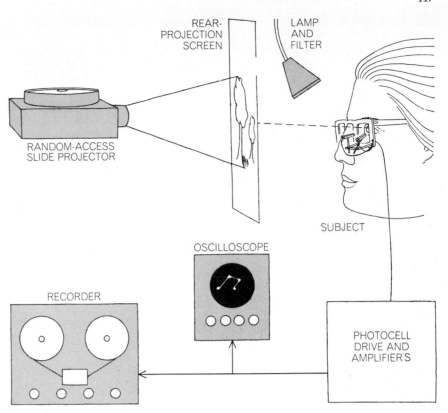

REAR-PROJECTION SCREEN   LAMP AND FILTER

RANDOM-ACCESS SLIDE PROJECTOR

SUBJECT

OSCILLOSCOPE

RECORDER

PHOTOCELL DRIVE AND AMPLIFIER'S

EXPERIMENTAL PROCEDURE employed by the authors is depicted schematically. The subject viewed pictures displayed on a rear-projection screen by a random-access slide projector. Diffuse infrared light was shined on his eyes; his eye movements were recorded by photocells, mounted on a spectacle frame, that detected reflections of the infrared light from one eyeball. Eye movements were displayed on oscilloscope and also recorded on tape.

low visibility and could be sure that the subject would have to look directly (foveally) at each feature that interested him, thus revealing to our recording equipment the locus of his attention.

Our initial results amply confirmed the previous impression of cycles of eye movements. We found that when a subject viewed a picture under these conditions, his eyes usually scanned it following—intermittently but repeatedly—a fixed path, which we have termed his "scan path" for that picture [see illustration on following page]. The occurrences of the scan path were separated by periods in which the fixations were ordered in a less regular manner.

Each scan path was characteristic of a given subject viewing a given picture. A subject had a different scan path for every picture he viewed, and for a given picture each subject had a different scan path. A typical scan path for our pictures consisted of about 10 fixations and lasted for from three to five seconds. Scan paths usually occupied from 25 to 35 percent of the subject's viewing time, the rest being devoted to less regular eye movements.

It must be added that scan paths were not always observed. Certain pictures (one of a telephone, for example) seemed often not to provoke a repetitive response, although no definite common characteristic could be discerned in such pictures. The commonest reaction, however, was to exhibit a scan path. It was interesting now for us to refer back to the earlier recordings by Zusne and Michels, where we observed scan paths that had previously passed unnoticed. For instance, in the illustration on page 115 fixations No. 4 through No. 11 and No. 11 through No. 18 appear to be two occurrences of a scan path. They are identical, even to the inclusion of the small reverse movement in the lower right-hand corner of the figure.

This demonstration of the existence of scan paths strengthened and clarified our ideas about visual perception. In accordance with the serial hypothesis, we assume that the internal representation of an object in the memory system is an assemblage of features. To this we add a crucial hypothesis: that the features are assembled in a format we have termed a "feature ring" [see illustration on page 119]. The ring is a sequence of sensory and motor memory traces, alternately recording a feature of the object and the eye movement required to reach the next feature. The feature ring establishes a fixed ordering of features and eye movements, corresponding to a scan path on the object.

Our hypothesis states that as a subject views an object for the first time and becomes familiar with it he scans it with his eyes and develops a scan path for it. During this time he lays down the memory traces of the feature ring, which records both the sensory activity and the motor activity. When he subsequently encounters the same object again, he recognizes it by matching it with the feature ring, which is its internal representation in his memory. Matching consists in verifying the successive features and carrying out the intervening eye movements, as directed by the feature ring.

This hypothesis not only offers a plausible format for the internal representation of objects—a format consistent with the existence of scan paths—but also has certain other attractive features. For example, it enables us to draw an interesting analogy between perception and behavior, in which both are seen to involve the alternation of sensory and motor activity. In the case of behavior, such as the performance of a learned sequence of activities, the sensing of a situation alternates with motor activity designed to bring about an expected new situation. In the case of perception (or, more specifically, recognition) of an object the verification of features alternates with movement of the eyes to the expected new feature.

The feature-ring hypothesis also makes a verifiable prediction concerning eye movements during recognition: The successive eye movements and feature verifications, being directed by the feature ring, should trace out the same scan path that was established for the object during the initial viewing. Confirmation of the prediction would further strengthen the case for the hypothesis. Since the prediction is subject to experimental confirmation we designed an experiment to test it.

The experiment had two phases, which we called the learning phase and the recognition phase. (We did not, of

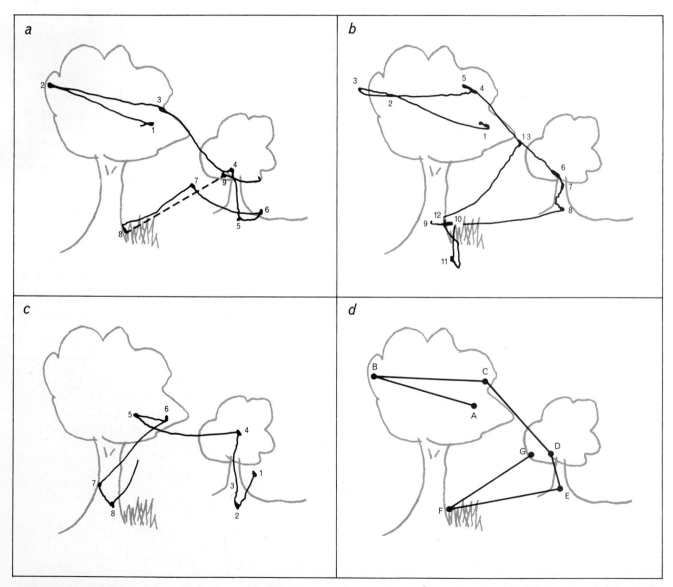

REGULAR PATTERN of eye movement by a given subject viewing a given picture was termed the subject's "scan path" for that picture. Two of five observed occurrences of one subject's scan path as he looked at a simple drawing of trees for 75 seconds are shown here (a, b). The dotted line between fixations 8 and 9 of a indicates that the recording of this saccade was interrupted by a blink. Less regular eye movements made between these appearances of the scan path are at c. Subject's scan path is idealized at d.

course, use any such suggestive terms in briefing the subjects; as before, they were simply told to look at the pictures.) In the learning phase the subject viewed five pictures he had not seen before, each for 20 seconds. The pictures and viewing conditions were similar to those of the first experiment. For the recognition phase, which followed immediately, the five pictures were mixed with five others the subject had not seen. This was to make the recognition task less easy. The set of 10 pictures was then presented to the subject three times in random order; he had five seconds to look at each picture. Eye movements were recorded during both the learning phase and the recognition phase.

When we analyzed the recordings, we were pleased to find that to a large extent our predictions were confirmed. Scan paths appeared in the subject's eye movements during the learning phase, and during the recognition phase his first few eye movements on viewing a picture (presumably during the time he was recognizing it) usually followed the same scan path he had established for that picture during the learning phase [*see illustration on following page*]. In terms of our hypothesis the subject was forming a feature ring during the learning-phase occurrences of the scan path; in the recognition phase he was matching the feature ring with the picture, following the scan path dictated by the feature ring.

An additional result of this experiment was to demonstrate that different subjects have different scan paths for a given picture and, conversely, that a given subject has different scan paths for different pictures [*see illustration on page 121*]. These findings help to discount certain alternative explanations that might be advanced to account for the occurrence of scan paths. The fact that a subject has quite different scan paths for different pictures suggests that the scan paths are not the result of some fixed habit of eye movement, such as reading Chinese vertically, brought to each picture but rather that they come from a more specific source, such as learned feature rings. Similarly, the differences among subjects in scan paths used for a given picture suggest that the scan paths do not result from peripheral feature detectors that control eye movements independent of the recognition process, since these detectors might be expected to operate in much the same way in all subjects.

Although the results of the second experiment provided considerable

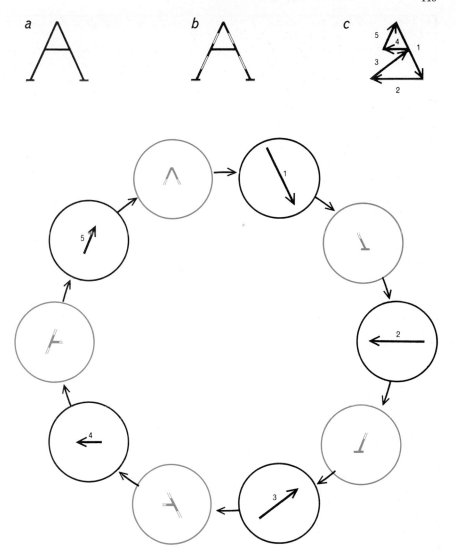

FEATURE RING is proposed by the authors as a format for the internal representation of an object. The object (*a*) is identified by its principal features (*b*) and is represented in the memory by them and by the recollection of the scan path (*c*) whereby they were viewed. The feature ring therefore consists of sensory memory traces (*color*) recording the features and motor memory traces (*black*) of the eye movements from one feature to the next.

support for our ideas on visual perception, certain things remain unexplained. For example, sometimes no scan path was observed during the learning phase. Even when we did find a scan path, it did not always reappear in the recognition phase. On the average the appropriate scan path appeared in about 65 percent of the recognition-phase viewings. This is a rather strong result in view of the many possible paths around each picture, but it leaves 35 percent of the viewings, when no scan path appeared, in need of explanation.

Probably the basic idea of the feature ring needs elaboration. If provision were made for memory traces recording other eye movements between features not adjacent in the ring, and if the original

ring represented the preferred and habitual order of processing rather than the inevitable order, the occasional substitution of an abnormal order for the scan path would be explained [*see top illustration on page 122*].

It must also be remembered that the eye-movement recordings in our experiments were made while the subjects viewed pictures that were rather large and close to their eyes, forcing them to look around in the picture to see its features clearly. In the more normal viewing situation, with a picture or an object small enough to be wholly visible with a single fixation, no eye movements are necessary for recognition. We assume that in such a case the steps in perception are parallel up to the point where an

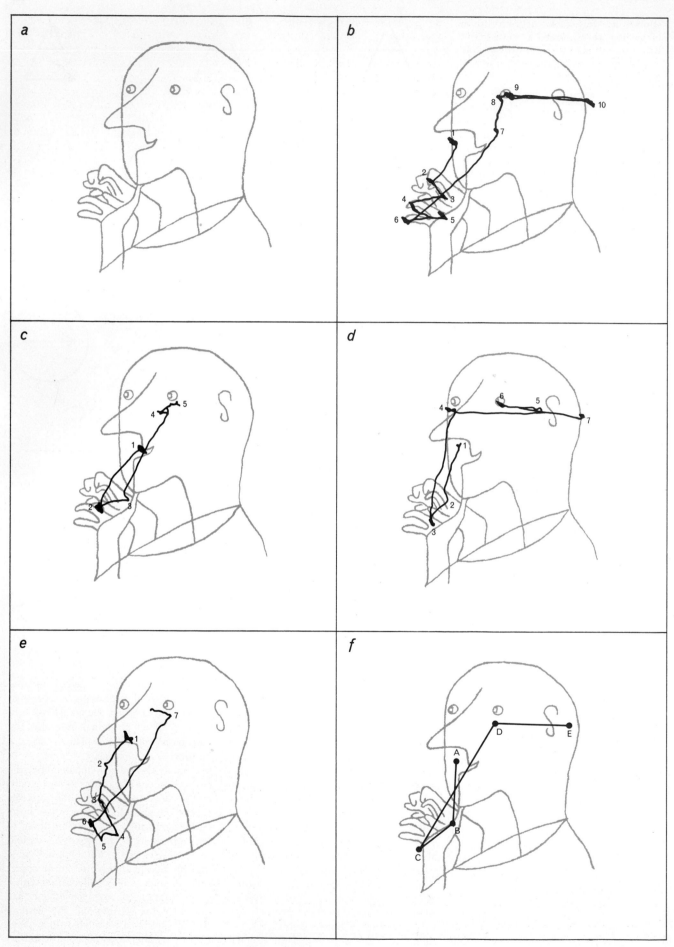

RECURRENCE OF SCAN PATH during recognition of an object is predicted by the feature-ring hypothesis. A subject viewed the adaptation of Klee's drawing (*a*). A scan path appeared while he was familiarizing himself with the picture (*b, c*). It also appeared (*d, e*) during the recognition phase each time he identified the picture as he viewed a sequence of familiar and unfamiliar scenes depicted in similar drawings. This particular experimental subject's scan path for this particular picture is presented in idealized form at *f*.

image of the object is formed in the visual cortex and that thereafter (as would seem evident from the experiments on recognition time) the matching of the image and the internal representation is carried out serially, feature by feature. Now, however, we must postulate instead of eye movements from feature to feature a sequence of internal shifts of attention, processing the features serially and following the scan path dictated by the feature ring. Thus

each motor memory trace in the feature ring records a shift of attention that can be executed either externally, as an eye movement, or internally, depending on the extent of the shift required.

In this connection several recordings made by Lloyd Kaufman and Whitman Richards at M.I.T. are of interest. Their subjects viewed simple figures, such as a drawing of a cube, that could be taken in with a single fixation. At 10 randomly chosen moments the subject was asked

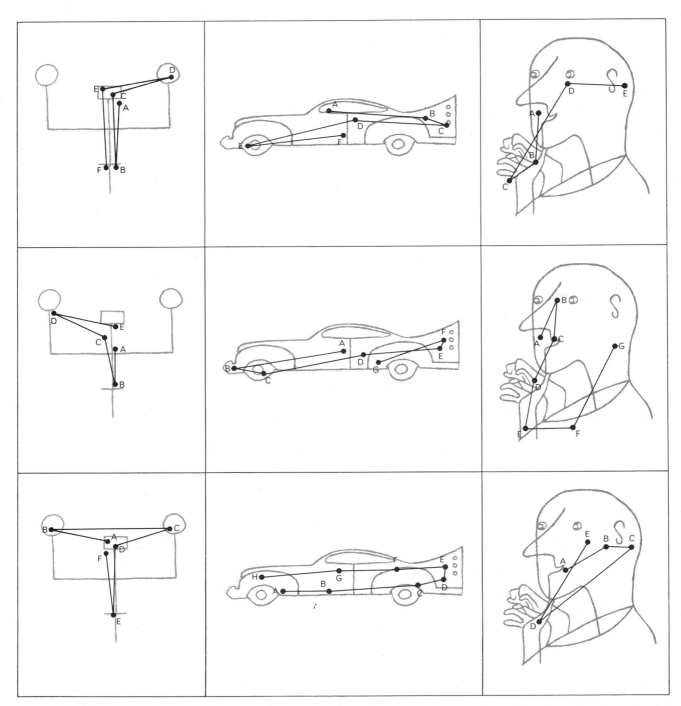

VARIETY IN SCAN PATHS is shown for three subjects and three pictures. Each horizontal row depicts the scan paths used by one subject for the three pictures. Vertically one sees how the scan paths of the three subjects for any one picture also varied widely.

to indicate where he thought he was looking. His answer presumably showed what part of the picture he was attending to visually. His actual fixation point was then recorded at another 10 randomly selected moments [*see bottom illustration at right*]. The results suggest that the subject's attention moved around the picture but his fixation remained fairly steady near the center of the picture. This finding is consistent with the view that smaller objects too are processed serially, by internal shifts of attention, even though little or no eye movement is involved.

It is important to note, however, that neither these results nor ours prove that recognition of objects and pictures is necessarily a serial process under normal conditions, when the object is not so large and close as to force serial processing by eye movements. The experiments on recognition time support the serial hypothesis, but it cannot yet be regarded as being conclusively established. In our experiments we provided a situation that forced the subject to view and recognize pictures serially with eye movements, thus revealing the order of feature processing, and we assumed that the results would be relevant to recognition under more normal conditions. Our results suggest a more detailed explanation of serial processing—the feature ring producing the scan path—but this explanation remains conditional on the serial hypothesis.

In sum, we believe the experimental results so far obtained support three main conclusions concerning the visual recognition of objects and pictures. First, the internal representation or memory of an object is a piecemeal affair: an assemblage of features or, more strictly, of memory traces of features; during recognition the internal representation is matched serially with the object, feature by feature. Second, the features of an object are the parts of it (such as the angles and curves of line drawings) that yield the most information. Third, the memory traces recording the features are assembled into the complete internal representation by being connected by other memory traces that record the shifts of attention required to pass from feature to feature, either with eye movements or with internal shifts of attention; the attention shifts connect the features in a preferred order, forming a feature ring and resulting in a scan path, which is usually followed when verifying the features during recognition.

Clearly these conclusions indicate a

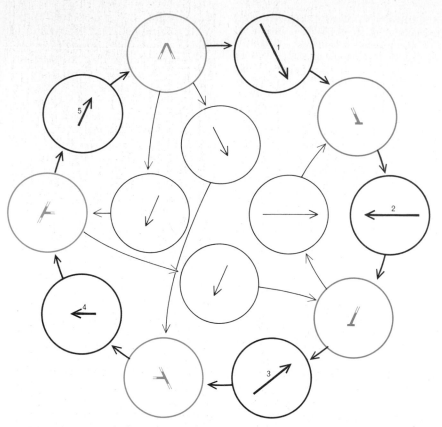

MODIFIED FEATURE RING takes into account less regular eye movements that do not conform to scan path. Several movements, which appeared in 35 percent of recognition viewings, are in center of this ring. Outside ring, consisting of sensory (*color*) and motor memory traces (*black*), represents scan path and remains preferred order of processing.

distinctly serial conception of visual learning and recognition. In the trend to look toward serial concepts to advance the understanding of visual perception one can note the influence of current work in computerized pattern recognition, where the serial approach has long been favored. Indeed, computer and information-processing concepts, usually serial in nature, are having an increasing influence on brain research in general.

Our own thoughts on visual recognition offer a case in point. We have developed them simultaneously with an analogous system for computerized pattern recognition. Although the system has not been implemented in working form, a somewhat similar scheme is being used in the visual-recognition system of a robot being developed by a group at the Stanford Research Institute. We believe this fruitful interaction between biology and engineering can be expected to continue, to the enrichment of both.

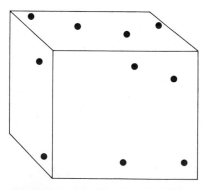
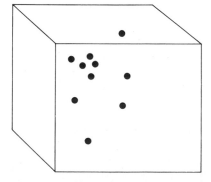

INTERNAL SHIFTS OF ATTENTION apparently replace eye movements in processing of objects small enough to be viewed with single fixation. A subject's attention, represented by statements of where he thought he was looking, moved around picture (*left*), whereas measured fixation point (*right*) remained relatively stationary. Illustration is based on work by Lloyd Kaufman and Whitman Richards at the Massachusetts Institute of Technology.

Eidetic Images

by Ralph Norman Haber
April 1969

Certain individuals report that they briefly retain an almost photographic image of something they have seen. Experiments with children suggest that such images are a real phenomenon

Many people believe they can retain a vivid image of something they have seen. When such people undertake to describe this ability, it usually turns out that the images are fleeting and lacking in true visual quality; the person describing the images is not quite sure that he is not merely remembering or imagining them. Certain individuals, however, report something rather different: a sharp visual image that persists for many seconds or even minutes. They speak of the image being localized in space in front of their eyes, usually in the same plane as the original stimulus. They maintain that it is so well defined that they can describe it in far more detail than they could from memory alone. They report that the image can be formed when their eyes simply flick over the original scene without fixating it, and also that the image can be scanned as it remains stationary in space.

Such reported images have been named eidetic, after the Greek *eidētikos*, meaning pertaining to images. Eidetic imagery was once the subject of considerable investigation; more than 200 experiments and studies on it have been published, most of them before 1935. This work indicated that whereas eidetic ability is relatively rare after puberty, it is common in young children (an average of 50 percent of the elementary-school-age children who were studied appeared to possess it). These findings were based, however, on widely divergent and often inconsistent methods. In spite of the seeming prevalence of eidetic imagery, the poor methods and an inability to explain the phenomenon tended to lead psychologists to ignore eidetic images, along with most of the other mental states that depend so heavily on subjective reports.

The past decade has witnessed a renewed interest in visual imagery of all kinds, particularly in connection with how images facilitate perceptual memory. It seemed only natural to look again at eidetic imagery, the most enduring and complete kind of imagery. Does it really exist? Can children (or adults) with this ability be found, and if so, in what other ways might their visual perception and perceptual memory be different? Exactly how do eidetic images differ from the ordinary visual memories reported by most adults? How does a child with eidetic imagery prevent his visual experiences from becoming a hopeless muddle? Is eidetic imagery a more primitive or developmentally earlier mode of perception and memory?

To answer some of these questions my colleagues and I (including from the beginning my wife and more recently Jan Leask Fentress) launched a large-scale effort to find eidetic children and examine aspects of their imagery and other perceptual abilities. Because of the elusive nature of the phenomenon, and because of the difficulty of finding a large number of eidetic children, we have conducted comparatively few formal experiments. Even so, we have found answers to a few of the questions listed above (although more questions have been raised). I shall describe how we conducted our search for eidetic children and some of the more outstanding results of the project. I shall also discuss, as I present the evidence, the visual character of eidetic imagery.

The basic procedures we followed in order to locate eidetic children were adapted from research of 40 years ago. Children from four elementary schools were tested individually, and as it became clear that eidetic imagery was going to be a rare phenomenon, we found it necessary to test large numbers of them. Our results are based on about 20 eidetic children, although more than 500 children have been screened in all.

The screening began with a test designed to elicit afterimages, which are a common phenomenon not to be confused with eidetic images. The subject sat before a table on which an easel of a neutral gray color was placed. His eyes were about two feet from the middle of the easel [*see illustration on page 127*]. A tape recorder transcribed the voices of the subject and the experimenter.

The first stimulus placed on the easel was a four-by-four-inch square of red paper mounted on a board of the same material as the easel. After 10 seconds the board was removed, and the subject then reported what he saw on the easel. At the beginning of this test he was instructed to stare at the center of the colored square as hard as he could, trying not to move his eyes. He was told: "After the square is removed, you will still be able to see something there. It is very much like when you stare hard at a light bulb and then look away. You can still see something out there in front of your eyes." If a child acted as if he was unfamiliar with this phenomenon, he was told to try it out with one of the overhead lights in the room. He was also encouraged to report, without waiting to be asked, what he saw after the square was removed and he continued to stare at the place where it had been.

During the exposure the experimenter watched carefully to be sure that the subject did not move his eyes. If, when the square was taken away, the subject said he saw nothing, he was encouraged by being assured that it was all right to see something. If he still said he saw nothing, he was reminded to stare hard and not move his eyes at all, and he was

TEST PICTURE was shown for half a minute to elementary school children; a few then reported eidetic images of it. For example, one boy saw in his image "about 16" stripes in the cat's tail. The picture, painted by Marjorie Torrey, appears in an edition of Lewis Carroll's *Alice in Wonderland* abridged by Josette Frank and is reproduced with the kind permission of Random House.

questioned about whether he knew what these instructions meant.

If the subject said he did see something, he was allowed to report spontaneously. Then he was questioned about items he had not reported. Was the image still visible? What was its color and shape? When the subject moved his eyes (he had been asked to try to look slowly toward the top of the easel), did the image move? How did it disappear? After the image had faded completely the experimenter repeated the initial instructions and another square, a blue one, was placed on the easel. The same procedure was followed with a black square and then a yellow one.

After the last square had been reported on, the test for eidetic imagery began. Four pictures were shown: two silhouettes of black paper pasted on a gray board (one showing a family scene and one an Indian hunter) and two illustrations in color taken from books for children. Each picture was presented for 30 seconds. For this test the subject was given the instructions: "Now I am going to show you some pictures. For these, however, I do not want you to stare in one place, but to move your eyes around so that you can be sure you can see all of the details. When I take the picture away, I want you to continue to look hard at the easel where the picture was, and tell me what you can still see after I take it away. After I take it away, you also can move your eyes all over where it was on the easel. And be sure, while the picture is on the easel, that you move your eyes around it to see all of the parts."

During the viewing period the experimenter watched to be sure that the picture was scanned and not fixated. After the first picture was removed the subject was reminded to continue looking at the easel and report whatever he could still see. He was also reminded that he could move his eyes. If a subject reported seeing something, the experimenter asked if he was actually seeing it then or remembering it from when the picture was still on the easel. The subject was frequently asked if he was still seeing something, since subjects would often fail to say that the image had faded and would continue reporting it from memory. The experimenter probed for further description of all objects still visible in the image. He noted the relation between the direction of the subject's gaze and details of his report. This process was repeated for all four pictures. The average time for testing var-

ied from four or five minutes for a young subject with no visual imagery to more than 30 minutes for an older subject with extensive imagery.

The tests were scored by encoding the tape recordings on data sheets. A different coding sheet was set up for each stimulus. The reliability of this condensation of the data was nearly perfect because there were categories for every object in the picture and most of their attributes. The coder rarely had to make a scoring decision.

We have introduced a number of variations in the screening, but these represent the main procedures. When a child was considered to be eidetic, further tests, demonstrations and examinations usually followed. I shall not present them in chronological or systematic order here, since most of the sessions did not constitute formal experiments.

Before discussing specific characteristics of eidetic imagery, let me make a few general comments. About half of the children screened said they saw something on the easel after the picture was removed, but nearly all these reports were of afterimages and the like, that is, the images were fleeting and indistinct. Between 5 and 10 percent of the children, however, reported images that lasted much longer (a half-minute or more) and that possessed some sharp detail. Without committing ourselves, we labeled these children eidetic and observed them further. Hereafter I shall refer to this group as eidetic, although you can judge for yourself whether they can be differentiated from the rest, and whether they have any visual imagery of noteworthy quality. I feel that the answer to both questions is clearly yes.

Let me start by offering an example (taken directly from a tape recording) of a report of an eidetic image. Not all eidetic reports are like this one; on the other hand, it is not atypical. The subject, a 10-year-old boy, was seated before a blank easel from which a picture from *Alice in Wonderland* had just been removed.

Experimenter: Do you see something there?

Subject: I see the tree, gray tree with three limbs. I see the cat with stripes around its tail.

Experimenter: Can you count those stripes?

Subject: Yes (*pause*). There's about 16.

Experimenter: You're counting what? Black, white or both?

Subject: Both.

Experimenter: Tell me what else you see.

Subject: And I can see the flowers on the bottom. There's about three stems, but you can see two pairs of flowers. One on the right has green leaves, red flower on bottom with yellow on top. And I can see the girl with a green dress. She's got blonde hair and a red hair band and there are some leaves in the upper left-hand corner where the tree is.

Experimenter: Can you tell me about the roots of the tree?

Subject: Well, there's two of them going down here (*points*) and there's one that cuts off on the left-hand side of the picture.

Experimenter: What is the cat doing with its paws?

Subject: Well, one of them he's holding out and the other one is on the tree.

Experimenter: What color is the sky?

Subject: Can't tell.

Experimenter: Can't tell at all?

Subject: No. I can see the yellowish ground, though.

Experimenter: Tell me if any of the parts go away or change at all as I'm talking to you. What color is the girl's dress?

Subject: Green. It has some white on it.

Experimenter: How about her legs and feet?

(*The subject looks away from the easel and then back again.*)

Experimenter: Is the image gone?

Subject: Yes, except for the tree.

Experimenter: Tell me when it goes away.

Subject: (*pause*) It went away.

The fact that only about 5 percent of the children reported images as prolonged and vivid as this one raised our immediate concern about the validity of eidetic imagery. How could it shrink in frequency so much in the 35 years since the early investigations? Perhaps it did not exist at all. The children might be faking or be strongly suggestible, giving us answers we led them to expect we want. Or could we as psychologists be fooled into thinking that these few children are describing their imagery when they are only telling us about their vivid memories? All of these have been difficult questions to answer or even to investigate. Furthermore, some of the most convincing evidence in support of visual images comes not from experiments but from incidental observations or comments made by the children that suggest the visual characteristics rather than the memory characteristics of the reports. Instead of listing such evidence

COMPOSITE PICTURES, closely resembling each other, provided a test of eidetic imagery. A child capable of maintaining eidetic images of both pictures would presumably be better equipped to distinguish between them accurately than would a child without such images who relied solely on his memory of the pictures. The montages were made by Leonard W. Doob of Yale University.

out of context I shall consider it in relation to some of the properties of eidetic imagery we measured.

First, who are the eidetic children? Those we labeled as such were distributed fairly evenly over the five grades from the second through the sixth. The absence of eidetics from the first grade and kindergarten (which were also tested) seemed due to the verbal demands of the task that was set, so that we have no way of being sure that younger children are less likely to be eidetic. The sex and racial makeup of the eidetic group mirrored the school populations as closely as such a small sample can. We tested I.Q., reading achievement and aspects of personality, but we could find nothing that differentiated the eidetic group from comparable noneidetic children.

The rather unsuccessful attempt to find some distinguishing characteristic of eidetic children has given us concern, although without further enlightenment. There is no question about the reliability of the testing for eidetic imagery, however. Once labeled this way, an eidetic child always produces such images. We have tested a few of the children four times over a five-year period, and have found no loss in the quality of their imagery.

One aspect of eidetic imagery we measured was the length of exposure time required for the formation of an image. For nearly all the eidetic children a five-second viewing of a picture will lead to an image of at least parts of it (the parts examined during that time). The better eidetic children (those who could more easily report long-lived and complete images) could occasionally form an image after only three seconds. Although we did not make careful measurements, it appears that three to five seconds of central viewing is needed to produce an image, and that the size of such an image is two or three degrees of visual angle. This is roughly the size covered by the fovea, the area of the retina that provides sharp vision. Thus to have a complete image of a typical picture measuring five degrees by five degrees at least four separate fixations would be needed. The children report that they do not have an image of parts of the picture they did not look at long enough, even though they may know and be able to remember what the parts contain. Moreover, the relation between duration of exposure and the production of an eidetic image holds even if the picture is totally familiar to the child. Hence his memory of it could be essentially perfect and complete and yet whether or not he has an image depends on how long his eyes dwell on the picture in the most recent viewing. Observations of this kind further suggest the visual character of eidetic images.

We wondered why eidetic children were not confused by the continual bombardment of images. The children described several ways they controlled the production of images. One way, of course, is not to look at anything too long. Moreover, most of the children indicated that exaggerated eye blinks could serve to "erase" an image. Nearly all the children said that if they moved their eyes from the original surface on which the picture was viewed, the image would disappear. This would further reduce the possibility of an eidetic child's picking up random images as he looks about the world.

By far the most intriguing method of control reported to us (again by most of the children) was based on naming the items in the picture. That is, if while the child is looking at the picture, he names, labels, rehearses or otherwise actively attends to the items, he will not have an image. After several children mentioned this spontaneously, we examined it more explicitly. In viewing some pictures a child would be asked to name each part; for other pictures the experimenter named the parts but the child was not asked to do so. We found a clear difference: no image or only a poor, brief image would form of those pictures for which the child had named the parts.

We have not yet been able to pursue

SUBJECT WAS TIMED as he inspected the picture; he was also watched to see whether he examined every part of it. After the picture was removed from view he reported to the experimenter what (if anything) he saw on the blank easel. His words were recorded.

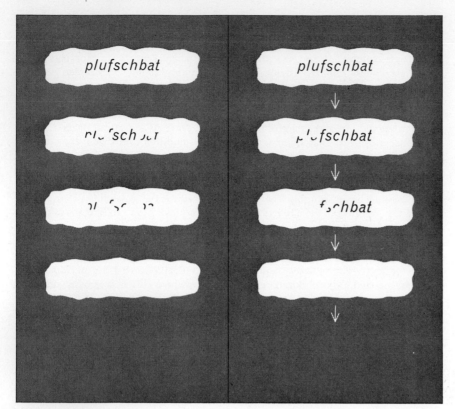

QUALITY OF EIDETIC IMAGES (reconstructed from verbal reports) varied from child to child. At left is the range of image completeness (of a nonsense word) for all the children with eidetic ability. Each reconstruction characterizes a different child most of the time. At right is the sequence of fading of all eidetic images. A perfect "image" is used as a model.

this finding further. It seems to imply at one level that eidetic children retain information either in the form of an image or in the form of a verbal memory or another kind of memory more similar to that in adults. The children do not seem to be able to do both at once. This can help to explain an earlier finding of ours. In one screening test, after an eidetic child had completed a description of his eidetic image and had said it had faded completely, he was asked to describe the stimulus from memory. Noneidetic children who had no images at all were also asked to describe the stimulus from memory. We expected the eidetic child to have a far superior memory, because he had had the opportunity to view not only the picture but also his enduring image, but we found that eidetic children were only slightly better than the others, and in some cases no better at all. It was as if the eidetic child paid no attention to his image in organizing his memory. Interpreting this behavior in the light of the later observations, it seems that if an eidetic child wishes to get an image, he can pay no attention to the picture in composing his memory, because trying to do so interferes with the image. The child asked to produce images sacrifices the memory. I shall re-

turn to this point. Let me note that here again we can make a distinction between the visual character and the memory character of the child's report, suggesting that the visual nature of eidetic imagery has some validity.

Can an eidetic child prolong his image or bring it back after it has disappeared? Does he have any control over its disappearance? Can he change the size or orientation of his image, or move it to another surface? The answer to each of these questions is in general negative. Few eidetic children seem to have any control over the images once they are formed.

The group of eidetic children we studied differed substantially among themselves with respect to the quality of their images. For example, the child with the most enduring images consistently reported them as lasting 10 minutes or more. Some eidetic children had good images that lasted no more than a minute. There was also variation among children in the completeness of the image, particularly for nonpictorial material such as printed letters. Some children could regularly see in their image all the letters of a very long nonsense word. Other children could see only some of

the letters, still others just a few letter fragments. There were eidetic children who could get images of pictures easily but could rarely see any print in an image. What is interesting about this is that the pattern of fading for a particular eidetic child seems to reproduce the spectrum of image completeness of the group as a whole [*see illustration at left*]. All the eidetic children reported that their images ended in the same manner each time, the image fading part by part in a comparatively independent fashion. As a good image begins to fade, first some fragments disappear and then more of them go until just a gray streak is left and finally nothing remains. The parallel between completeness and fading suggests that the mechanism responsible for the completeness of an eidetic image is similar to the one for its subsequent fading.

None of our eidetic children maintained that he could by any action prolong his image. One girl reported the ability to bring an image back after it had faded. She was asked to do this over periods of several weeks and reported being able to do so.

We explored somewhat more fully whether the eidetic child can move his image or change its size or orientation. The apparent size of an afterimage varies with the distance of the surface on which the image is projected (an effect known as Emmert's law). No such effect can be tested with eidetic imagery because the eidetic child cannot move his image off the original surface without losing it. The image could be moved over the surface, but nearly all the children said that when they tried moving the image over the edge, it "falls off." Only the girl who was able to bring her images back could move her image off the surface. (She said she could move it anywhere and even turn it upside down.) With this one exception the image seems to be related in specific ways to the picture that produced it. It has the same size, orientation and shape. It moves on its "own" surface but not into space or onto a "foreign" surface.

We had used pictures selected to be interesting to children in our screening procedures, because the older studies suggested that these elicited better eidetic images. We were also most interested in images of letters and how much information was maintained in these images. This was significant in its own right and also because eidetic imagery might facilitate or hinder reading. Although all the eidetic children were able to develop images of print (we used long nonsense words, strings of digits or misspelled words), these images were in general poorer than images of pictures. They were less complete and distinct, and did not last as long. The quality of the image did not differ according to the kind of printed material. The duration of exposure also seemed to be irrelevant. An eidetic child with only a partial image of print would not get a better one if he looked longer.

One procedure we followed was to show a subject letters or digits one at a time through a small viewing window in a screen. The most striking result was the nearly uniform statement by the children that as each new item appeared in the window they moved their image of the preceding one along the surface to the left [see illustration below]. When the image of the first letter exposed reached the left margin of the surface, it would (if it had not yet faded with the passage of time) "fall off" the edge and disappear. Note again the visual character of this description given by nearly every eidetic child.

Regardless of whether the child scanned a group of letters from left to right or from right to left, the items seen last exerted a strong effect. This was clearly due to the fact that the images of the first items scanned were fading before the last ones were scanned. Since in a task of this kind the first items viewed would normally be remembered better, the finding again seems to indicate that the children are seeing something rather than just remembering it.

We were disappointed in how few letters (or digits) can be maintained in a visual image. For a relatively good eidetic child an average of only about eight of 10 letters (one presented every three seconds) remained in an image after the 30 seconds of total exposure, and this held only under optimum conditions. A few of the children could probably have done better had we given them more letters, but for most of the children items of this kind do not persist in images for nearly as long as parts of pictures. Although we did not try to use a page of printed words as a stimulus, it was clear that none of the children would have had an eidetic image of even part of it.

In an attempt to learn the amount of information retained in an image, we tried two tests utilizing pictorial items. For one test we designed a "rogues' gallery," showing a group of letters and a series of digits in conjunction with the shoulders and head of the "wanted" man [see illustration on following page].

Only four of the eidetic children could develop an image of even part of the gallery, and these images were so incomplete that the children were unable to report much information. None of the children felt he could have maintained better images with longer exposures. (The exposure time was about three seconds per rogue.)

In the second test montages made up of familiar objects were presented to the children. The montages were in pairs, one member of the pair rather closely resembling the other [see illustration on page 126]. We expected (and showed) that from memory alone children and adults often tended to confuse which element belonged in which picture of the pair, assuming that they could remember all the elements to start with. An ei-

detic child, however, if he could have a good image of both members of a pair, should have no trouble describing them accurately. Unfortunately when first one and then the other montage was shown to the eidetic group, only one child was able to maintain an image of the two pictures side by side. Several children could retain images of the second montage shown, but the first image would disappear. None of the eidetic children could report any more detail or accurate positioning of detail than noneidetic children could.

We therefore have been unable to determine how much information an eidetic image can contain, because eidetic children do not achieve satisfactory images of either high-information stimuli or even simple nonpictorial stimuli. One

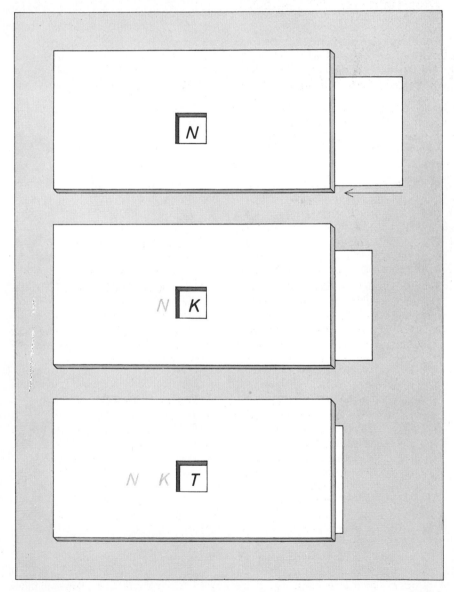

SEQUENCE OF LETTERS appeared one at a time in an aperture of a screen as children who had previously displayed eidetic ability watched. They reported that the image they formed of a letter (gray letter) moved to the left as a new letter appeared in the window.

dandyhall   hutvopsly   quarstilo   axlerfnan   hamnersby

00-6114   84-9270   53-0624   79-3516   90-4265

"ROGUES' GALLERY" STIMULUS was designed to provide a basis for estimating the amount of information contained in an eidetic image. In addition to the name and the number associated with a rogue there are binary dimensions that could be used descriptively, for example the presence or absence of hair or a hat. The rogues (together with 20 others) were shown as a group to the children.

reason for the poor response to letters may have been the tendency to name them, which we already know interferes with the formation of a good image. These results are somewhat in contrast with the seemingly better images from complex but cohesive pictures.

We have also tried to elicit eidetic imagery with a few three-dimensional objects. Three of the eight children so tested reported images of everyday objects, at which they looked for 30 seconds. They were able to move their images and reported that they had clear three-dimensional qualities. The children were also shown the visual illusion known as the Necker cube, a line figure that spontaneously reverses in apparent depth [see top illustration, facing page]. During the 30 seconds of scanning time all the children reported reversals of depth; only three (the same three mentioned above) could report reversals in their image. The number of reversals in the image was about four per 30 seconds compared with seven per 30 seconds during the viewing of the drawing of the cube. Since (barring deliberate faking) a report of a reversal requires a three-dimensional view, a few of the eidetic children seem to be capable of forming three-dimensional eidetic images. A reversal also requires a visual experience. There is nothing in the memory of a Necker cube that would cause its orientation to alternate.

At several points in this article I have raised the question of whether eidetic imagery could merely be vivid memory. This is a crucial aspect of the research. Some criticisms of the earlier studies of eidetic imagery focused on the lack of evidence that the eidetic children were reporting a visual image rather than just describing their memory of the stimulus. Whereas many in-

credibly detailed reports of eidetic images have been described in these studies, there is no reason to doubt that some children may have superb memories and be quite capable of the same feats from memory alone.

I believe that resting the case for eidetic imagery on the fidelity of reports is the wrong approach. Our own evidence suggests that the amount of detail an eidetic child can report from his image is in general not phenomenally good (although we have had some amazing exceptions). I see no reason to assert that an eidetic image has to be complete or contain all the content of the original stimulus, or that it must last long enough to enable the eidetic child to describe all the content before it fades.

If we are not to depend on the criterion of accuracy, then what does differentiate eidetic images from other kinds of images or from memory? The only distinction with respect to other images is in their location. Afterimages seem to be the result of differential adaptation of retinal receptors and neural units. The image, once formed, is "burned on" the retina and cannot be moved in relation to the retina. Moreover, during the formation of an afterimage reasonably stable fixation is required to produce the differential adaptation. The likelihood of an afterimage's being produced should thus vary inversely with the amount of scanning during inspection and with the degree to which the image itself can be scanned once it is formed. Since in all our work with eidetic images we demand scanning during inspection of the stimulus and check further to be sure the child moves his eyes during his report of his image, it seems almost certain that this image cannot simply be retinal in origin.

We still leave open the possibility that an eidetic image is not an image at

all. The child may not be seeing anything in front of his eyes. It is always possible that these children are trying to fool us when they say they see the image; that our questions effectively structure their answers to be as if they saw images; that since they think we want them to talk about images, they do; that they are so suggestible they "think" they see images even if they do not, or that the distinction between seeing and remembering is so difficult for a child (let alone an adult) that he is innocently confused. All of these are possible explanations and are likely to be true for perhaps one or two children most of the time and for many of the children occasionally.

Still, sufficient evidence is available to support the argument that these are images that are visual in nature and not dependent on memory in any way (except perhaps negatively). Whereas this argument cannot be settled to the degree we would wish, let me repeat some of the observations or comments that support the visual character of eidetic imagery: (1) An eidetic child can remember parts of the picture he cannot see in his image, and he says he did not have an image of those parts because he did not look at them long enough. (2) A conscious attempt to label the content of the stimulus interferes with the formation of an image. (3) Nearly all the eidetic children report the same pattern of fading in their images, even though that is only one of a number of possible sequences. (4) When asked to move their image from one surface to another, eidetic children report spontaneously that when it reaches the edge it falls off. (5) When the child forms an image of letters exposed individually in a window, he moves his image to the left as a new letter appears in the window. Furthermore, when the image reaches the edge of the surface, it too falls off. (6) Children are most capable of seeing details that they scanned most recently, a result contrary to normal organization in memory. (7) At least some of the eidetic children are able to develop three-dimensional images. This was particularly true with the Necker cube, for which reversals cannot be the result of anything other than a visual three-dimensional image.

This list should be longer, and there are certainly a large number of other observations that could be made to help verify the distinction proposed here. At present this represents the nature and amount of evidence we have.

We have tried only one direct test of the visual character of eidetic imagery. This has been very difficult to work out, and our first step is only a beginning. We wanted a test for the screening of eidetic imagery that did not depend on verbal facility and could not be biased by memory. The best solution we have found so far is to use a sequence of pictures that together form another picture [see illustration below]. The first picture shown to the child is designed in such a way that, although it is cohesive in its own right, if it is superimposed on a second picture, a third picture (a face) is formed by the combination. Assuming that the combination picture is unpredictable from either picture alone, the only way the eidetic child could know what the combination is would be if he could superimpose one picture on the other visually. If he viewed the pictures separately, this could be accomplished only by maintaining an image of the

first picture long enough to superimpose it on the second one.

We have given this test to 20 eidetic children. Only four (who were among the best four in other criteria as well) were able to "see" the combination face picture. The reaction of one child was quite impressive to us. After developing a good image of the first picture, he superimposed his eidetic image of it on the second and at first persisted in reporting the various separate elements of each picture. Suddenly, with obvious surprise, he reported the composite face and exclaimed that the experimenter was pretty "tricky" to have fooled him that way.

Although a few adults appear able to see the outline of the face in the first picture alone, children do not seem able to. Nevertheless, many more versions of the test need to be tried. It is a stringent test, since not only does it require a fairly complete image of the first picture lasting long enough for it to be superimposed on a second picture but also it assumes that the first image will not be erased and can be lined up with the second picture. The instance mentioned above seems to be one where an initially poor alignment stood in the way of a meaningful result. The child suddenly saw the composite after nearly a minute of viewing, when presumably he achieved a better alignment of image and picture.

This test cannot be faked, nor does it depend on memory or on any distinction between memory and imagery. All the child has to do is describe what he can

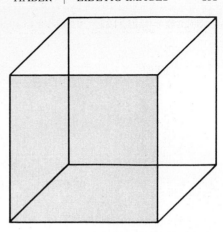

VISUAL ILLUSION was presented to children to explore their ability to form three-dimensional images. The area of the cube in color can appear as a front surface or as a rear surface, producing (in some children's images) a reversal in the cube's orientation.

see when the second picture is presented. The test could in fact be used with very young and preverbal children (and could be adapted for animals, if anyone thought they might be eidetic).

Much more work needs to be done with eidetic imagery. We know very little about eidetic children as individuals and have only an inkling of what their imagery is like, but the shunning of an interesting psychological phenomenon for 35 years should be ended. Imagery is an important characteristic of many cognitive tasks, and it should be further opened to serious scientific investigation.

 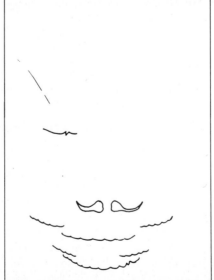 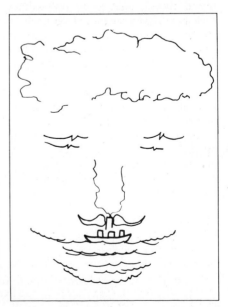

RECOGNITION TEST posed the problem of visually superimposing an image of a picture on another picture. The eidetic children first were shown the picture at left; it was then removed and the middle picture was exposed to view. Some children then "saw" a face. At right is the picture formed by combining the other two pictures. None of the children saw a face in the picture at left.

BIBLIOGRAPHIES

1. The Processes of Vision

THE KINETIC DEPTH EFFECT. H. Wallach and D. N. O'Connell in *Journal of Experimental Psychology*, Vol. 45, No. 4, pages 205–218; April, 1953.

THE RELATION OF EYE MOVEMENTS, BODY MOTILITY AND EXTERNAL STIMULI TO DREAM CONTENT. William Dement and Edward A. Wolpert in *Journal of Experimental Psychology*, Vol. 55, No. 6, pages 543–553; June, 1958.

THE SENSES CONSIDERED AS PERCEPTUAL SYSTEMS. James J. Gibson, Houghton Mifflin Company, 1966.

COGNITIVE PSYCHOLOGY. Ulric Neisser. Appleton-Century-Crofts, 1967.

I   COLOR AND CONTRAST

2. Contour and Contrast

MACH BANDS: QUANTITATIVE STUDIES ON NEURAL NETWORKS IN THE RETINA. Floyd Ratliff. Holden-Day, Inc., 1965.

LINEAR SYSTEMS ANALYSIS OF THE LIMULUS RETINA. Frederick A. Dodge, Robert M. Shapley and Bruce W. Knight in *Behavioral Science*, Vol. 15, No. 1, pages 24–36; January, 1970.

CONTOUR AND CONTRAST. Floyd Ratliff in *Proceedings of the American Philosophical Society*, Vol. 115, No. 2, pages 150–163; April, 1971.

INHIBITORY INTERACTION IN THE RETINA OF LIMULUS. H. K. Hartline and F. Ratliff in *Handbook of Sensory Physiology: Vol. VII/Part IB*. Springer-Verlag, in print.

3. The Perception of Neutral Colors

BRIGHTNESS CONSTANCY AND THE NATURE OF ACHROMATIC COLORS. Hans Wallach in *Journal of Experimental Psychology*, Vol. 38, No. 3, pages 310–324; June, 1948.

SOME FACTORS AND IMPLICATIONS OF COLOR CONSTANCY. Harry Helson in *Journal of the Optical Society of America*, Vol. 33, No. 10, pages 555–567; October, 1943.

A THEORY OF DEPRESSION AND ENHANCEMENT IN BRIGHTNESS RESPONSE. A. Leonard Diamond in *Psychological Review*, Vol. 67, No. 3, pages 168–199; May, 1960.

THE WORLD OF COLOUR. David Katz. Kegan Paul, Trench, Trubner & Co., Ltd., 1935.

4. The Perception of Transparency

GESETZE DES SEHENS. Wolfgang Metzger. Verlag von Waldemar Kramer Frankfurt am Main, 1953.

MARGINI QUASI-PERCETTIVI IN CAMPI CON STIMOLAZIONE OMOGENEA. Gaetano Kanizsa in *Rivista di Psicologia*, Vol. 49, No. 1, pages 7–30; January-March, 1955.

ZUR ANALYSE DER PHÄNOMENALEN DURCHSICHTIG KEITSERSCHEINUNGEN. F. Metelli in *Gestalt und Wirklichkeit*. Duncker und Humboldt, Berlin, 1967,

AN ALGEBRAIC DEVELOPMENT OF THE THEORY OF PERCEPTUAL TRANSPARENCY. F. Metelli in *Ergonomics*, Vol. 13, 1970.

II SPATIAL DIMENSIONS OF VISION

5. Visual Illusions

SENSATION AND PERCEPTION IN THE HISTORY OF EXPERI-
MENTAL PSYCHOLOGY. Edwin Garrigues Boring.
D. Appleton-Century Company, 1942.

OPTICAL ILLUSIONS. S. Tolansky. Pergamon Press, Inc.,
1964.

EYE AND BRAIN. R. L. Gregory. McGraw-Hill Book
Company, Inc., 1966.

WILL SEEING MACHINES HAVE ILLUSIONS? R. L. Gregory
in *Machine Intelligence I*, edited by N. L. Collins
and Donald Michie. American Elsevier Publishing
Co., Inc., 1967.

THE ANALYSIS OF SENSATIONS AND THE RELATION OF
THE PHYSICAL TO THE PSYCHICAL. Ernst Mach,
translated from the German by C. M. Williams.
Dover Publications, Inc., 1959.

ORIENTATION AND SHAPE I AND II in *Human Spatial
Orientation*. I. P. Howard and W. B. Templeton.
John Wiley & Sons, Inc., 1966.

SIMILARITY IN VISUALLY PERCEIVED FORMS. Erich Goldmeier in *Psychological Issues*, Vol. 8, No. 1, Monograph 29; 1972.

ORIENTATION AND FORM. Irvin Rock. Academic Press,
1974.

6. Texture and Visual Perception

BINOCULAR DEPTH PERCEPTION WITHOUT FAMILIARITY
CUES. Bela Julesz in *Science*, Vol. 145, No. 3630,
pages 356–362; July, 1964.

THE OPTICAL SPACE SENSE. Kenneth N. Ogle in *The
Eye, Vol. IV: Visual Optics and the Optical Space
Sense*, edited by Hugh Davson. Academic Press,
Inc., 1962.

STEREOPSIS AND BINOCULAR RIVALRY OF CONTOURS.
B. Julesz in *Bell Telephone System Technical Publications Monograph 4609*, 1963.

TOWARDS THE AUTOMATION OF BINOCULAR DEPTH PER-
CEPTION. B. Julesz in *Information Processing 1962:
Proceedings of IFIP Congress 62*. North-Holland
Publishing Company, 1962.

7. The Perception of
Disoriented Figures

RECOGNITION UNDER OBJECTIVE REVERSAL. George V.
N. Dearborn in *The Psychological Review*, Vol. 6,
No. 4, pages 395–406; July, 1899.

8. Pictorial Perception and Culture

GEOGRAPHY AND ATLAS OF PROTESTANT MISSIONS.
Harlan P. Beach. New York Volunteer Movement
for Foreign Missions, 1901.

THE STUDY OF THE PROBLEM OF PICTORIAL PERCEPTION
AMONG UNACCULTURATED GROUPS. William Hudson
in *International Journal of Psychology*, Vol. 2, No.
2, pages 89–107; 1967.

DIFFICULTIES IN PICTORIAL DEPTH PERCEPTION IN
AFRICA. Jan B. Deregowski in *The British Journal
of Psychology*, Vol. 59, Part 3, pages 195–204;
August, 1968.

PERCEPTION OF THE TWO-PRONGED TRIDENT BY TWO-
AND THREE-DIMENSIONAL PERCEIVERS. J. B. Deregowski in *Journal of Experimental Psychology*, Vol.
82, No. 1, Part 1, pages 9–13; October, 1969.

RESPONSES MEDIATING PICTORIAL RECOGNITION. Jan B.
Deregowski in *The Journal of Social Psychology*,
Vol. 84, First Half, pages 27–33; June, 1971.

III FORM ANALYSIS

9. Multistability in Perception

THE ANALYSIS OF SENSATIONS AND THE RELATION OF
THE PHYSICAL TO THE PSYCHICAL. Ernst Mach.
Dover Publications, Inc., 1959.

AMBIGUITY OF FORM: OLD AND NEW. Gerald H. Fisher
in *Perception and Psychophysics*, Vol. 4, No. 3,
pages 189–192; September, 1968.

TRIANGLES AS AMBIGUOUS FIGURES. Fred Attneave in

The American Journal of Psychology, Vol. 81, No.
3, pages 447–453; September, 1968.

10. The Recognition of Faces

SOME ASPECTS OF RECOGNITION OF HUMAN FACES. L. D.
Harmon in *Pattern Recognition in Biological and*

Technical Systems: Proceedings of the Fourth Congress of the Deutsche Gesellschaft für Kybernetik, edited by Otto-Joachim Grüsser and Rainer Klinke. Springer-Verlag, 1971.

IDENTIFICATION OF HUMAN FACES. A. Jay Goldstein, Leon D. Harmon and Ann B. Lesk in *Proceedings of the IEEE*, Vol. 59, No. 5, pages 748–760; May, 1971.

MAN-MACHINE INTERACTION IN HUMAN-FACE IDENTIFICATION. A. J. Goldstein, L. D. Harmon and A. B. Lesk in *The Bell System Technical Journal*, Vol. 51, No. 2, pages 399–427; February, 1972.

MASKING IN VISUAL RECOGNITION: EFFECTS OF TWO-DIMENSIONAL FILTERED NOISE. Leon D. Harmon and Bela Julesz in *Science*, Vol. 180, No. 4091, pages 1194–1197; June 15, 1973.

11. Eye Movements and Visual Perception

PATTERN RECOGNITION. Edited by Leonard M. Uhr. John Wiley & Sons, Inc., 1966.

CONTEMPORARY THEORY AND RESEARCH IN VISUAL PERCEPTION. Edited by Ralph Norman Haber. Holt, Rinehart & Winston, Inc., 1968.

A THEORY OF VISUAL PATTERN PERCEPTION. David Noton in *IEEE Transactions on Systems Science and Cybernetics*, Vol. SSC-6, No. 4, pages 349–357; October, 1970.

SCANPATHS IN EYE MOVEMENTS DURING PATTERN PERCEPTION. David Noton and Lawrence Stark in *Science*, Vol. 171, No. 3968, pages 308–311; January 22, 1971.

12. Eidetic Images

THE EIDETIC CHILD. Heinrich Klüver in *A Handbook of Child Psychology*, edited by Carl Murchison. Clark University Press, 1931.

EIDETIC IMAGERY, I: FREQUENCY. Ralph Norman Haber and Ruth B. Haber in *Perceptual and Motor Skills*, Vol. 19, pages 131–138; 1964.

EIDETIC IMAGERY: A CROSS-CULTURAL WILL-O'-THE-WISP? Leonard W. Doob in *The Journal of Psychology*, Vol. 63, pages 13–34; 1966.

INDEX